# BELONGING

CAROLINA ACADEMIC PRESS
European Anthropology Series
Pamela J. Stewart and Andrew Strathern
Series Editors

Bear Country:
Predation, Politics, and the Changing Face of Pyrenean Pastoralism
Bryan Cummins

Believing in Belfast:
Charismatic Christianity After the Troubles
Liam D. Murphy

Landscape, Heritage, and Conservation:
Farming Issues in the European Union
Pamela J. Stewart and Andrew Strathern

Minorities and Memories:
Survivals and Extinctions in Scotland and Western Europe
Andrew Strathern and Pamela J. Stewart

Belonging:
The Social Dynamics of Fitting in as Experienced
by Hmong Refugees in Germany and Texas
Faith G. Nibbs

# BELONGING

## THE SOCIAL DYNAMICS OF FITTING IN AS EXPERIENCED BY HMONG REFUGEES IN GERMANY AND TEXAS

Faith G. Nibbs

Carolina Academic Press
Durham, North Carolina

Copyright © 2014
Faith G. Nibbs
All Rights Reserved

Library of Congress Cataloging-in-Publication Data

Nibbs, Faith G.
 Belonging : the social dynamics of fitting in as experienced by Hmong refugees in Germany and Texas / Faith G. Nibbs.
     pages cm. -- (European anthropology series)
 Includes bibliographical references and index.
 ISBN 978-1-61163-288-0 (alk. paper)
 1. Refugees--Laos--Social conditions. 2. Hmong (Asian people)--Cultural assimilation--Germany. 3. Hmong (Asian people)--Cultural assimilation--Texas. 4. Group identity. I. Title.

 HV640.5.H58N53 2014
 305.8959'72043--dc23

2014003201

CAROLINA ACADEMIC PRESS
700 Kent Street
Durham, North Carolina 27701
Telephone (919) 489-7486
Fax (919) 493-5668
www.cap-press.com

Printed in the United States of America

# Contents

| | |
|---|---|
| List of Figures | ix |
| Series Editors' Preface | |
| *Negotiating Life and Displacement: Refugees, Identities, and Emplacement* | |
| Andrew Strathern & Pamela J. Stewart | xi |
| Acknowledgments | xv |
| List of Abbreviations | xvii |
| Introduction | 3 |
|     Why Belonging? | 6 |
|     Refugees: Helpless Victims or Active Agents? | 10 |
|     Locality, Intersections and Scale | 12 |
|     Methods | 14 |
|     An Outline of Chapters | 17 |
| Chapter 1 · The Hmong: Pre-Resettlement History of Movement, Belonging, and Culture | 19 |
|     Early Historical Accounts | 20 |
|     Migration into Southeast Asia and Laos | 22 |
|     The Beginning of Refugeehood | 26 |
|     Liminality and the Thai Refugee Camps | 28 |
|         Registration | 30 |
|         Clearance | 31 |
|         Approved Entry | 32 |
|         Exit through Bangkok | 33 |
|     Hmong Concepts of Belonging | 34 |

Chapter 2 · Two Hmong Resettlement Communities:
The Context of Reception                                            43
    Gammertingen, Germany                                           44
    The Dallas/Fort Worth Metroplex                                 53

Chapter 3 · Policies, Politics, and National Belonging              61
    Background to U.S. Refugee Policy                               63
    Background to German Refugee Policy                             65
    From Nationals to Citizens                                      68
    Rights, Responsibilities, Belonging, and Location: A Complicated Rela-
        tionship                                                    75
    Reconciling Citizenship and Belonging                           85

Chapter 4 · Making Members: Institutional Constraints,
Agency, and Local Belonging                                         89
    Sponsorship                                                     94
    Local Discourses and Public Assistance                         106
    Ingenuity and Agency                                           122

Chapter 5 · Religious Institutions: Intervening Mechanisms
of Belonging                                                       125
    Hmong Traditional Religion                                     126
    Gammertingen and Religious Member-Making                       128
    DFW and Religious Member-Making                                136
    Flexibility and Improvisations                                 140
    Localized Identity in Expressions of Faith                     146
    Making It or Being Made?                                       149

Chapter 6 · Growing Pains: Negotiating Co-Ethnic Belonging         153
    Gammertingen                                                   155
    Dallas/Fort Worth                                              168
    A Doubleness of Similarity                                     177

Chapter 7 · Mapping Hmong Networks: Diasporic Belonging            179
    The Hmong Diaspora                                             182
    Political Activism in the Diaspora                             183
    Media Technology                                               190
        Video                                                      191

|   |   |
|---|---|
| Satellite Television | 196 |
| Cyberspace | 197 |
| Celebration, Ritual, and Festival Performances | 204 |
| Wedding Ceremonies | 205 |
| Funeral Rituals | 209 |
| New Year's Celebrations | 212 |
| Being Hmong: An Ongoing Formation | 214 |
| **Chapter 8 · Implications: Belonging, Place, and Scale** | 219 |
| **Appendix** | 225 |
| **References** | 227 |
| **Index** | 247 |

# List of Figures

| | | |
|---|---|---|
| Figure 1.1 | Map of Hmong Camps | 29 |
| Figure 1.2 | Camp "Mug Shots" | 30 |
| Figure 1.3 | Traditional Hmong Ball Toss | 39 |
| Figure 2.1 | Map of Gammertingen | 45 |
| Figure 2.2 | Ethnic Composition, Gammertingen 1980 | 48 |
| Figure 2.3 | Gammertingen Village | 51 |
| Figure 2.5 | Initial German-Hmong Refugees | 52 |
| Figure 2.4 | Refugee Dormitory | 52 |
| Figure 2.6 | Map of DFW | 53 |
| Figure 2.7 | Map of DFW Townships | 54 |
| Figure 2.8 | Ethnic Composition Dallas/Fort Worth Area 1980 | 55 |
| Figure 3.1 | Self-Described Hmong Identity | 81 |
| Figure 4.1 | Evening Walks with Germans | 104 |
| Figure 4.2 | Dinner with Sponsors | 105 |
| Figure 4.3 | Hmong Homes in Gammertingen | 111 |
| Figure 5.1 | Evangelisch Hmong Celebration | 132 |
| Figure 5.2 | Membership Service at Evangelisch Church | 133 |
| Figure 5.3 | Pa Ndau Hanging in Evangelisch Church | 134 |
| Figure 5.4 | German Hmong House Church | 136 |
| Figure 5.5 | Hmong Cultural Church Items | 148 |
| Figure 7.1 | Hmong Videos for Sale at a Sport Festival Event | 213 |

SERIES EDITORS' PREFACE

# NEGOTIATING LIFE AND DISPLACEMENT: REFUGEES, IDENTITIES, AND EMPLACEMENT

*Andrew Strathern & Pamela J. Stewart*\*

Refugees, in one sense and another, are a salient part of the global flow of persons today. They are a very special part of that flow for at least two reasons. First, they are displaced from their homes and do not, in principle, have access to return there. Second, they have to seek a special status in the places they migrate to, one that marks them out as marginal persons, particularly

---

\* Prof. A.J. Strathern and Dr. P.J. Stewart are a husband and wife research team in the Department of Anthropology, University of Pittsburgh, and were the 2012 DeCarle Distinguished Lecturers at the University of Otago, Dunedin, New Zealand. They are also Research Associates in the Research Institute of Irish and Scottish Studies, University of Aberdeen, Scotland, and have been Visiting Research Fellows at the Institute of Ethnology, Academia Sinica, Taipei, Taiwan during parts of every year from 2002–2013. Their long-term, diverse, and creative research work has been published in over 45 books and over 200 influential articles on their research conducted throughout the Pacific, Asia (mainly Taiwan), and Europe (primarily Scotland and Ireland, also on the European Union). Their most recent co-authored books include *Witchcraft, Sorcery, Rumors, and Gossip* (Cambridge University Press, 2004); and *Self and Group: Kinship in Action* (Prentice Hall, 2011). Their recent co-edited books include *Exchange and Sacrifice* (Carolina Academic Press, 2008), *Religious and Ritual Change: Cosmologies and Histories* (Carolina Academic Press, 2009) and *Ritual* (London: Ashgate Publishing, 2010). They have broad interests which embrace and engage with global issues, utilizing their cross-cultural linguistic skills, a powerful comparative and interdisciplinary approach, and a uniquely engaged scholarly gaze. Their current research and writing is on the topics of Political Peace-making and the new arena that they are developing on Global Disaster Anthropology Studies. Their webpages are: (http://www.pitt.edu/~strather/sandspublicat.htm), (http://www.pitt.edu/~strather/), and (http://www.StewartStrathern.pitt.edu/).

dependent on those who take them in. Do refugees in fact find refuge? And how do they recreate their lives?

One concept that we have deployed in this rich arena of studies is that of transplacement (Strathern and Stewart 2006; Stewart and Strathern 2005, 2007). What we label as migration entails not just a movement of people through space, but their movement from one place to another, in search of work, money, freedom, community or whatever aims they may have for their future. There is also a dimension of time, with the idea that the migrant is moving from a past which they seek to leave behind towards a future that they are seeking to find or make for themselves. Since such a future can be made only by recreating their emplacement in the world and since they are always leaving a specific place, the ritual of migration, like a classic rite of passage, has a tripartite structure, from emplacement to displacement to re-emplacement. This whole process we call transplacement. It is full of contingencies, hazards, sometimes failures, and compromises, and varies with the conditions of placement and the determination and resources of the migrants.

Such a model of transplacement lends itself well to a comparative study such as Dr. Nibbs has carried out in the present volume. The novelty and strength of her contribution is that she has studied Laotian Hmong refugee resettlement communities in two very different places: Gammertingen in Germany and Dallas/Fort Worth in the USA. She focuses on the migrant refugees' own senses of belonging in their places of resettlement. With this focus, she also pays attention to the agency of people because the sense of belonging is not something given or passively accepted but has to be actively constructed by the settlers themselves, in dialectic with state structures and local cultural practices. Scaling is important here, because people exercise agency within, and are constrained by, different scales of relationships depending on the contexts of interaction. At what scales, for example, is belonging most crucially developed? Language capacities also make a big difference. Nibbs found that it was important for her work to marshal a lexicon of some 20 key words through which immigrants could express their feelings of belonging, either in a German village or in the Texas, USA context. She realized, too, that religion was a factor in determining how the refugees achieve belonging, and that they had to learn to exercise flexibility in adapting their own indigenous religious ideas to Christian cultural modalities. Finally, the politics of power and placement play a big role. Scattering Hmong in pockets separated from one another with varying access to resources works to negate Hmong indigenous understanding of locality and power, because they are not on their own land. Nevertheless, the refugees in Gammertingen were able to use aspects of their own material culture to integrate themselves in with the local church there, by giving a large piece of embroidered fabric showing Hmong history and value orientations as a present to their local pastor, who then hung the cloth in the church. Conflicts remained, in both localities, on the questions of veneration for ancestors and the healing roles of shamanic specialists.

In nuanced context after context Dr. Nibbs explores the cross-currents of influence that enhance or constrain the trends of belonging available to the refugees. Because one set are based in a European village and the other in a U.S. city (Dallas/Fort Worth), macro-differences of history and culture between the receiving populations entail continuous thoughtful exposition on the author's part. In terms of the study's theoretical impact, the discussion of scaling stands out, but it does so only because it is a product of extensive and intensive fine-grained local ethnography. In the theoretical terms that we ourselves have used here, transplacement seen as a process of initiation is gradually turned by a myriad of practical, material actions into forms of embodied emplacement. Dr. Nibbs' study of this process which she calls "belonging" will place it in the forefront of scholarship on resettlement and re-scaling of relationships, and the many poignant aspects of her account make it comparable to a classic work, Anne Sigfrid Grönseth's monograph *Lost Selves and Lonely Persons* (2010).

# References

Stewart, Pamela J. and Andrew Strathern. 2005. Body and Mind on the Move: Emplacement, Displacement, and Trans-Placement in Highlands Papua New Guinea. *Asia-Pacific Forum* (Centre for Asia-Pacific Area Studies, Academia Sinica, Taipei, Taiwan) No. 27 (March): 205–217. Available *online* at http://www.rchss.sinica.edu.tw/capas/publication/newsletter/N27/2704_03.pdf.

Stewart, Pamela J. And Andrew Strathern (2007), *Transplacements and Indigenous 'Cosmopolitanism' among Taiwan's Indigenous Population*. For the session 'Landscape Interrupted: Reflections on Experiences of Place and Displacement'. 2007 American Anthropological Association annual meeting, December.

Strathern, Andrew and Pamela J. Stewart. 2006. Foreword to Collection (JRS 20.2, 2006). Ritual: Transplacements and Explanations. *Journal of Ritual Studies* 20(2): i–v.

Gronseth, Anne Sigfrid. 2010. *Lost Selves and Lonely Persons*. Durham, N.C.: Carolina Academic Press.

# Acknowledgments

I would first and foremost like to thank the many people who were gracious and generous enough to share their stories and lives with me during my fieldwork and in shaping this project. In the Dallas/Fort Worth area I received warm help and encouragement from the Hmong community; without their willingness to share, this research would not have been possible. Thoa Phia Xaykao, Executive Director of the Hmong American Planning and Development Center, especially, provided me with an enormous amount of information and entrance into the Hmong community at large. My sincere gratitude also to the entire Gammertingen Hmong community who made my intrusion in their lives seem like a welcome inclusion, especially the Lo family, who took my family in as their own. I am deeply thankful to Chue Lo, for her research assistance in Gammertingen, continued friendship, and for paving the path to higher education for other German-Hmong as she is the first in that country to pursue a university degree. I am especially excited that she has chosen to study anthropology. In Gammertingen, Germany, the former mayor, Erwin Hirschle, provided me with an enormous amount of information about the Hmong's resettlement process, to which I will be forever grateful.

A special thanks to the National Science Foundation for their generous sponsorship of this research under grant BCS 0849055, and Hunter and Stephanie Hunt for their support of this work. I would like to thank Nina Glick Schiller for her guidance and support of this research, particularly in regards to laying the groundwork for the exploration of scale, and to Chia Youyee Vang for her guidance on understanding the history of the Hmong. I owe the deepest debt of gratitude to my mentor and friend, Caroline Brettell at the Department of Anthropology at Southern Methodist University in Dallas, Texas, for her unending support and advice in all stages of this project from its inception, through the fieldwork, and in the writing and editing phases. Her wealth of knowledge on migration and her cheerful willingness to impart it serve as an inspiration on how to mentor young scholars and will never be forgotten. I am also grateful for Alexander Betts and Anne Sigfrid Gronseth for their thoughtful reviews, and the support of Carolina Academic Press and Series Editors Pamela and Andrew Strathern for their interest in this project and all their assistance, advice and encouragement in moving this book to press. And, finally to my parents, my husband David, and my sons Jonathan and David Jr., for their support and encouragement all along the way, and who, without even reading a word of this manuscript, constantly assured me that, to them, I would always be "the best writer in the world."

# LIST OF ABBREVIATIONS

| | |
|---|---|
| AFDC | Aid to Families to Dependent Children |
| DFW | the Dallas/Fort Worth Metroplex |
| ESL | English as a Second Language |
| GSL | German as a Second Language |
| ICE | Immigration and Customs Enforcement |
| INS | Immigration and Naturalization Service |
| IRC | International Rescue Committee |
| MAA | Mutual Assistance Agency |
| MAPDC | Hmong-American Planning and Develop Corporation |
| NGO | Non-Governmental Organization |
| ORR | Office of Refugee Resettlement |
| SES | Social Economic Service |
| SPD | Social Democratic Party of Germany |
| SPSS | Statistical Package for the Social Sciences |
| UNHCR | United Nations High Commissioner for Refugees |
| VOLAG | Voluntary Resettlement Agency |

# BELONGING

# Introduction

*Today began like so many before for Lu X., Kang Y., and their families. They didn't know each other, but could have as they were from the same general forested area in the high elevations of Laos and lived similar lives steeped in the colorful traditions that had been passed down to their clans for centuries as minority swidden farmers. They were Hmong. Waking that morning in their separate make-shift assigned sleeping births in the infamous overcrowded shelters of the Thai Ban Vinai refugee camp, Lu X., in Row 12, House 14, and Kang Y., in Row 4, House 9, had learned to tolerate the poor conditions, trusting that one day their applications for resettlement in another country would be approved. Today was the day for both of them.*

*Like a giant net tossed out by a fisherman into the sea, the UNHCR scattered among the crowds of people hundreds of pieces of paper with lists of names on them. Lu X. and Kang Y., who couldn't read, were told their names were on the list. Then like fish caught in the net, they and their families were separated from the throngs of other Hmong in the refugee camp and put on busses that would sort them into separate destinations in the West. Kang Y. and his family would fly to Southern Germany, Lu X. and his family to the Southern United States. While bound for separate destinations, they shared a fear of the unknown ahead of them: unknown people, faces, customs, climate, food, and institutions. As they rested their foreheads against the windowpanes of their separate buses, they contemplated what would be expected of them in their new lands. What tradeoffs would they be making for their refuge? Would they ever connect with their clan members again? As individuals in this move, one that is yet another in a long history of migration and displacement for the Hmong people, they also wondered who now would have the power to decide if they could belong, and to what?*

\* \* \*

The narrative of refugees Lu X. and Kang Y. alludes to the uncertainties that are experienced in the process of reconstructing uprooted lives, and speaks to the ways in which refugees conceptualize belonging, fitting in, or becoming members of the new societies where they have been resettled. It also raises a number of questions about the nature of belonging: its location, who can know it, what it looks like, when it has happened, and how it could be manipulated. These questions are particularly noteworthy because according to the United Nations (UNHCR 2012), there were 43.3 million displaced people worldwide in 2011, most of whom remain in camps or are internally resettled, but 128,000 of whom were resettled in the West as refugees. With a million and a half more projected to be resettled in Western societies over the next ten years, large receiving countries such as those in North America, Europe, and Australia struggle to effectively include them, setting for themselves bench marks for what successful integration, belonging, or social inclusion should look like.

For the purposes of this book, identity is taken to mean who a person is, or a self-representation of someone's interests, relationships, social activities, et cetera, whereas belonging is the state where that self-representation is perceived to fit. Sometimes the one leads seamlessly to the other, but more often the two intersect in more disruptive ways; either aspects of one's self-representation are sacrificed in order to belong, or belonging is sacrificed in order to preserve aspects of self-representation. Because of the interdependence of identity to belonging, the two of them are often discussed in tandem throughout this book.

Scholarship on identity has moved past thinking of this concept as a fixed point in people's lives to one that resides between a number of moving and intersecting discourses (Hall 1992), whereas belonging in migration studies, is still understood as an one-dimensional phenomenon that is measured by certain social indicators of perceived togetherness. Thus, much of the scholarly work on the construction of belonging has focused on a singular movement of the immigrant from being deterritorialized to becoming reterritorialized, or being detached from a host community to becoming attached (see Probyn 1996; Fortier 2000; Mandel 2008; Reed-Danahay & Brettell 2008; Getrich 2008; Crul & Schneider 2010). However, immigrant decision-making in the course of resettlement is never one-dimensional. In the same way that James Clifford (1988:344) challenged us to rethink identity "not as a boundary to be maintained but as a nexus of relations and transactions actively engaging a subject," this book challenges us to rethink immigrant belonging as influenced by the intersection of multiple factors at different scales in different contexts that go beyond the immigrant/host dichotomy. Refugees, in particular, are often engaged in multi-sited lives with active diasporic social networks that span numerous countries and cities at the same time. Through this book, I propose a framework for reconceptualizing belonging as a multifaceted phenomenon that overlaps, intersects, and often conflicts with other social arenas where perceived togetherness is also desired, arguing that a more thorough understanding of its processes requires unpacking the social dynamics of fitting in as they are simultaneously represented in immigrant experiences across different scales—local, regional, national and global. By doing so, it exposes ways that refugees can construct a sense of belonging that do not correspond to either local or national policies nor reflect notions of national identities.

Scholars have called for more consideration of relative positioning in migration research (Schiller & Caglar 2011). Unpacking the process of *belonging* is one area that can benefit from this approach. This book is a comparative case study of Hmong refugee resettlement in Texas and Germany that examines their experiences in processes of belonging in a multilevel environment. Through its pages, I hope to advance our thinking regarding how different kinds of belonging at multiple social scales are produced and intersect, and the effect these processes might have on integrative efforts and migrant identity. When I began thinking about this process, I gave some consideration to the various social arenas at play. Who were the stakeholders involved? How does each of them perceive togetherness and with what effect to the other? How do they negotiate the often intersecting and complex relationships that accompany belonging? And, what can we learn about the process of how refugees restructure and reposition themselves in the course of upheaval by examining belonging at different scales? These are the questions that guided this work. I address them through a cross-continental comparative case study of two little-known Hmong refugee communities that originated from the same Lao-Hmong refugee group but resettled in communities with markedly different approaches to welcoming them—one that draws more on the assistance of Non-Governmental Agencies (NGOs) and that encourages a rapid transition to autonomy and independence (Texas, United States) and the other involving more active state processes (Gammertingen, Germany). These two countries have both been labeled "magnet societies" attracting large numbers of immigrants and refugees. As such, comparisons of processes of immigration settlement and immigrant incorporation between the two are becoming increasingly valuable, especially in relation to a broader understanding of immigration in advanced industrial societies (Heisler 2007).

Heisler argues that the institutional differences between the United States and Germany offer different opportunities and constraints for immigrants whose subsequent levels of social interaction with other ethnic minorities and within the wider society need to be more systematically explored (19). Recent multisited research on diasporic communities has started to investigate concepts of incorporation in multiple locations—for example, between refugees in the United States and Canada (Bloemraad 2006), Salvadorans in Miami and Washington, D.C. and Toronto (Landolt 2001), Kurdish refugees in Britain and Finland (Ostergaard-Nielson 2001), and Nicaraguan transnational migrants in

Zurich and Miami (Wimmer 1998). Other comparative works tie issues of integration and reception with place and identity (see Daniel & Knudsen 1985; Delanty et al., 2008; Fuglerud 1999; and Grnseth 2010). This body of work suggests differences in the way in which refugees are received, and the divergent structural forces and conditions provided by different locations that shape the character of their transnational practices including how they utilize their social networks. Others have advocated for more place-based comparisons, suggesting that a locality analysis can assess multiple ways that migrants negotiate belonging and restructure place in different contexts (Karanovic 2011; Glick Schiller 2010). This book will reminds us that, while immigrants experience relationships at different scales, they are also resettled into localities of scale. Both communities of Hmong in this study were resettled into localities nested in the social hierarchies of two different nation-states: one country resettled them in a village, and the other in a city. Thus, while this study focuses on belongings of scale, another important contribution it makes is its vital insights into the structural constraints and opportunities that cause different obstacles and opportunities for refugees placed in various communities of scale. It is hoped that this examination will play a role in widening public debate about the social dimensions of belonging and be of value not only to migration scholars, but the many North America, European, and Australian social partners, nongovernmental and grass-root resettlement organizations, and policy makers with a vested interest in creating flexible and creative incorporation programs for extremely diverse populations.

Throughout the book, I will refer to the Hmong who resettled in these two localities as an "ethnic community" and "co-ethnics." I do not do so in any attempt to construct or impose a national or shared cultural boundary on them, or because I presuppose they share the same ancestry, or history. They do not. I use this descriptor because it is their perception of their own identity. Early in this book I will introduce the process of network building and leadership that has led to this collective identification and how and when the Hmong began to view themselves in this way. The global process of how this sensibility spread throughout the Hmong diaspora and its key implications for understanding the multidimensions of belonging will be discussed in greater detail throughout the chapters.

## Why Belonging?

At the close of the twentieth century, Wahlbeck (1999) called for more adequate theories and more clearly defined concepts to describe the resettlement experiences of refugees.[1] The first conceptions of this process were colonial and thought of in terms of Anglo-conformity or "the expectation that immigrant groups should swallow intact the existing Anglo-American culture while simultaneously disgorging their own" (Alba & Nee 2003:17). This sentiment was later articulated in the term, *assimilation,* which comes from the Latin word *assimilates,* meaning "absorbed, or incorporated." First used by the Chicago School of Sociology in 1921 as a paradigm for understanding immigration (Park 1921), assimilation was defined as "a process of interpenetration and fusion in which persons and groups acquire the memories, sentiments, and attitudes of other persons and groups, and, by sharing their experience and history, are incorporated with them in a common cultural life." With the publication of *Beyond the Melting Pot* (Glazer & Moynihan 1963), sociologists began repudiating the concept of assimilation, realizing that U.S. ethnic groups persisted across generations. When anthropologists began looking at immigration in conjunction with the growth of peasant and urban studies (Mayer 1961; Plotnicov 1967; Mangin 1970), they, too, were uncomfortable with the hegemonic process this term represented and wanted to convey a greater degree of tolerance and respect for ethnocultural differences than the notion of assimilation implied. Moreover, assimilation theories failed to account for the "second" and "third" generation of immigrants who still maintained their cultural characteristics. Anthropologists therefore began to conceptualize the processes of migration from the standpoint of cultural pluralism.

In the pre-desegregated United States, scholars began referring to the inclusion and exclusion of migrants through models of *integration.* While the term *integration* has been used to cover a broad range of policies and ideologies, it generally refers to the same one-way "process in which a minority group adopts the values and patterns of behavior of a majority group" as the term *assimilation* implies (Jary & Jary 1991:31). In this sense, integration is understood as more assimilationist in nature. This is the case when it is associated not with the maintenance of group uniqueness, as Jenkins (1988) suggests, but with its dissolution, "as when integration is measured by the degree of normative consensus and intermarriage with the indigenous population" (Vermeulen & Pennix 2000:3). The use of this concept began to wane in the United States as it was associated with another process—the dismantling of the Jim Crow system that segregated and isolated African Americans in the post-Civil War era. That began to be challenged in the period after World War II, culminating

---

1. As refugee theory is broadly incorporated into the immigration literature, the term *refugee* and *immigrant* appear interchangeably throughout this section.

in the Civil Rights Act of 1964. In the early 1980s, scholars in the United States moved toward a discourse that was perceived as less prejudiced and more in favor of access and equity, settling on the term *incorporation*, which was defined as "a process through which a social unit is included in a larger unit as an integral part of it" (Isajiw & Perera 1997:82; see also Portes & Rumbaut 1996, Glick Schiller et al., 2006).

Incorporation is occasionally used in the European context but it means something altogether different. For instance, in German scholarship it connotes an aggressive one-way process more akin to "ultra-assimilation" (Glick Schiller et al., 2006). There are structures, including the state, that work to either integrate or incorporate migrants into the body of the state and society. As such, governments in both North America and Europe often use the terms assimilate, integration, inclusion, adaptation, insertion, or incorporation, interchangeably as "politically correct words to convey an agenda meant to produce a unitary society" (Lucassen 2005). In all cases, the words are generally embedded in some sort of hegemonic narrative of race and nation where the "Other" enters the dominant domains of state life. Despite the confusion and discomfort, some continue to see current migration scholarship to be "shaped not only by these past approaches, but also by the current historical conjuncture in which the leaders of migrant-receiving states are emotively legitimating national discourses and narratives" (Glick Schiller 2010:30–31).

The way that the concepts of integration, assimilation, and incorporation are broadly applied, and seem to have multiple meanings in different national contexts, make them all problematic as an analytical framework for international comparative research. For this reason, cross-national attempts at comparing forms of immigrant integration are usually limited to various quantifiable domains where "successful outcomes" such as employment numbers (Bradley 2004), income levels (Yuval-Davis 2004), school results (Boyd 2002), housing patterns (Balakrishnan & Hou 1999), and numbers of intermarriages (Liang & Ito 1999; Coleman 2004) can be measured. While these models may favor governments that want statistical data to evaluate desired outcomes of their policies, such models present a "tidier than life" account of social reality, and ignore questions of "whether, when and how far the actor identifies with those who share the same categorical status" (Wallman 1986:223–224); that is, whether or not they perceive success or failure along the same nodes by which they are being measured. Moreover, this raises the question of what and who precisely defines success. Simply including immigrant or refugee voices to get at these questions becomes problematic. Concepts like integration, assimilation, or incorporation hold little meaning to displaced peoples who, in my experience, are altogether bewildered by them and often have no equivalent translation in their native languages.

Integration or incorporation, when conceived as social and cultural processes, need to consider the hard to quantify and harder to obtain data that stems from the lived experiences of the immigrant or refugee, something difficult to do when conceived with such top down terminology. Such research would require bottom up language that gives voice to considerations of the newcomer, and whether or not they think they belong, fit in, or have become full members in a particular society; or how important these factors are, if at all, to their own understanding of group membership. Because of the hegemonic and historical baggage associated with concepts such as integration, assimilation, and other related terms, there is a need for an analytical concept that not only accords more agency to the immigrant or refugee newcomer, but also gives equal weight to interactions within a variety of social fields encompassing aid workers, local nationals, local co-ethnics, dispersed kin, and the broader diaspora. Without such a concept, we are left, as Heisler notes, with "no analytic thread" or "attempt to develop new hypotheses that contribute to theory" (2007:2), and on a more applied level, policy makers and resettlement programs looking to handle the complex needs of incoming refugees are left without important pieces of the puzzle that aid in cultural sensitivity.

This is why, in this book, I focus the process by which refugees reestablish their lives in a new context in terms of constructs of *belonging,* and propose this as a cross-national framework for thinking about perceived togetherness. This term has a long history in both political and social theory and has recently begun to resurface in discussions of migration (Lovell 1998; Fortier 2000; Mandel 2008; Reed-Danahay and Brettell 2008; Delanty et al., 2008). It has been suggested that a framework of belonging allows "for an understanding of how transient, sometimes unclear relationships can contribute to an individual's position vis-à-vis a collective identity" (Jones & Krzyżanowski 2008:41). The concept is often included in discussions around identity, allowing for "a range of attachments, subjective feelings, preferences and memberships" outside of the not-so-fixed boundaries of nation-state (42). I find this term useful, particularly as it pertains to refugees, because it draws attention to emic understandings of how those who are displaced conceptualize being "in the right place," "members," or "fitting in" to the various social fields within which they must now act and with the diversity of people with whom they must now interact. In other words, belonging can account for associative feelings with several collective identities in several different social fields at the same time, thus, avoiding the one-way connotation of integration, assimilation, and sometimes even incorporation. Jones and Krzyżanowski's theory of belonging posits that "identities are constructed both internally—by us through our self-representation and alignment with others—and externally—by the power of "others," such as institutional gatekeepers, who set threshold criteria for entry to groups either through membership in a formal sense" or "symbolically" (2006:44–45). From this vantage point we can assess whether or not programs are "successful," not in terms of making one group like the other—as assimilation suggests—but in terms of assessing whether or not the newcomer feels a part of the other as a direct result of the programs, or for other reasons altogether. The concept of belonging also allows room for researchers to account for how a group negotiates various memberships simultaneously—such as with local nationals and their own co-ethnics—and also at multiple scales—local, national, and global. The concept of belonging moves us beyond the examination of normative models of integration to explore the refugee's orientation to connecting in specific contexts and points in time. Informed by this vantage point, the research on which this book is based sought to offer insights into where perceptions of membership derive from, how they are codified in the process or resettlement, and who has the power to define who can belong, and under what conditions.

# Refugees: Helpless Victims or Active Agents?

Academic debates on the category of refugees and how they are to be distinguished from other migrants are longstanding and ongoing (See Malkki 1995; Adelman & McGrath 2007; Cohen 2007; DeWind 2007; Hathaway 2007). One of the elements used in defining them is the involuntary character of their movement, prompted by "a well-founded fear of being persecuted for reasons of race, religion, nationality, membership of a particular social group or political opinion, is outside the country of his nationality" (UNHCR 1968). This is most often coupled with characterizations of traumatized victimhood. Maja Korac suggests that the "longstanding, highly politicized, and often heated debate on asylum rights in many parts of the world revolving around the issue of 'bogus' versus 'genuine' refugees seems to generate further the need to essentialize refugees and represent them as 'ultimate victims,' hence, deserving international (state) protection" (2009:7). Consequently, the multiple levels of social disruption experienced by those forcibly displaced bring about the perception that refugees are perpetual victims who will live in a permanent sense of disempowerment, or victims with pathologies, such as PSTD that need interventions and treatment to become "normal."

However, uncertainty and loss do not necessarily connote an absence of agency. Malkki (1995) was one of the first among migration scholars to point out that the process of resettlement involves both disempowering and empowering experiences, noting that third-country resettlement, while traumatic, can open up new social spaces and opportunities for refugees, spaces that in specific circumstances and contexts can be experienced as freedom from sociocultural norms that had previously constrained them. While the process of refugeehood sidelines a refugee's own skills, ambitions, and entrepreneurship, Alexander Betts (2012:9) notes that it can also create new opportunities for refugee innovation, entry into new markets, and space to create unique adaptive and transformative strategies toward less dependent livelihoods (see also Ramsden & Ridge 2013; Marfleet 2013; Deluca & Rhoades 2009; Grabska 2006). For example, gender roles may be reshaped (Berghahn 1995; Franz 2003; Ui 1991), caste systems abandoned, and new understandings of biomedicine adopted that allow for cures to a host of infectious diseases previously thought incurable.

Agency and empowerment are generally recognized as a response to both institutionalized (Foucault 1978) and everyday (Scott 1985; Scott & Kerkvliet 1986) forms of power, and there has been much debate over what constitute forms of agency and self-will. As Ortner explains:

> Michael Adas, for example, constructs a typology of forms of everyday resistance, the better to help us place what we are seeing (1986). Brian Fegan (1986) concentrates on the question of intention: if a relatively conscious intention to resist is not present, the acts not one of resistance. Still others (Stoler 1986; Cooper 1992) suggest that the category itself is not very helpful and that the important thing is to attend to a variety of transformative processes, in which things do get changed, regardless of the intentions of the actors or the presence of very mixed intentions (1995:175).

While I acknowledge that those conversations exist, the interest of this book is less in deciding what constitutes self-will, then in understanding how different forms of resistance are embedded in the psychological and socio-political complexity of the refugee experience and their individual realities. In this way I find agency a useful category to highlight the presence and play of power in relationships that exist within those realities. This book begins from the assumption that those realities are complex "bricolages" that Ortner describes as "borrowed from or imposed by others ... woven together through the logic of a groups' own locally and historically evolved" (1995:174). For the refugee, that means subjectivities evolved from a combination of subordinations imposed by those with different interests—such as French colonists against the Southeast Asian colonized; the refugee against its U.S./German host country; resettled Hmong against those left behind; insider against outsider. This call to rethink the refugee experience by acknowledging it as a process entailing both disempowering and empowering experiences is to make an analytical distinction, which implies simultaneous experiences of victimization and practices of overcoming it. Throughout this book, the experiences of refugee resettlement are seen as a dialectic relationship between agency and victimization, between "making it" and "being made," and of both structure and agency.

## Locality, Intersections and Scale

Bourdieu and Wacquant (2000) have cautioned that migration cannot be fully understood apart from its historical and international relations, both material and symbolic, urging scholars to begin the process with an understanding of the historical and structural conditions of the sending communities. Refugees, for example, often negotiate relationships between and among social spaces that include a world of resettlement sites and temporary camps. While not all immigrants or refugees identify or participate in these diasporic networks, some groups, such as the Hmong, organize themselves around important networks of communication and shared ethnic identity and experiences of oppression (Rivera-Salgado 1999). The diasporic experience of these refugees has been defined as living in a global community, either real or imagined, where their social networks have been established outside of their home country due to expulsion (Safran 1991; Sheffer 1996; Clifford 1997). In many cases, the traditional way the nation-state and its citizens are understood cannot be easily transferred onto the transnational social organization that these groups display. Cohen argues that refugees represent a challenge to the exclusivist claims of modern nation-states. It may be that these forms of social organization "have pre-dated the nation-state, lived within it and now may, in significant respects, transcend and succeed it" (1995:16). For this reason, Wimmer and Glick Schiller (2002) have heavily critiqued the presupposing of nation-states as the natural units of social life or analysis, something they call methodological nationalism. They argue that this approach to migration "confines discussions of social processes within national boundaries" (Glick Schiller & Caglar 2011:9), and therefore, does not effectively allow us to get at the "sociospatial nodes within transnational fields of power" (37).

Sociologist Neil Long (1992:14) suggests that immigrant strategies for "making it" are shaped by even "larger frames of meaning and action" formed through the links between the "small" worlds of actors, and large-scale "global" structures. The newcomer's social position, for example, could be simultaneously influenced by the local dynamics of the resettlement site and intersections with resettlement policies, those who implement resettlement policies, co-ethnics in the broader diaspora who have been resettled in countries of different economic positions, and pre-settlement worldviews that include a stateless existence. Geographer Becky Mansfield (2005) suggests that one way to explore these intersecting nodes is with a concept of *scale*. Scale first emerged in the 1990s when geopolitical economists noted that regional, national, and transnational units of modern capitalism were connected to local processes, a phenomenon Swyngedouw (1997) referred to as "glocalization." Glick Schiller and Caglar adopted a scalar approach to migration studies, redefining it as "the ordering of sociospatial units within multiple hierarchies of power" (2011:44). Scale differs from size in that the social practices that take place within its spaces are connected with a conception of power emanating from the global opportunities within each level. They have proposed applying a scale-attuned approach to understanding the "nexus between localities and migration," suggesting it will help us understand the "relationship of specific places to migrant experiences and identity and the way the different positioning of locality contributes to variations in migrant experience" (2011:44). An important contribution of their work is in its attention to how the local variations between cities of reception and their ensuing policies, and broader positions in the global economy affect immigrant belonging. They argue that new comparative perspectives that build on the intersection of migration studies and the scholarship of scale are needed to understand the significance of the different scaled localities that migrants are increasingly settled in.

By theorizing resettlement locations through a scale-attuned approach, it becomes easy to imagine how refugees dispersed from a single location, and resettled among a host of countries with vastly different histories, resources, and global positioning, might, in the process of resettlement, become engaged in a rescaling of the social and economic hierarchies of their pre-resettlement world. This book continues, as Glick Schiller and Caglar would put it, to "theorize locally" by acknowledging that the process of integrating immigrants locally is critically shaped by layers of hierarchical regional, national, and global relationships passing through that locality (2). This approach allows us to consider how the process of refugee belonging is entangled in multiple social arenas that are negotiated directly with regional or globally connected institutions. Does the fact that some Hmong have settled in a large metropolitan areas while others have settled in a more remote village make a difference in how they construct their sense of belonging? In how they interact with local institutions and national institutions? In how they engage the diasporic community? These questions will guide this ethnography in understanding the process of how refugee groups renegotiate those local positions for advantage, or reach beyond local networks outside to those in other arenas as a means of ethnic survival—a process some theorists call "jumping scale" (Glick Schiller & Caglar 2011:4; see also Swyngedouw 1992; Smith 2003). A critical argument of this book is that by rethinking refugee experiences in more agentic terms of belonging, and including a concept of scale in the analysis, we have the potential to generate new perspectives on the growing body of literature concerned with rethinking the spatialities and forms of membership experienced in the migration process.

## Methods

I first came to be involved with the Hmong population in Texas during the 1995 resettlement of Hmong refugees from the Wat Tham Krabok camp in Thailand. Though living in Texas at the time, I was not native to it and had little support system in this area of the United States. A New Englander at heart, I have found the State's particular character difficult at times to interpret and adjust to. Reading a newspaper article one day on the fifty Hmong families to be resettled from that camp in the Dallas/Ft. Worth area, I took pause. From my own alienated position, I wondered how this population would fare. I began a short-term research project following some of these arrivals. In its course I found something more fascinating—that the previously resettled Hmong who were living in Texas since the early 1980s had taken on a wonderfully Texan/Hmong hybrid identity distinctively different from forms of Hmongness identified in the larger U.S. Hmong resettlements. Moreover, these Hmong were socializing their newcomers into this subjectivity. This led to larger questions of how differences in place of resettlement can affect senses of agency in forming belonging and identity.

I had lived in Germany as a U.S. military wife for five years and had grown quite fond of the country, its language, and delicious breads. I thought of refugee resettlement in its quaint country villages as a completely different context in which to explore how to rethink specialties and forms of memberships experienced. There are, of course, differences between a U.S. urban area and a small German town as locales to study comparative processes of incorporation. However, I chose these areas because I believed their differences enhanced the research design of the project as they were fundamental to varying refugee resettlement policies of the U.S. and Germany. The U.S. resettles refugees in major urban immigrant gateways where myriad services, largely through volunteer agencies (VOLAGs), and employment opportunities are available. Germany, by contrast, typically resettles refugees in small towns were the local community is asked to actively participate in their integration. Recently, scholars of immigration (Gozdiak & Martin 2005; Brettell 2003; Singer et al. 2008, Massey 2008) have turned their attention not only to new areas of refugee and immigrant settlement, but also to understanding how the characteristics of different immigrant receiving areas affect newcomers. I was under the impression that the comparison of these two locations could add new material and insights to this discussion precisely because the scale of host context is fundamental to resettlement policy. At the same time, because of their differences, care was taken to develop reasonable reliable indicators for belonging that can be tested across the different localities. Further, it is important to emphasize that within these two distinct places the Hmong populations are of comparable size and with similar clan structure making them good populations on which to focus of the research. I was convinced that the comparison, while challenging, would be poised to make an important contribution to an understanding of processes of immigrant belonging.

An elder in the Texas Hmong community with whom I had established a trusted relationship sent the small Hmong community in southern Germany a letter telling them about my research and how I was a "trusted friend" of the Hmong. Even though the German Hmong did not know the Texas elder, out of respect for their clansman, they welcomed me into their lives. In exchange, I spent many hours working with the Hmong in both field sites, helping them sort through mail, fill out forms, cook and clean, and offering my services in any way I could. While I tried not to insert my Westernness, I was always aware that the American Hmong saw me as a privileged elite in a system that held power over them, and the German Hmong saw me as a curious stranger from a country that did not treat them so well during the Vietnam War. Because of those positionings, I took extra care to give them deference while understanding that whatever they would tell me would likely be filtered through that subjectivity. I used triangulation between the observed and the spoken to reconcile some of their filtered statements during the first few months. Yet, somewhere along the way, and I'm not sure when, those who I had seen as research subjects and informants became family and friends—they accepted me into their inner circles, ceremoniously dressing me in Hmong clothes and giving me a Hmong name. I am still both humbled and honored by their continued presence in my life.

Doing research in areas characterized by their different scale—village, city, and global diaspora—posed particular methodological challenges. First and foremost, it required long-term fieldwork among all of the three research populations at multiple sites, which I tackled in three consecutive stages: At various times between May 2006 and May 2010, in the DFW area, and in 2009 in Gammertingen, Germany. Interspersed were observations through modes of engagement between Hmong in what Lok Siu (2005) refers to as the "third space," or the diaspora. These "third space" events were the 4th of July Hmong international soccer festival in St. Paul, Minnesota, and Hmong New Year celebrations in Strasbourg, France, as well as weddings and funerals. At these events people spoke almost exclusively in Hmong. In Texas, all but the very eldest of Hmong spoke fluent English; however I traveled with a Hmong college student interpreter in case language nuances better expressed in Hmong were beyond my own bilingual limitations. In the German context, the Hmong spoke German as well as I. However, I traveled in the field as well as to third-space events with a Hmong college student as interpreter for the same reasons. I was also fortunate to witness many impromptu diasporic events that happened in Texas and Gammertingen when large numbers of Hmong from other countries had visited. I also overheard several international clan-wide conference phone calls, diasporic church events, and observed the use of social networking websites as places where the diaspora routinely came together. Finally, in 2010, I worked on the comparative analysis of the data collected from both field sites and re-interviewed some DFW and Gammertingen Hmong to compare unanticipated things that had been observed within the multiple contexts.

I reviewed and analyzed archival government documents on Southeast Asian refugee resettlement in both communities to get a thorough understanding of the integration policies and their implementation strategies in place during the resettlement years. These documents were used to establish a common framework that allowed for systematic comparison of how the different official dimensions of belonging were articulated at the two field sites—specifically, the legal circumstances of first entry, rules regarding acquisition and rights of citizenship, rules regarding family reunification, security of residence, labor market access, social security rights, and welfare benefits.

Once a framework was established, a controlled comparative amount of data was collected from each research population within the two field sites using: structured and semi-structured interviews, archival data research, a pile sort exercise, a media content analysis, focus groups, and ethnographic decision models. The decision models consisted of a series of questions that asked thirty-eight individual Hmong representing the various clans, gender and age sets (nineteen in each field site) a series of questions about their most recent behavior. The questions asked how and where they looked for a spouse, a job, a loan, and cultural materials or to whom they would go for parenting, marriage, legal, personal, or medical advice. Each answer was followed up by asking under what circumstances they would seek these services elsewhere (that is, outside of their immediate family, local ethnic group, diaspora, or host nationals). This was designed to determine at what scale they choose to operate, under what circumstances, and the way in which they think about scale.

After three months in each field site, I comprised a lexicon of twenty key words I heard repeatedly in conversations about refugee incorporation. This lexicon was drawn from conversations with local nationals, the Hmong, and those who had worked with them. From those words I comprised a pile sort exercise where participants were asked to rank in order the twenty words in terms of how salient they thought they were to "belonging" or "fitting in." This method was helpful in identifying the range of variation and areas of overlap in the concept of "fitting in" that is attached to belonging within and between groups of actors and field sites.

In addition to these more formal methods, ethnographic participant-observation was performed over the course of three years and was critical to providing some of the most essential and valuable data for this book. I ate dinner and shared afternoon tea in the homes of almost all the Hmong informants and became a regular at Hmong "third space" events such as weddings, birthdays, religious services, sporting events, Hmong New Years, and other local community gatherings such as backyard barbeques, baby showers, picnics and holiday parties. In Germany, I went grocery shopping with them, to the movies, on evening walks, and often on sightseeing and excursions to local historic attractions. As a resident of the village of Gammertingen, and because of the German curiosity about the nature of my visit and all things American, many villagers also befriended me. I was often invited to people's homes for afternoon tea or on sightseeing outings. I ran into them at village-wide events, festivals, and over the course of everyday life. While participating in community events, I was particularly sensitive to the relationship between all the independent research populations of this book to see how they interact with one another and affect processes of belonging at various social intersections. As such, these community-wide events, when attended by the Hmong, became important sites of observation to explore how behavior stays the same or is altered in relation to particular contexts. As fieldwork in the Dallas/Ft. Worth Metroplex required less footwork and more "car fieldwork," it also provided an experiential idea of some of the differences in the structures and face-to-face relationships faced by refugees resettled in communities of varying scale.

## An Outline of Chapters

To convey a sense of the process of belonging and identity making, I have developed composite narratives of the two fictitious families of Lu X. and Kang

Y. that will introduce each chapter. Although based on actual incidents, their stories are a blend of a number of individuals and experiences in each field site. I did this because it allowed me to introduce the chapters with a combination of narratives of many different individuals without telling all ten or fifteen stores to draw the same picture. Throughout the body of each chapter, I continue to indent text that is an actual quotation. The chapters of this ethnography are drawn from a year of fieldwork in each of two different sites of Hmong refugee resettlement. Chapter 1 offers a brief historical account of the Hmong's history of movement and their conceptions of belonging prior to Western resettlement, then Chapter 2 describes the two resettlement communities of Gammertingen, Germany, and the Dallas/Fort Worth Metroplex. Chapter 3 introduces belonging in the national arena, offering a brief but important description and analysis of the different refugee resettlement policies in Germany and the United States, and how the politics of national membership are reinterpreted and implemented in association with regional and localized ideas of belonging, as well as the refugee's pre-settlement experiences with belonging under statelessness. Chapter 4 moves to the local arena, unpacking how local nationals go about "making members" through their actions and local discourses that exemplify local identity. Attention is paid to the way refugees perceive that reception, and how they exert agency by jumping scale. Chapter 5 offers a look at the role religious institutions play as intervening structures of belonging and the flexibility and improvisations demonstrated in the refugee belief systems, while Chapter 6 focuses on intre-ethnic belonging, examining the growing pains of refugees who are resettled in areas with no particular prior relationship to each other apart from their shared ethnicity. Chapter 7 takes a look at diasporic belonging and the ways in which scatter-placement policies that dispersed the Hmong to areas with unequal access to resources and power have challenged this ethnic group's pre-resettlement understandings of belonging. The final chapter provides a summary of the book's arguments while considering both its theoretical and applied implications.

CHAPTER 1

# The Hmong: Pre-Resettlement History of Movement, Belonging, and Culture

*It was the freedom that came with the openness of the hills that Kang Y. and Lu X. liked most. It was a world without fences, where their backyard stretched as far as their children could run, and there were few roofs to box in their spirits or thoughts. They spent most of their time outdoors filling their lungs with the warm, moisture-dense Southeast Asian air that therapeutically hugged their insides. There were no calendars, clocks, watches, magistrates, mayors, state systems, or any such constricting devices in their lives. Relationships were the rice of life, and every ebb and flow in it accommodated that priority.*

*Every morning they traveled the hillsides at will to cut down the brush and farm a plot of land, burn it, and till the ashes in the ground. Afterwards they returned to their open village where they raised chickens, told stories, and sewed threads of tree bark into colorful clothing outside their bamboo homes. Although these small villages of 40 to 60 people were somewhat isolated from each other, Kang Y. and Lu X. would each find a way to connect to the others for purposes of harvest celebrations, marriage, funerals, or other spiritual events. Living this lifestyle for the past century might make it hard for Kang Y. and Lu X to imagine Hmong life any other way. But it wasn't. Every evening by the fire their parents would pass on to them the stories told by their parents—the folklore that reminds them that every aspect of their freestyle life that they so enjoyed was a cultural adaptation derived from their peoples' willingness to survive a long and arduous history of expulsion and migration.*

\* \* \*

When I first went to my field sites, I was less concerned with history or pre-resettlement cultural norms than their current manifestations. Nonetheless, the Hmong I met evoked their past daily as justification for almost everything they did in the present, including their local identity, sense of belonging, and diasporic connections. These experiences substantiate that constructs of belonging cannot be fully understood apart from the Hmong's early migratory history.[1] This chapter begins by introducing that story, and then moves from the general to the particular by tracing the path of those who became the participants of this study through the beginning of refugeehood with their exit to the West. As historically emic forms of membership and ideologies are critical to any exploration of post-settlement ideas of belonging, I end by outlining how the Hmong experienced relatedness and interdependence prior to Western resettlement.

# Early Historical Accounts

The exact origins of the Hmong are unknown. While concrete archaeological or written proof is elusive, legends abound. One popular legend suggests that the Hmong came from a land of ice and snow to the far north, which may have been Mongolia, Siberia, or even Turkestan. Other legends suggest that the Hmong are part of an early northward migration of peoples from Indonesia. It is certain, however, that at a date which preceded the beginnings of the Christian millennium, at the earliest beginnings of the Chinese state, the Hmong—which they called Miao—were known by the Chinese as a "savage barbaric people" that needed suppressing (Tapp 1986).

The Chinese name *Miao*, by which the Hmong are often known, was a broadly generic term referring to many non-Han people in China. This term designates a large set of minority ethnic groups, all belonging to the same linguistic sub-family—the MiaoYao—from which the Hmong of the Indochinese Peninsula have descended. At one point during the Ch'ing Dynasty, the term *Miao* "became as broad as the character Man, embracing all the southern and southwestern barbarous peoples" (De Beauclair 1960:270). Several ancient Chinese texts from the Hisa Dynasty (2207–1766 BC), the Chou Dynasty (1121–256 BC), the Han Dynasty (140–87 BC), and the Five Dynasties (907–960

---

1. Migrant memories may be shaped by nostalgia, making accurate historical reconstruction difficult and informant accounts of history and cultural traditions problematic. Some of the scholars cited in this section are Hmong themselves; others are refugee scholars with historical accounts taken from Hmong; and others are regional scholars with the ability to step back a little bit and be more objective on what is considered Hmong 'traditions.' I want to acknowledge these problems in the accounts given of Hmong traditions in this chapter.

AD) all mention conflicts with the Miao peoples (Savina 1924:115–170). However, because there are many ethnic groups called Miao, there is much confusion about the exact identity of the Hmong population and the historical value of Hmong origin stories remain speculative.

Scholars generally attribute Hmong migration into Southeast Asia as the result of the Chinese encroaching on the mountainous areas that the Hmong were occupying.[2] The Chinese annals record a significant growth in China's population that coincided with the introduction of corn in the mid-seventeenth century. As population numbers grew to more than three hundred million, people started searching for available farmland. Since the Han masses in the lowlands could grow corn in the mountainous areas with less rich soil and poorer irrigation, they began expanding upward to the mountain ranges where the Miao lived. Some Hmong responded by migrating further south, some chose to move into the higher mountain ranges of Guizhou, Sichuan and Yunnan, while others left the Chinese empire altogether for the scarcely populated mountain ranges that would later become the Indochinese countries. Other Hmong chose to fight. Chinese annals note that during the uprisings in 1668, 1732, 1794, and 1855, the "Miao scattered in all directions, initiating the migratory movement of the modern period" (Wiens 1954:90).

It is also then that the Hmong believe their language split into multiple dialects that divided them into different social groups. The two predominant dialects spoken among the Hmong refugees who have resettled in the West are *Hmong Der* (white Hmong) and *Mong Leng* and *Mon Njua* (green Mong). There is no official written evidence of when or why various dialects emerged from what scholars generally acknowledge was a homogenous linguistic group. Oral histories of this separation have passed on from one generation to the next, an example of which was expressed by an elder who, appealing to his memory of stories passed on to him, explained that

> Many years ago we were all one people together in the Yunnan province of China and spoke a version of green Hmong. But we were becoming too many in number and the Han Chinese feared that we were becoming too powerful. The Chinese began to persecute and kill many of the Hmong. Some of us broke off from the others and changed our dress and dialect to fool the Chinese into thinking we were another group. One of these dialects became known as white Hmong, and those of us who speak it, came from this group that broke away.

---

2. See McAleavy 1958.

The word *Leeg,* from *Hmong Leeg or Leng* (green Hmong), means "to admit" because the green Hmong might have stayed and admitted their ethnicity to the Chinese. Others suggest that it was the Chinese who had divided them, giving each group a derogatory name and mandating different clothes and dialect usage under threat of death. Chinese ethnographers support this rendition suggesting that the different Hmong group names came from Han insults (*Hmong Leng* can imply dark or evil, and *Miao,* dirty), which were eventually accepted by local non-Han peoples, and eventually by the Hmong in China themselves.[3]

Current demographic data on the Hmong in China and the Indochinese Peninsula, however, suggest that only a small fraction (fifteen percent) of these dialect groups were aggressively pushed by Han expansion out of China into Southeast Asia into the mountainous zones of refuge. It is a part of this migrant group fleeing the Han state from which the research population for this book is derived.

## Migration into Southeast Asia and Laos

It is recognized among Hmong scholars today that not until the second half of the nineteenth century did large numbers of Hmong swidden agriculturists move from China and settle in the Indochinese Peninsula "where they got as far south as the 17th parallel near Tak, in Thailand, following roughly a northeasterly and southwesterly route from French Tonkin" (Culas 2004:71). This southern expansion is generally believed to have been led by small groups of Hmong looking for high altitude forest to clear when the soil in their plots were exhausted. They mostly settled in highlands situated above 500 meters elevation. Another factor that served as a catalyst for the continued move farther down into Southeast Asia was confrontations between the Hmong and the Europeans in the 1880s. When the French and British were searching for new safe ways into South China, fighting that erupted pushed many mountain people to travel as far south as the Indochinese Peninsula in search of more peaceful and less crowded opportunity zones of refuge to continue in their traditional life ways.

A timeline for the Hmong's arrival in what is modern-day Laos was put together through oral history by Dao Yang in 1975. Triangulating oral history with accounts of an English observer in Siam at the end of the 19th century,

---

3. See Tapp 2001; Ling & Ruey 1947.

he concluded that they first moved into Laos between 1810 and 1820. One observer noted "thousands of emigrants ... and a growing population of Meo [Hmong] and Yao ... Eight years ago, the Meo were not to be found on the right bank of the *Nam-kawng* [Mekong], but, in the interval, they have been swarming down" (McCarthy 1894:71). Additionally, the Iu Mien branch of the Yao, who are close relatives of the Hmong, have written records in their own script that illustrate the migration of the Hmong as "having left the Chinese province of Guangdong around 1860 and crossed Yunnan and Laotian territory to finally settle in Nan province around 1880" (Culas and Michaud 2004:74). This translates to a 650-mile migration journey spread over just twenty years.

Little attention was paid to these highland peoples by lowland monarchs until the French occupation of Indochina in the 1880s. During this time, French troops explored the mountain highlands of Laos in an effort to learn more about these "savage" populations under their control (Michaud 2009:28). Of particular interest to the French was how to encourage the production and trade of opium that was well suited for these mountainous areas. It is estimated that at one point "the Laotian highlands produced ninety percent of the total French opium output" (Lucke 1995:59). Accounts of relations between the hill people Hmong and the French during occupation suggest that they were ruled by an indirect colonial system that established a racial hierarchy placing the French at the top, followed by the Vietnamese, the Thai, Lao, and at the very bottom, the Hmong highlanders (McCoy 1972:78). "In Laos under French colonialism, the Chinese word 'Miao' degenerated into 'Meo,' a term that ... with a slight change in intonation, can be pronounced to mean "cats." (Vang 2010:48) This insulted the Hmong who did not want to be associated with wild cats living in the forested mountains. Nevertheless, the French left the Hmong to self-rule, establishing a system of administrative districts in Nong Het. While granting them some autonomy, it did not end their exploitation, as some appointed leaders used their positions to gain an economic advantage over their ethnic peers. Thus, the introduction of state-like political structures into these previously stateless peoples resulted in a new kind of heirarchy that had not been previously experienced (58).

It was during this time that some of these families with French contact began moving out of the mountains to the lowland where they could afford to send their children to French schools. The first handful of Laotian Hmong attended school in 1922, one of which then attended college at the school of Law and Administration at Vientiane (133). While those Hmong who moved to the lowlands saw their efforts as leverage to gain concessions to schools, other Hmong viewed these aspirations as "hopelessly utopian." Despite their presence in the lowlands, the Hmong were held as second-class citizens by the ethnic Lao and exploited by Laotian officials. As one author put it:

It was particularly humiliating to the proud Hmong to have to literally grovel before Laotian bureaucrats, crawling on hands and knees, head down, up the steppes of the official's office to his desk where they had to kneel patiently until the Laotian recognized their presence. Trade with the Laotians was a constant reminder to the Hmong of their inferior status. They were charged several times more for goods than Laotians, and when they sought employment in lowland towns their wages were invariably half of what a native Lo received for the same work. Few Hmong expected this to change. The general perception was that the most that could be hoped for was an increase in village autonomy so that the Hmong might get by with as little contact with Laotian officials as possible (Qunicy 1988:135).

While what most Hmong hoped would result was an increase in village autonomy so that "the Hmong might get back with as little contact with Laotian officials as possible" (135), there were a few Hmong who aspired to political positions. One particular Hmong, Touby Lyfoung, was educated in French law and administration in the Vientiane school system and aspired "to build a Hmong power base that enjoyed French confidence and then use it as a lever to gain concessions for schools and government positions for the Hmong so that they could enjoy political autonomy in the lowlands and in the hills" (Quincy 1988:134). This migration has been attributed to the highlander Hmong essentializing the white Hmong as "more educated." As rumors of these characterizations spread, social divisions between the dialect groups emerged. After his education, Lyfound returned to the mountainous area of Nong Het. It was also during this time that a serious clan dispute arose between the lowland Lo and Ly clans as Lyfound's colonial education favored him in an election for the villages vacant administrative post over Ly Found who thought the post should be his. Things became so contentious that the French authorities had to divide the leadership of the lowland French district of Nong Het, where the Hmong lived, between the two clans. While the details of that dispute are not central to this thesis, the fact that the conflict drove an indelible wedge between these two Hmong groups is. The Lo, under the leadership of Faydang publically vowed that "whatever Touby Lyfound and his men do, I and my men will do the opposite."

The introduction of state forms of governance have been attributed to creating rivalry's and divisions that grew to new heights during the second World War, and "pitted the two most powerful clans in Nong Het, the Ly and Lo, against each other ... ultimately foreshadowing how the Hmong became entangled on both sides" of the war that would eventually lead to their dispersal (Vang 2010:58). Other French-inspired rivalries between a Hmong prophet and Vang Pao, a Hmong military leader and political broker of the Royal Lao Government, would also entangle the Hmong on opposite sides of the U.S. Secret War that would last until the end of the Vietnam War in 1975.

Historian Michaud states that "until the communist takeover of 1975, minorities in mid- and upland Laos were not subject to clear national policies" (2009:29). It has been suggested that the most powerful recruiting tool the CIA used to enlist the Hmong was the promise of an autonomous Meo state in return for their help (Scott 1990). It is also noteworthy that the goal of reattaining a form of self-governance has motivated the Hmong's early involvement with the state, even if this meant first supporting the French. Political Scientist, James Scott, in his controversial thesis, *The Art of Not Being Governed* (2009), has assessed the two-millennium long history of movement and migration of Southeast Asian hill people as purposely fleeing state-making projects.

Concerning this Southeast Asian Massif region he calls *Zomia,* he posits:

> A strong, and, I believe, more accurate political description is that the hill populations of Zomia have actively resisted incorporation into the framework of the classical state, the colonial state, and the independent nation-state. Beyond merely taking advantage of their geographical isolation from centers of state power, much of Zomia has "resisted the projects of nation-building and statemaking of the states to which it belonged."[4] This resistance came especially to light after the creation of independent states after World War II, when Zomia became the site of secessionist movements, indigenous rights struggles, millennial rebellions, regionalist agitation, and armed opposition to lowland states. But it is a resistance with deeper roots. In the pre-colonial period, the resistance can be seen in a cultural refusal of lowland patterns and in the flight of lowlanders seeking refuge in the hills (19).

Scott argues that virtually everything about highland Hmong culture—their pre-settlement livelihood as swidden agriculturists, egalitarianism, social organization, belief system, and ideologies can be read as strategies designed to keep state-like concentrations of power at arm's length. I am not implying, as Scott does, that a stateless mindset was a categorical certainty for all Hmong refugees who came to the West; indeed the lowlanders who fled as refugees had been incorporated by the Laotian state. Vang Pao had at one time

---

4. Van Schendel (2002), "Geographies of Knowing" (12).

engaged in nation-building trying to proclaim an independent Hmong nation, creating a Hmong anthem, flag, and naming a would-be cabinet (Garrett 1974:89). However, the huge literature on the resettlement of Hmong refugees does not even allow for the potentially important identity-informing possibility that among the highland populations, who came as refugees to the West, was a stateless mindset. Migration scholars have noted that many European migrants first learned of their national identities when they arrived in the United States, particularly those who arrived in the late 19th and early 20th centuries when many European countries were just becoming nation-states. Oddly, this never was considered in migration scholarship on the Hmong. Scott's thesis does not account for the many Hmong who moved to the lowlands. My position is that these refugees were more complex than what Scott imagined in his Zomia thesis, but also more complex than we have imagined in the nationalist-centered methodologies that have typically guided Hmong refugee research. By investigating which Hmong, if any, that migrated to the West had identities that were informed by deliberate or relative statelessness, or deliberate or relative incorporatedness as lowlanders, we can better understand how those perceptions might have shaped resettlement experiences. This book will consider this history as a factor in understanding the Hmong's reactions to and strategies against member-making in their resettlement sites, and to their concept of belonging in general. In fact, I will argue that they cannot be understood apart from it.

## The Beginning of Refugeehood

Throughout the 20th century, the Hmong increased in numbers. By the early 1970s, "there were an estimated two hundred thousand Hmong in Laos residing in nine northern and central provinces" (Lucke 1995:57). With the Viet Minh invasion on the Plain of Jars, Laos was thrown into a civil war that split the Hmong into several factions. The Pathet Lao formed a coalition with the communist forces from Vietnam. It is estimated that nearly one-third of the lowland Hmong during this time allied themselves with or fought for the Pathet Lao (61). By the early 1970s, conflict in the Vietnam War (1954–1975) passed through the hill people's territories via the Ho Chi Minh Trial. The American CIA, who recognized their knowledge of the difficult highland terrain, recruited hill Hmong as soldiers for their secret involvement in this war to both cut-off supplies and rescue downed pilots. Hmong Vang Pao, recognized early as a great leader and strategist, rallied many hill Hmong to this cause and was elevated by the CIA to the rank of General in the war effort.

General Vang Pao held the highest military position in the Royal Lao Government forces and remained an important and influential figure among U.S. Hmong until his recent passing.[5] A third group of Hmong in both the highland and lowland tried to remain neutral.

It was also during this Vietnam War era that tremendous changes were forced upon the Lao Hmong hill people. The way of life that they had known for generations was almost obliterated. Their homes were destroyed by bombs, mine fields, and chemical weapons. Many groups were driven into areas that were no longer suitable for swidden farming. Where good plots of land could be found, many congregated and eventually the land could not support them. Some groups were displaced before a full harvest (Lucke 1995:63). The security and self-sufficiency of their small villages was replaced by large gatherings known as "safe villages" with better access to resources, often supplied via airdrop by the Americans. The largest such village was Long Cheng (64).

Long Cheng was known as a military staging area and the CIA field headquarters for the offensive in 1966. It was estimated that at one time between 30 and 60 thousand Hmong, Khamu and Mien highland peoples came through the area on any given day (Cooper 1986). Life in these "safe areas" did not resemble traditional life. Many customs could not be practiced. For example, the makeshift shelters that were constructed were not positioned in accordance with their ancestor worship. There was often no space in the house for traditional altars or to perform ceremonies, and there was a perpetual lack of animals for sacrifices. Moreover, many religious specialists were involved in the war, or had been killed. Polygyny increased as levirates—the custom of brothers marrying a brother's widow—became more common as a result of men losing their lives in the war, and brothers took second and third wives (Keown-Bomar 2004:65).

In February 1973, a ceasefire was signed and in 1973 a coalition government of the Pathet Lao and the royal political organization was established. The fall of Saigon in Vietnam had a direct impact on Laos, resulting in the communist Pathet Lao taking firm control of the Laotian government. Royalists' lives were threatened if they did not join forces with the Pathet Lao by government statement in the May 9, 1975, *Khaoxane Pathet Lao* newspaper, declaring "We must eradicate the Meo minority completely." This included many lowland Hmong who had been recruited as officers. As the situation deteriorated, 40,000 Hmong fled to an airbase where the U.S. CIA only airlifted

---

5. General Vang Pao, 81, passed away of pneumonia in Clovis California on January 7, 2011.

General Vang Pao and other high-ranking officers out of Laos, leaving the others behind. Aided by "distance-demolishing technologies" such as roads, bridges, bomb-dropping airplanes, and modern weaponry, the Laotian state began immediate retaliatory campaigns to incorporate the peripheral hill people from stateless zones to areas of state control (Scott 2009:10). The Pathet Lao associated those Hmong who allied with the U.S. as traitors. As the Pathet Lao army's massive air and chemical weapon campaign bombarded the hills, particularly those in the Long Cheng area, the Hmong began to flee the hills to Thailand in large numbers. Some Hmong were lured out of the mountains under the promise of a ceasefire only to be gunned down; many were sent off for "reeducation" or just disappeared; some stayed in the mountains to fight under the nickname of "freedom fighters." However, most fled through the jungle on foot, evading gunfire and bombs, and made their way toward the Mekong River in hopes of crossing to the safety of yet another zone of refuge — Thailand. The research population for this study came from those who made it to the Thai refugee camps.

## Liminality and the Thai Refugee Camps

The Thai government did not agree to permanent resettlement for large numbers of refugees so the United Nations High Commissioner for Refugees (UNHCR) setup "camps of first asylum," where the refugees had to remain until they received permission to emigrate to another country of permanent resettlement. UNHCR contracted with the Thai government to provide food, shelter, water, electricity, medical care, supplies, education, and self-reliance projects for the refugees. Moreover, the UNHCR was responsible for seeking a more permanent solution for the refugees; whether in local settlement, repatriation, or resettlement outside the country. Victor Turner's (1967:93) concept of liminality is expressed in the idea of being "betwixt and between,"— a state between separation from one social situation or group and reincorporation into another. The legal, social, economic, and psychological uncertainty of camp has led some scholars to characterize this time in a refugee's life as liminal.[6]

Thailand had fifteen refugee camps in 1979, with a population that totaled over 140,000; eight of these were for the Hmong and lowland Lao. Many refugees were shuttled from camp to camp in the government's effort to keep all the

---

6. See Harrell-Bond & Voutira 1992; Long 1993; Horst 2007; Korac 2009.

Laotian Hmong together. The population that first resettled in Gammertingen, Germany, and DFW, Texas, had stayed in Nong Khai and Ban Nam Yao camps, which were later split due to overcrowding into what became Ban Vinai.

**Figure 1.1 Map of Hmong Camps**

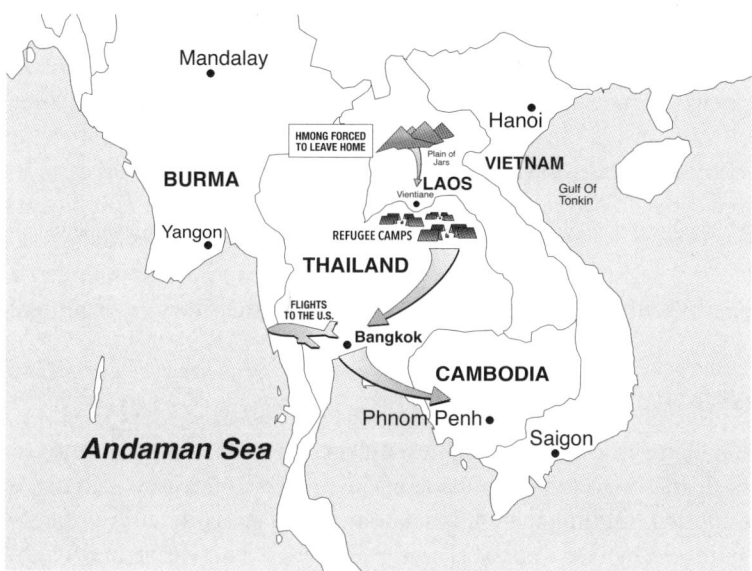

The UNHCR provided each refugee a blanket, mosquito net, and an assigned space in a very overcrowded long hut-style shelter. According to congressional records, each of the shelters at Nong Kahi, for example, contained at least 250–300 refugees at a time (Congressional Research SVC Library 1979:32). One Hmong in the study spoke of sectioning off their area with cardboard and string to bring some semblance of privacy in a crowded and noisy atmosphere where "getting any sleep was nearly impossible." Most Hmong I talked to still remembered these living arrangements vividly, one recalling, for example, that he stayed in "Row 2, House 18."

The refugees I talked to generally considered this camp a temporary stop on their way to another country, thus, tolerating the overcrowded living conditions, poor food rationing, boredom, and often abuses by the Thai government. For example, even though the Thai Ministry of Education had been contracted by the UNHCR to bring free education to the people in the camps, many of my research participants remembered having to pay Thai officials for this "luxury," or go without.

The process that Hmong went through from entrance in the camps to resettlement was a detailed one performed by various organizations through translators. It was characterized by four stages; registration, clearance, approved entry, and exit through Bangkok. While a liminal existence is often viewed as disempowering, it is also a space where great agency is employed (Korac 2009). The Hmong were goal-oriented in that they were trying to get from the camp into a new zone of refuge, a resettlement country. Unlike in their previous history, a zone of refuge could not be found by walking to another mountain. This time they would have to maneuver the UNHCR system to get into an asylum country. For most, it was their first experience with this kind of membership. The hills welcomed anyone who could negotiate its terrain, whereas in the camps, membership was negotiated by the International Rescue Committee (IRC) who sorted people by specific criteria of who belongs where. How the Hmong were introduced to and negotiated these sorting mechanisms is important in understanding their post-resettlement strategies for making it in their new environments.

## Registration

In Thailand, the process began with the IRC registering all refugees who expressed a desire to resettle outside of the first asylum country. Refugees were photographed holding a small blackboard with an assigned number written on it followed by what many Hmong described as invasive and frightening medical examinations.

Figure 1.2 Camp "Mug Shots"

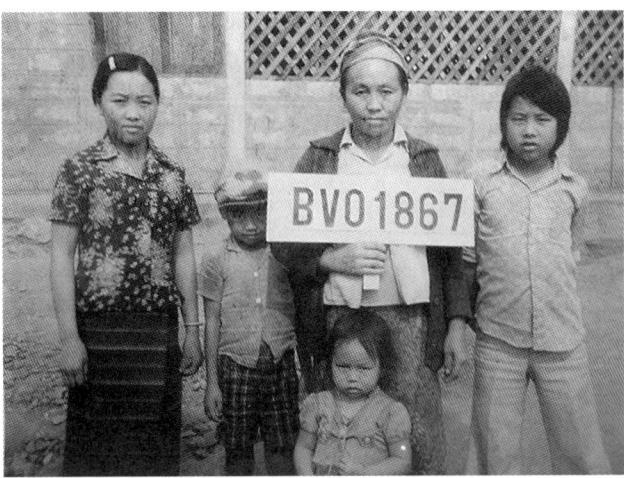

Photo by Nou Yang

Biographical data was collected from each family and sent to Bangkok where families were separated into three categories:

**Category 1**—Those having immediate family in the country they wished to resettle in.
**Category 2**—Those not in category 1, and were not accepted for permanent resettlement by their first asylum country and should be granted asylum as a group (called Humanitarian Parole in 1977) in a third country on humanitarian grounds (because they were part of a group fleeing war or other violence).
**Category 3**—Those not in category 1 or 2 (such as an economic migrant) and therefore were not eligible for resettlement under this program.

If the refugee wanted resettlement in the United States, there were additional sorting categories such as "Worked for the U.S. government in a meaningful capacity," or "associated with U.S. policies or programs."

# Clearance

After sorting, the refugee's dossier was sent to intelligence and immigration agencies in the country where they wished to resettle. That country would then have approximately twenty days to verify the refugee's claim to a specific category status. After clearance and verification of evidence, an immigration officer from the country of resettlement would interview each applicant through a translator to try to sort through their claim. This proved difficult with the Hmong hill people that did not live by a calendar, did not keep dates, did not celebrate birthdays, and had no formal education or medical records. To illustrate these difficulties, I offer the following transcript from one woman who was the second wife of her husband who divorced her to go to the United States with his allowed first wife.

> A mother and her four children waited for the caseworker to interview them. He took a few minutes to study their file. He then went to get the ex-husband's file from the registrar because the information in her file was inconsistent. The three older children crawled around on the floor. The mother nursed the youngest while they talked. "How many brothers and sisters does she have in the U.S.?" The young interpreter held up his finger in response after asking the question in Hmong. The caseworker continued, "What's the second's name? It really is her sister? Same mother, same father?" The interpreter translated, the woman nodded. Realizing suddenly that the same person had been listed under two names, the caseworker used white-out to correct the

form. "Was she ever in Nong Khai?" "Yes," replied the interpreter. "Does she know her date of arrival in Nong Khai?" Silence. "Same date as arrival in Thailand." The interpreter explained and the women nodded. "Does she know any of the months of date of birth of her children?" This was translated but the woman did not reply. "How about Young Sue?" To this translation, she shook her head. "How about Non?" Again, she gave the same response. "All right, for the rest of them I'm going to assign a year and month—2/2, 3/3, 4/4, 5/5," the caseworker replied listing the dates off and pointing to each child as he assigned a birth date. The children would need these dates for school, hospital, immigration, and welfare forms. "Does anybody have two names?" the caseworker asked. The interpreter drew a blank, all Hmong have several names. The caseworker covered the form with more white-out. "How old was she when her mother died?" The woman stared uncomprehendingly. "She doesn't know." "Her mother died before Vang Pao left?" the caseworker asked, referring to the Hmong leader. "Yes," replied the interpreter after helping the woman to remember. "Did her family ever adopt anybody?" "No," he translated. "Does she have any idea about when she married her first husband?" Again, the woman stared. "No." "How old is she?" "She doesn't know," the interpreter explained. "Doesn't know how old she was when she got married?" "Doesn't know," he repeated. The caseworker decided that she must have been about sixteen then and is now about thirty-three. He wrote that on the form. "Ok, I think I have this all figured out. If she gets called to get on the bus, is she ready to go?" When this was translated, the women nodded (Long 1988:319–20).

The refugees in my research talked about the long and uncertain wait for their name to be called.

> There were so many people coming and going. It was very confusing and no one really knew what was going on. Family tried to stay with family and village with village, but it was not possible. In these camps, we were like a school of fish in the sea, and every now and then a big net would come and scoop up a bunch of us, put us on a bus, and send us off. It seemed just that sudden and random.

## Approved Entry

The biographical history of approved refugees without known family in any country were put in a pool along with the Vietnamese refugees and divided among all six countries participating in resettlement: Australia, France, Argentina, French Guyana, Canada, and the United States. The United Kingdom and Germany also participated in resettlement, but only for the so-called Vietnamese "boat people." From there the Intergovernmental Committee for European Migration (ICEM) or the Immigration and Naturalization Service of the United States (INS) would secure sponsorship in their respective countries and then notify the refugees that they should prepare to leave for their country of resettlement.

Both a town in Argentina and the Dallas/Fort Worth area of Texas in the United States were designated resettlement sites for Hmong refugees without known family in the country. The Hmong populations that participated in this study were among those who arrived in the refugee camps within the first year of flight from Laos, and therefore had no known family ties in resettlement. This wasn't uncommon; as families and villages first fled to Thailand, they often lost track of other clan members and were without knowledge of who had even made it across the Mekong. Families that were fortunate enough to have traveled together or who found each other in a camp requested only that they get placed together, although this often was not the case. In what seemed like random fashion, the names of my Hmong informants were called and they boarded buses that would take some of them to Argentina, and others to Texas.

The UNHCR arranged with the Thai Ministry of Interior for the transportation of refugees from the camps to Bangkok for out-processing.

## Exit through Bangkok

This story of exit moves from the general to the particular, told in this section through the eyes of the Hmong informants who became the research population for this study. They noted that once they were in Bangkok City, the ICEM conducted a final medical screening. Those heading for Texas passed their physicals, were boarded on a plane and headed to the Dallas/Ft. Worth International Airport. Five of the families heading to Argentina, however, tested positive for tuberculosis and were told they would have to stay in a hospital for a few weeks before they could join the rest of the passengers flying out. At this juncture, a daughter was separated from her parents, and a brother from brother, elders from sons. "We'll see you soon!" they assured one another as they went their separate ways.

Five weeks later, after receiving medical clearance, the five Hmong families going to Argentina were told that the country had reached their quota of refugees and "would not be taking anymore." They waited another week in liminality as the Intergovernmental Committee for European Migration tried to find another country willing to take them. Finally, they were told that Germany, a country that was not participating in Hmong resettlement, but rather chose to concentrate on resettling 20,000 Vietnamese "boat people," had agreed to take these five Hmong families, and no more. "Germany?" one Hmong man recalled. "We didn't even know what a Germany was." As they boarded the plane, their thoughts fluctuated between the unfamiliar and frightening expectations of air travel, living in a country they had never heard of, and the family members who would now be a world and "many mountains" away.

## Hmong Concepts of Belonging

It's this disconnection of home and place that affects the way Hmong assign their new localities of resettlement with any significance of belonging. It is also this "plasticity of ethnicity" that Jenkins (1997:169) refers to which "permits us to appreciate that although it [ethnicity] is imagined it is not imaginary; to acknowledge its antiquity as well as its modernity." Its within Jenkins' perception that I conceive the Hmong as an ethnic group, "somewhere between irresistible emotion and utter cynicism, neither blindly primordial nor completely manipulable, ethnicity and its allotropes are principles of collective identification and social organization in terms of culture and history" (170). Their history, however, cannot be understood simply in terms of political resistance, but must also be considered as what Scott refers to as "a life of cultural refusal" (2009:20). Scott notes that "the hill populations do not generally resemble the valley centers culturally, religiously, or linguistically … the languages spoken in the hills are, as a rule, distinct from those spoken in the plains. Kinship structures, at least formally, also distinguish the hills from the lowlands." This is in part what Edmund Leach had in mind when he characterized hill society as following a "Chinese model" while lowland society followed an "Indian or Sanskritic model" (1954:21).

Out of these histories, the Hmong have developed certain ideologies of relatedness that are important not only to processes of belonging in both DFW and Gammertingen, but also to the construction and use of diasporic networks. Hmong social organization is not static and has undergone adaptation and change in the course of contact with other cultures over time. These adaptive behaviors have continued during refugee resettlement in the West. This section will outline the supra-national identity constructed through the Hmong kinship system and its role in cultural reproduction, while the specific adaptations of this system in Gammertingen and DFW will be considered in a later chapter. I begin with a popular Hmong folktale that is sometimes used to explain the origin of their connectedness.

A long time ago, a lot of water fell from the sky. All living things were killed: No fathers, no children, no mothers, no pigs, no babies, no oxen, no buffalo, no horses, no insects, no squirrels, and no birds. Only two people—one boy and his sister who had taken refuge in a large wooden barrel. After the waters receded, the brother said to his sister "Marry me and we can have children and make more people." But the sister said, "I cannot marry you. You are my brother." Every day the brother asked this again. After many days the girl said, "If you really want to marry me, we must each bring a stone and climb up on that mountain. When we get to the top, we each roll a stone down opposite sides. The next morning, if both stones have gone back up the mountain and we find them lying together, then I will agree to marry you." When it was dark, the boy went and found the two stones and brought them back up the mountain. The next day he said, "See, they have come together as we should. Now you can marry me." So the brother and sister married. After a while they had a baby that did not look like an ordinary baby. It was round like a big soft egg with no arms and legs. "Maybe this baby is a seed," they said. "Let's cut it into pieces and scatter it around." So they cut the baby seed into little pieces and scattered them in all directions. Some pieces fell into the garden and made people. They named one group of people Vang, because it sounds like the Hmong word for garden. Some pieces fell in the weeds and grass and these people were named Thao, because Thao sounds like the Hmong word for weeds and grass. Some pieces fell in the goat house, and the people from these pieces were called Li. Other pieces fell in the pig house, and those people were named Moua, for the Hmong word for pig house. Three days later, the village was full of houses for every family group. Then the brother and sister said, "Now we aren't sad. We're not alone anymore." This is how the world was filled with Hmong families or clans (Hmong Folk Story).

This broad idea of shared descent as articulated in this folklore underlies Hmong identity. A patrilineal clan system has dominated Hmong social organization since the period of the Chinese Sung Dynasty (Tapp 1986:167) when it is believed that the folktale originated. Besides this legend, another explanation offered for the derivation of clans is the early influence of the Chinese. In fact, anthropologist Gary Lee suggests that Chinese records imply "Hmong clan names were borrowed from Chinese family names, presumably for registration of Chinese officials and to raise the Hmong's social position" (1982:5). No matter its origin, since its inception, the patrilineal clan system has served as a primary integrating mechanism for Hmong culture as a whole. A Hmong child becomes a member of a clan at birth when she is given the father's clan name. The Hmong have traditionally lived without a calendar, so rites of passage from one age set to another are more important than acknowledging actual birthdays. Everyone sharing the same clan name in the same age set, even strangers, are considered cousins. This relationship is signaled "with the form of address *kuv ti/kuv tyo* literally meaning elder/younger sibling" (Weinstein 1986:69). Older age sets are considered aunts and uncles, or grandparents. The everyday use of these kinship terms helps to reproduce Hmong identity and cohesion from generation to generation.

The Hmong have twenty clans. Each of these traces its origin to a common mythological ancestor. When two members of a clan meet for the first time, they will compare genealogies to see if they are from the same lineage; that is, if they can trace their connection back to any common ancestor. "*Koj yog ces twg*," or "Whose branch do you belong to?" is the first question asked between two Hmong members of the same clan meeting for the first time. The traditional answer would be the most prominent ancestor that they know from oral tradition. From there they would ask "*Koj yog paws twg*" or "Whose group do you belong to?" which requests the name of a living clan leader. This establishes the pre-Vietnam War village or cluster of villages from which one has come (Weinstein 1986:70). Finally, a question is asked about current place of residence. As kinship relations are the primary features of a Hmong person's identity, these formalities serve to establish relatedness at the outset of a meeting, as well as set the ground rules for the kinds of social and material obligations that people may have toward one another. This exchange was recently witnessed in Gammertingen when a U.S. Hmong visited the village.

> When I knocked on the door, the Hmong man only opened it a sliver. He began asking who I was, and we went through the Hmong ritual greetings tracing our ancestry. Finally he said "OK, You are good Hmong. I respect you." He then opened the door and let me in.

The smallest social unit of the Hmong is the household, which includes everyone under the authority of its head, whether or not they live under the same roof. This unit usually consists of a husband and wife, their unmarried daughters, and their sons and their wives and children. This patrilineal unit only changes when a daughter marries (and thus, becomes a member of her husband's clan and household) or a son moves to another village or city and then is considered to be a separate household. These kinship conceptions were problematic for the Hmong during resettlement in Texas and Gammertingen because Western social welfare systems are organized around the notion of the nuclear family—a subject that will be more thoroughly examined in Chapter 3.

Hmong clans are exogamous and the woman is expected to join her husband and as a result receive the benefits and privileges of being a member of his clan. As a new member, she is treated more equitably as she takes on more household responsibilities and adds to the family's overall production. Any children the couple may have are considered a part of his clan, even in the case of divorce. Thus, having children, especially sons who can carry on the patrilineage, gives the female the most status in her husband's clan.

According to my respondents, this was one reason for the high fertility rates of their women in Laos. In a society where family means everything, children are celebrated as a gift. Not only does a large family guarantee the continuation of the lineage but, according to my informants, lightened the heavy workload in the fields and household of Laos. There is, however, another explanation for high fertility. In the past, it was not uncommon for highland Hmong women to give birth to ten children and have none survive. Since a family could never be sure who would live and who would die, having many children was an assurance against infant and childhood mortality. In Western countries, by the 20th century, biomedicine had effectively reduced the rates of infant mortality, but when Hmong refugees resettled in Western societies, they did not understand that their children were more likely to survive, or the financial practicality of having smaller families, or that large families do not necessarily confer high status in the West. These separate understandings of childbirth and child survival carry implications for the processes of their perceptions of belonging. Both will be discussed at more length in Chapter 4.

As could be imagined living in areas with no social safety nets in place, Interdependence was an essential element in pre-settlement Hmong life. In times of crisis, a Hmong person is expected to turn to members of his/her household and to a "close group" of relatives—the *ib tsev neeg* and the *ib cuab kwv tij*—for help. In Laos, mutual support—*ib cuab kwv tij*—came from the village lineage (Hall 1990:29). When these villages of kin were separated through refugee resettlement, often members of the *ib cuab kwv tij* no longer live next door or even in the same country as one another. During resettlement, the local nationals often misunderstood this ideology of interdependence, especially in Gammertingen and DFW, Texas whose models of stability relied on Western independence and the ability to "pull oneself up by the bootstraps." But for Hmong refugees, interdependence became an adaptive strategy that led them to search out their "close group" across the global diaspora, and use it as a means to re-create their village of mutual help. The Germans and Americans often mistook diasporic reliance as a sign of instability when, in fact, such reliance was a move *toward* stability and considered by the Hmong as essential for survival. A more detailed discussion of how these support systems brought over with the Hmong were mobilized in response to lack of local resources available in their new environment will be discussed in a later chapter.

In light of Hmong history and way of life which has scattered them over southern China, northern Vietnam, Laos, Thailand, and nine countries of refugee resettlement, it is surprising that a collective identity distinct from non-Hmong has remained as strong as it has. This has been attributed to their continued tradition of marrying within Hmong society (Millett 2002). As a result of their strong emphasis on marrying within the group, they became more or less genetically closed, and shared a special biological bond with each other. It is this biological bond that sets them apart in their minds from other groups. As one informant told me when asked about his identity:

> I was born from Hmong parents. I have Hmong blood. I am Hmong. Where I live can never change who I am. Because of this blood I will always be first and foremost Hmong.

Pierre van den Berghe argues that this perception of ethnicity is, at its core, "made up of people who know themselves to be related to each other by a double network of ties of descent and marriage" (1987:24). This "myth of ancestry" (Horowitz 1985:52) is perpetuated through folktales and stories of their origin, such as the one mentioned earlier. Therefore, inter-marrying is a powerful force that perpetuates ethnic identity that Manning Nash (1989) has called "blood, bed, and cult." Hmong marriage is usually framed in relation to Nash's conceptualization. For one, it unites a man and woman into a social unit for the purposes of procreation and economic production (bed). Marriage also creates reciprocal economic, political, and ceremonial ties between clans (blood) (1989). Traditionally, it is the man who seeks a wife, and the woman who waits to be sought after. This was exemplified when asking Hmong women who were married in Laos how they found their husbands. The response was often laughter followed by "Hmong women don't look for a husband. They wait to be found."

Relatives of an eligible man are often called upon to suggest a suitable partner. According to my informants, suitability is determined first by reputation of the family, history of criminal activity, extreme poverty, or history of disease, then by the woman's reputation for obedience, industry, congeniality, and attractiveness. The bachelor follows the suggestion of his extended kin with a visit to this relative who has arranged for the two to meet. This visit is usually followed by a short period of contemplation, and then if the woman is seen as a good "fit," the man asks her to marry him. Nancy Donnelly suggests that the limited range of acquaintances in the Lao mountains led to a preference toward marrying into family already related by marriage, suggesting such bonds "might argue well for a couple's future, and in case of marital dispute might provide sympathetic counselors for both husband and wife" (1994:125). Here is an account of an ordinary marriage that has followed this pattern, as shared by a Hmong man resettled in Texas:

> The grandmother of my wife was also an aunt-like figure for me. When I was looking for wife, I asked my grandmother if she knew of an available woman who would make a suitable wife. My grandmother told me about this woman related to another of her grandchildren. She arranged for us to meet. After a few weeks, we married and she moved to my village.

Another traditional source of finding a spouse before resettlement was at large gatherings centered around the harvest new year. These New Year celebrations lasted for a couple of weeks and were visited by all Hmong within traveling distance. During this celebration, the single people would dress in their best clothes hoping to meet a future spouse. Special events, such as a traditional ball toss served a purpose like modern day speed dating. Eligible men and women would line up opposite each other and toss a ball back and forth while getting to know each other.

**Figure 1.3 Traditional Hmong Ball Toss**

After a while, the participants shift positions and begin tossing the ball with another and the process continues. Here is an account of how one man found his wife though this event:

> I was sixteen or maybe seventeen years old in Laos and working for the United States CIA in their war effort. My wife was just thirteen at the time. I met her at a Hmong New Year's celebration while we did the ball toss. I liked her. We talked for a while. A month later I asked her to marry me. We were married six months later.

The courtships in Hmong agricultural society were short, during which "premarital sexual involvement is strictly prohibited because a daughter's promiscuous sexual behavior would bring the biggest shame and loss of face to herself and the good name and reputation of her parents, extended family, and clan" (Moua 2003:15). During this time the father or, if there is none, the older brother of the groom brings a formal request to the prospective bride's parents. Once they accept, formal negotiations between delegate teams representing the two families begin. Among the negotiations is the bride-price, dowry, and costs of the wedding ceremony. In Laos, the bride-price served as the marriage contract or security between the bride's family and clan and the groom's family and clan. The dowry, on the other hand, was to assist the newlyweds start their new married life together in the groom's extended parental house. Negotiations also included decisions for the couple's social welfare—who would take care of the bride in case of the groom's death, for example, or provide for them in times of financial hardship.

Traditionally, after a couple marries, they move to live with the groom's family but are still not considered adults until they have children, at which point their names change to signify this new status. When the number of children becomes too large to be accommodated in the house, the nuclear family moves out to a nearby unit, but are still considered a part of the groom's family's household. There was incentive to stay in the same village as the couple's means of economic production was still dependent and secured through joint efforts with extended family members. Beyond the need for ongoing economic support, there were obligations of shared rights and responsibilities to support each other for life. In Laos, the last-born married son is bestowed a special duty. He and his nuclear family would remain permanently in the house of their extended family and become the eventual caretaker of their aged parents and grandparents until their death. This tradition provided an important social safety net for the care of elderly Hmong.

Another important way the Hmong were traditionally interconnected is through their animistic spiritual beliefs and ritual practices, or what Manning

Nash (1989) would consider the "cult" aspect of ethnicity that accompanies "blood" and "bed." For the Hmong who lived in Laos, many of the most important spiritual, life-supporting ceremonies could only be conducted jointly by members of the entire extended family. Moua suggests that these ceremonies make the nuclear family less significant in Hmong society while privileging kinship over individuals (Moua 2003:25).

Prior to contact with Western missionaries, the hilltribe Hmong were primarily animists who held strong beliefs in spirits and the supernatural world. As these practices did not occur in a central place of worship, clan and extended family members participated in rituals performed in the home. These ceremonies usually required the aid of a shaman and frequently entailed animal sacrifices of chickens, pigs, or cows, followed by a time of feasting together.

All these traditions practiced by the Hmong prior to resettlement, their folklore, conceptions of kinship, residence patterns, and supernatural belief support a form of relatedness that is seen as quintessential to being Hmong. It is how they experienced belonging. However, the practicality of continuing those forms of belonging would prove problematic in Gammertingen and Texas, leaving way for new expressions of group connectivity to emerge.

CHAPTER 2

# TWO HMONG RESETTLEMENT COMMUNITIES: THE CONTEXT OF RECEPTION

*After many hours of plane and bus rides, Lu X. and his family boarded their final bus ride to Gammertingen. The ride took them through hilly terrain and the bus climbed one steep mountain after the other. While there was a lot of greenery, Lu X. noticed the absence of the lush, lime-colored jungle greens he was used to. The trees were much darker and the vegetation altogether strange. He looked at the ground rolling beneath the bus and wondered if they could plant in that soil. As the bus wound its way up the mountains the air became considerably colder and the ground covered with heaps of cottony white snow. He was sure they couldn't plant in it now.*

*Meanwhile, Kang Y. and his family were met at the Dallas/Ft. Worth Municipal Airport by some white people who drove them to their home. The white people talked and smiled a lot, showing their big teeth. This made him uncomfortable because he didn't fully understand the intention of these smiles or what they were saying. They drove Kang Y. and his family through ribbons of pavement with more cars on it than he had ever seen. Everyone was driving very fast. It seemed dangerous. Unlike where they had come from, there were very few people walking about outside and little forest—just lots of cars racing on pavement past short and even-heighted grass trapped between columns of pavement. He could see the city of Dallas ahead of him with its tall buildings clustered together and pushing up toward the sky. He thought of how many households they consisted of and muttered to himself, "That must be where they keep all the people."*

\* \* \*

This research is concerned primarily with the Hmong's reorientation in two specific resettlement localities—the village of Gammertingen, Germany, and the metropolitan city group (Metroplex) of Dallas/Ft. Worth Texas (DFW), and with how that reorientation affects and is affected by the social relationships that develop at different scales—local, national, and global. As stated previously, the purpose of working within these two different field sites is to define what is unique about them, and what might be unique about the administration of resettlement programs operating within them, and then see how the refugee experiences of belonging are shaped by the overlapping and fluid social territories of different scale that intersect with them. To do this, it is important to understand in which ways the village and city have their own identity formed in part by their respective landscape, industry, history, and traditions. De Certeau (1988) observed that each city, town, or village projects "a recognizable sensibility" as well as the sense of the "phantasmagoric," by which he means its own constantly changing, yet signature assemblage of images. This section will draw a picture of the two different environments into which the Hmong resettled by their "signature assemblages" of late 1979.

## Gammertingen, Germany

Gammertingen, Germany, is a small village located in the southwest corner of Germany in the State of Baden-Wuerttemberg. The village occupies approximately thirty-four square miles and is nestled like an inverted bowl in the valley and up the sides of three steep hills. In fact, getting to and from this village demands driving up and over the mountains. Gammertingen serves as the central transportation hub and school district for six smaller villages within a seventeen-kilometer radius. The village itself has a population of roughly 13,000 but serves a greater population of 20,000. Its official classification is that of "city" but it is not considered densely populated or large by German standards.

The center of town is located in the basin of the bowl as are the municipal offices housed in an old castle dating back to 1775. The original and operational castle moat forms a ring of water around "Old Gammertingen" with buildings dating back to the 1600s and where parts of the city's original wall are still intact. The main street of Gammertingen, on which lie the town's only two traffic lights, is dotted with an array of small shops and businesses. Gammertingen prides itself on being a self-contained village that does not require its residents to travel outside of it. It includes three doctor's offices, two dentists, three pharmacies, four bakeries, four butchers, an office supply store, a travel agency, two ice-cream shops, three beauty parlors, a book store, three clothing shops, three small grocery stores, a tailor, a hardware store, an appliance store, an optometrist, a fair trade and bio-food store, two photo shops, a post office, liquor store, an auto dealership, one gas station, a cabinetry shop, a housewares store, two banks, a real estate agent, and an arts and crafts supply store.

### Figure 2.1 Map of Gammertingen

There are also several gathering spots such as hotels, restaurants, pubs, churches, a park, library, and the castle whose ballroom is used for cultural performances and town meetings. While none of these businesses are large in and of themselves, they are centrally located at the bottom of the bowl, as is the public rail and bus station, all six schools, and all municipal and social service offices.

Another aspect of the town is the multiple footpaths and staircases built into the landscape that offer pedestrian shortcuts from any section or elevation of the mountainside to the center of town. The nature of the foot traffic, the close proximity of houses, the centrally located business and gathering spots all provide a context for heightened face-to-face contact among Gammertingen's inhabitants. This is expressed in local traditions such as greeting every passerby with a friendly "*Gruss Gott*," (translated "Godly Greetings!"), and stopping by a neighbor's house, a café, or pub for communal cake and coffee at 3:00 PM.

Gammertingen is part of a distinctive geographic region known as the Swabian Alb, a high plateau with rolling hills and dense forests made out of limestone that sits 400 meters above the rest of Baden-Wurttemberg. Up on this plateau, small villages of half-timbered houses, old grocery stores and Mom and Pop gas stations dot the landscape. In between villages, herds of sheep graze on the mountainside, reminiscent of a time when herding was a way of life. The large expanses of hilly land have made it possible for most (80 percent) Gammertingens to own property and live in single-family homes. There are few apartment buildings and few buildings over three stories tall. Unlike other land-locked and more populous areas of the country, Gammertingen describes itself as a "community of homeowners."

Most communities of this size in Southern Germany were almost entirely agricultural until World War II. The soil quality on the Alb, however, has never been suitable for raising crops and consequently, raising sheep became a more popular way for its people to earn a living. The large herds and development of a railway led to thriving textile mills that clustered in Gammertingen. In the late 1970s, the textile industry collapsed and factories closed or moved overseas. City planners immediately zoned a small industrial center that attracted a few new manufacturing businesses, fourteen of which remain today. The largest employer in the village, however, is not manufacturing, but government. The city employs over 1,000 people as schoolteachers for its six district schools, in the retirement home, at a special school for the mentally handicapped, in public works, police, fire, and in municipal administration. Because of Gammertingen's scenic location in the beautiful Alb, the village also has a small tourist industry as a popular outdoor recreation site for its twenty different Nordic hiking trails, ten biking trails, and a scenic rail system. Other community members not employed by the city, manufacturing, or in village shops, travel thirty minutes north to Reutlingen and Stuttgart, both of which have reputations as among the largest and most stable industrial zones in Germany. As such, Gammertingen has historically had one of the lowest unemployment rates in the country. Because of its low cost of living and high employment rates, women in this town have traditionally been full-time *hausfraus,* and the men the providers of the family.

Archeologists have discovered remains of a first-century AD Roman settlement in Gammertingen. The claim that the village was a stop on a major Roman road, and the archaeological find of a gilded Roman helmet that proves it, is known to every Gammertinger. The town's written history goes back to 1101 AD, when it belonged to the Counts of Gammertingen and was mentioned in a monastery document (Gammertingen.de, 1988). The people of the Swabian Alb were participants in the Thirty Years' War (1618–1648), and the toll taken on the citizens of Gammertingen was large. Death as a result of starvation or disease was common. During its last years as an independent kingdom, Gammertingen suffered permanent occupation by French troops. In 1806, Gammertingen began to develop into a small town with its own district court, land registry, and newspaper, all three of which remain to this day. When the railroad was established in the early 1900s, it gave Gammertingen an economic boost and a local textile industry was born. After WWII, the need for more workers in this growing industry coincided with the return of large numbers of German expellees who fled the Soviet Union's Red Army in 1945. These two factors led to strong population growth and Gammertingen's central place for civic management, operation of the school system, and regional retirement center (Gammertingen.de 2008).

According to the town's historian, Gammertingen has had a steady foreign-born population of just fewer than 10 percent since the 1950s, beginning with Hungarians fleeing communism. In the 1960s immigrants from Italy, Spain, and Portugal came as guest workers, many of whom worked in the Gammertingen textile mills. In the 1970s, Turkish guest workers made their way to the village working in the construction industry. The Hmong were the first refugees to be placed in the town, which made them somewhat of a novelty, and as the mayor described, "the towns first official compassion project." Taken from town hall statistics, Figure 2.2 on the next page illustrates the ethnic composition of Gammertingen in 1980.

Although Germans, in general, do not self-ascribe as being particularly religious, Germany's tax laws that require everyone to designate a portion of their taxes to either the Catholic or Protestant (known in Germany as *Evangelisch*) Church place everyone in relationship to these two recognized churches. However, when asked to describe their village identity, of the 100 German village residents I interviewed, "religious" was mentioned 85 percent of the time, often with the caveat "because of the role it played in this area," referring back to the Thirty Years War. Because Gammertingen's churches were located at the center of town and acted as social hubs responsible for organizing many village-wide festivities and perform public functions, I was unable to tell whether they were really identifying themselves with Catholicism/ Protestantism, the institution of the Church, or with the Thirty Years' War. In any event, most (90 percent) of Germans in the village I interviewed were either members or attended one of these churches regularly and it could be assumed that religious history, as taught in these institutions, has contributed to their identity in myriad ways. An example of how local people think in terms of religious stereotypes was demonstrated by the village historian, herself a lifelong resident, who said that Catholicism has garnered a love for government and an

Figure 2.2 Ethnic Composition, Gammertingen 1980

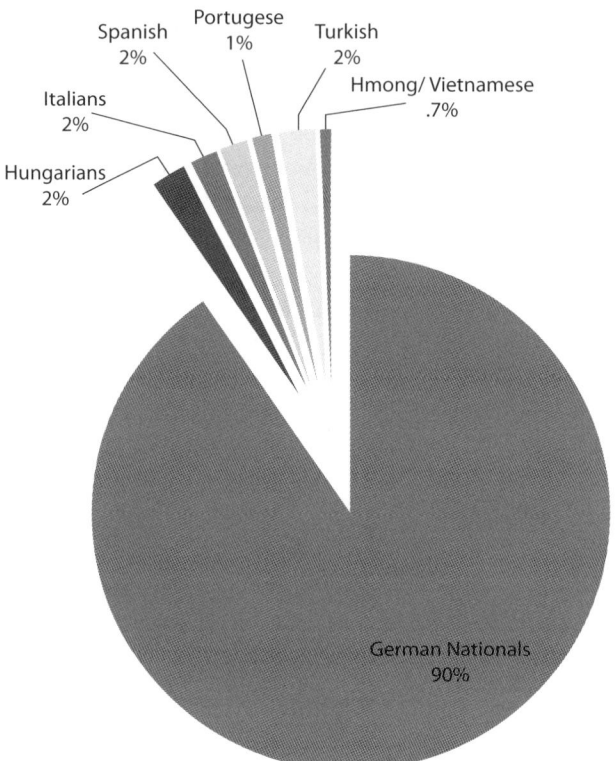

acceptance of bigotry in the people of Gammertingen, while its Protestant influence has led to a deep-seated belief in work and frugality. These virtues were evident in many conversations I had with locals where laziness and financial frivolity were spoken about with the same contempt as sensual sin is in DFW.

The residents of Gammertingen speak a regional version of German known as Schwaben. It is considered a peasants' dialect and ascribes a lower status than "proper German" in Germany at large. The villagers, however, identify strongly with this language, which is illustrated in their popular colloquialism "We can do anything except speak proper German." Gammertingen is devoted to celebrating this distinctiveness in poetry, song, and in a special weeklong carnival in February dedicated to scaring away its harsh winters. The rule of all speeches, comedians, and other festival performers is that they *must* speak in this dialect, making the celebration a museum for Schwaben language.

Traditional food eaten in this village is also perceived as a reflection of Gammertingen's history and identity. A renowned favorite is their unique version of macaroni and cheese known as *Spaetzler*. While other regions also claim it as their own invention, I was told on several occasions that it was invented locally out of protest to Italy's encroachment during the 1800s. It is still featured in every restaurant and we (my husband and I) were proudly served each family's heirloom recipe in every German Gammertingen's home we visited, with each boasting theirs was the best in town. I was given tutelage by an elderly woman on how to make the dish and, upon leaving the field, was given a spaetzler maker from the town's mayor "to remember them." Another local cuisine that is representative of this area is *Maultascheem,* or large pork-filled ravioli served with brown gravy. The folklore behind this dish relates directly to their Catholic heritage. It is said that the church wouldn't allow them to eat meat on Fridays, so the Schwaben hid it beneath the layers of pasta and gravy where "God couldn't find it."

While small, Gammertingen is not without its artistic traditions. It has music lessons, choirs, and community orchestra clubs and the village takes turns with larger regional cities to host world-class musical performances in its castle ballroom. The village is home to several different sport clubs, of which soccer is the largest. Gammertingen has its own soccer stadium (about the size of a football stadium found in American public high schools) and an indoor swimming pool. Gammertingen has three major festival traditions that they host. In winter, they celebrate the winter-chasing festival *Fashcing*. While this is celebrated almost everywhere in Germany, Gammertingen is known for its parade featuring troops of wood-masked scary creatures and a talent pageant featuring Schwaben dialect and self-loathing skits and monologues.

On Palm Sunday of each year, this particularly Catholic region also has a church service that is followed by a parade of children down the center of town carrying their regionally distinct, large, elaborate columns made of palm fronds and hallowed Easter eggs. Its third festival tradition is called Gammertingen Days, a weeklong festival of bands, food, games, and fun. This is not unlike most towns across Germany that host similar festivals, but is distinct in its showcase of local flavor and its representations of the village and its inhabitants.

I found one of the most public statements of Gammertingen's identity in a local newspaper article entitled "The friends of pietism. The Schwaebische Alb and its inhabitants of fantastic and lone rebels" (*Sueddeutsche Zeitung* 2008). The author claims the inhabitants of this village have an identity informed by its unique culmination of history, environment, and tradition, claiming its often difficult living conditions and limited resources have made hard work, resourcefulness, and a sense of community essential values.

They know they are distinctive and take pride in it, self-identifying as frugal, hardworking, religiously pious, close knit, home owners, neighborly, conservative, and above all—Schwaben.

Germany and Laos have had cordial diplomatic relations since 1958 (Federal Ministry of Economic Cooperation and Development 2008). Germany has never officially occupied or taken part in a war on Laotian soil. The French Foreign Legion, however, is said to have heavily recruited former German SS members and used WWII German artillery in their occupation of Indochina (Salazar 2006). During the cold war years when the communist Pathet Lao gained control, West Germany broke relations with them and East Germany emerged as a priority partner location for Laos. During this time, Laos sent many students to attend East German universities to study socialist military science and socialist economics. In 1990, after the fall of the Berlin Wall, diplomatic cooperation was reestablished between Laos and a united Germany where they became a sustainable rural development partners seeking to reduce poverty through the introduction of new agricultural products and vocational instruction in new viable forms of employment in the largely inaccessible highland regions where the hill Hmong live. Today, Germany is one of the country's largest financial donors. In addition, Germany has been providing economic policy advice to the Lao government since 1980 and supports its efforts to promote private enterprise (Federal Ministry of Economic Cooperation and Development 2008).

The country of Germany did not officially take part in the resettlement of Hmong refugees, choosing instead to focus on resettling the Vietnamese after the Vietnam War. As previously explained, Germany agreed to take the five stranded Hmong families who were supposed to go to Argentina and no more. The German authorities at the Federal Ministry of the Interior were in the process of dividing their quota of Vietnamese refugees and the five Hmong families in proportion to the size of each German state. The Hmong were assigned to the Southern State of Baden Württemberg. They were placed in a group processing home with other Indochinese refugees in the town of Goppingen. From there the Interior Ministry of Baden Württemberg divided the Southeast Asian refugees into different districts and specific townships in proportion to the towns' populations. The Hmong, through a translator, explained the nature of their clan life and kinship system and pleaded that they be allowed to stay together in one location. Gammertingen had not yet taken any refugees, and were anxious to do their part in the ongoing and very public crisis of "boat people." The Mayor of Gammertingen, was given a call asking if his

### Figure 2.3 Gammertingen Village

Photo courtesy of DN/Omega Productions.

village could accommodate this special group request. Because of the recent collapse of Gammertingen's textile industry, the town happened to have an empty dormitory that used to house foreign mill workers. It had many private rooms with a shared kitchen and common great-rooms that he thought suitable for group orientation and classes. He also thought the self-contained nature of their village—the availability of doctors, a school system, a wide array of social clubs, and its pedestrian-friendly setup—provided an ideal setting to accommodate the group. After working out a deal for the village to acquire the dorm, the Mayor called the central processing center in Goppingen and agreed to take the Hmong families, as well as five Vietnamese families for resettlement in the town. In December of 1979, within two days of the phone call, the five Hmong refugee families were placed on a bus to their permanent location: a dormitory house in this distinctively Schwaben village in southern Germany—the village of Gammertingen.

### Figure 2.4 Refugee Dormitory

Photo courtesy of DN/Omega Productions.

### Figure 2.5 Initial German-Hmong Refugees

Photo courtesy of the Lo family.

# The Dallas/Fort Worth Metroplex

The Dallas/Fort Worth *Metroplex* (DFW) is a copyrighted term (1972) that designates the urbanized area surrounding the cities of Dallas and Fort Worth, Texas. The Metroplex occupies twelve counties of over 9,286 square miles and according to 1979 figures at the time of Hmong refugee resettlement had a combined population of over two million (Pass 1980). The cities of Dallas and Fort Worth anchor the Metroplex with 1979 populations of one million and 500,000 respectively. They were in 1979, and still are, surrounded by smaller cities and towns ranging in population size from over 100,000 to less than 1,000. The DFW Metroplex is located in the northeast section of the state and is a hub for trade, distribution, and transportation (both rail and air). In the late 1970s, the area's recreational and cultural facilities included some of the nation's leading museums, professional and amateur athletics, large lakes, theaters, and recreational parks. It was home to eight institutions of higher education and also home to multiple recreation sites such as Six Flags amusement park, a wax museum, as well as national baseball and football teams. Its geographic loca-

Figure 2.6 Map of DFW

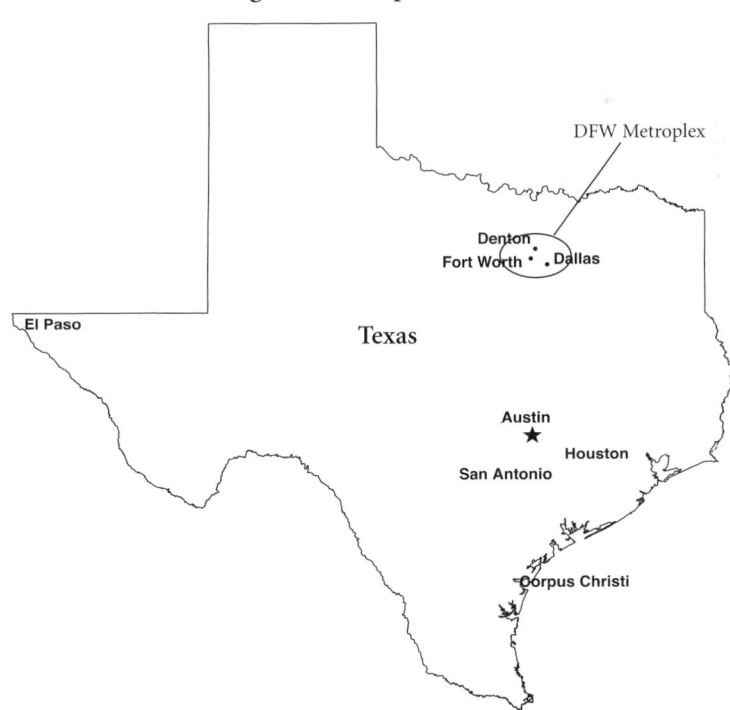

tion is considered to be in the interior lowlands of the state, which are characterized by its flat land and dense red clay soil. As part of the southernmost part of the Great Plains, the area maintains a hot, dry climate for most of the year.

In late 1979, the United States took over 50,000 Hmong refugees and scatter placed them across the country. DFW was one of those locations. The Hmong were mostly put in the northwest to southeast suburbs surrounding the two anchor cities that were, at the time, considered to have the lowest cost of living and most affordable housing. Thus, small concentrations ended up in the towns of

Figure 2.7 Map of DFW Townships

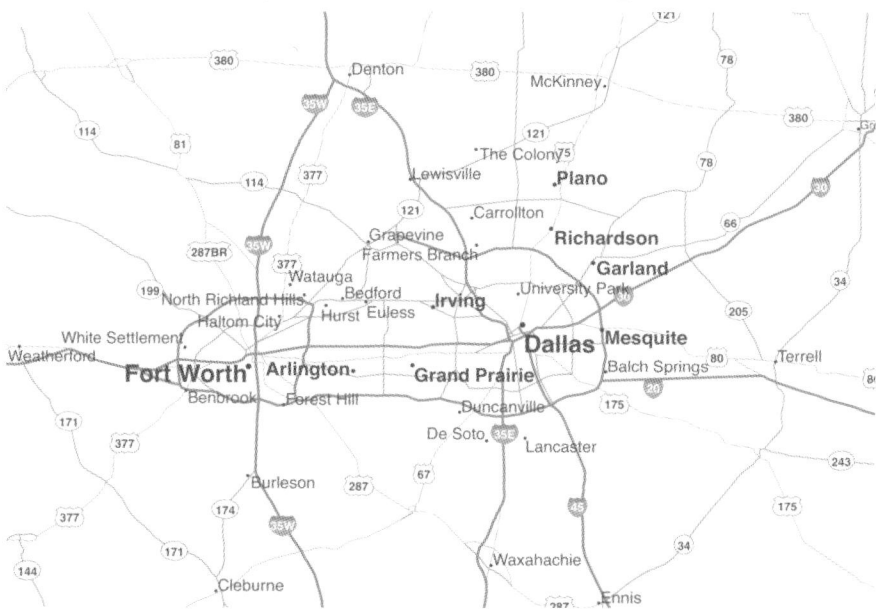

Arlington (1979 pop. 122,000), Irving (1979 pop. 103,700), Grand Prairie (1979 pop. 58,000), Duncanville (1979 pop. 22,000), North Richland Hills (1979 pop. 18,900), Cedar Hill (1979 pop. 4,900), and Keller (1979 pop. 1,900).

The 1979 racial and ethnic composition of these areas was predominantly Anglo-American, 18 percent African-American and approximately fifty thousand people who identified as Mexican-American. At the same time as the Hmong resettlement was going on, large numbers of Vietnamese were also being resettled in a similar scatter-placed distribution throughout the Metroplex. In fact, U.S. statistics show that by 1980 there was already a population of 5,000 Vietnamese in the area (Commerce 1983). Figure 2.9 illustrates the ethnic composition of the Dallas/Fort Worth Metropolitan statistical area in 1980. Note that the category of "Asian" is comprised of Vietnamese, Cambodian,

**Figure 2.8 Ethnic Composition Dallas/Fort Worth Area 1980**

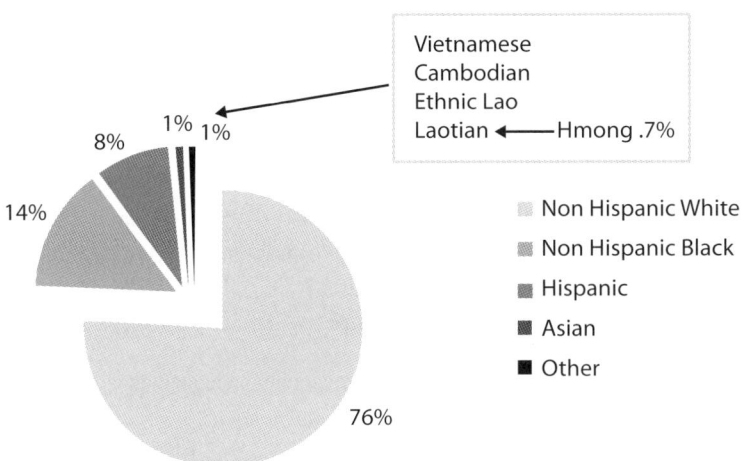

and Laotian. The Hmong are a subset of the Lao, and therefore exact numbers were not recorded. Community estimates put them in the range of .2 and .3 percent of the DFW population.

The character of the DFW Metroplex changed after the opening of the Dallas Central Expressway in 1956, when the cities of Dallas and Fort Worth began to experience suburban sprawl. The houses in these suburbs followed the "new urbanism" development design of its time with ranch-style homes on small lots, with back alleys that led to rear garages. The streets without alleys often had L-shaped garages attached to the front of the home and driveways that swept in front of the home. This "smart growth," as it was called by city planners, was designed to promote environmentally friendly land use, and to promote a sense of community (McDonald 1986). Consequently, children's activities like biking, basketball, and jump rope, began to take place in the back alleys instead of the front of the house. This left the front of people's homes abandoned and became the site of meticulously manicured lawns not meant for playing or walking on. These neighborhood changes coincided with a time when planning boards were excluding sidewalks in their new neighborhood designs. These design trends of the late 1970s resulted in neighborhood developments that were not pedestrian friendly, and have been credited by city planners as contributing to the decline of face-to-face relationships in the area.[1]

This was also the time of shopping mall and super-store development, when mega-retail zones were created on the outskirts of town leaving the traditional

---

1. This information was garnered from a personal conversation with Barbara Becker, Ph.D., FAICP, Executive Director and Dean, School of Urban and Public Affairs, University of Texas at Arlington.

downtown shops empty in favor of larger, often less-expensive chain stores. Foot traffic in the downtowns ceased in favor of driving out to the malls. In general, the late 1970s saw a transition in planning and zoning that reduced foot traffic and took people out of daily consequential contact with their neighbors and into a more auto-dependent and secluded lifestyle.

Despite these distancing developments, there were two places where the community continued to gather in ritualistic celebration, at church and at high school football games. Football frequently involved the total participation of school and town, and cheerleaders, marching bands, and pep rallies all served to intensify its importance. Historian Archie McDonald describes Texas football as a spectacle event where emotions "erupt in a crescendo of civic pride that helps define the boundaries of the community both geographically and psychologically" (1986:159). Churchgoing, on the other hand, has been a part of Texas' social fabric ever since white settlers believed that such acts demonstrated "the triumph of civilization over the heathen wilderness" (Pritchard 1988).

DFW's economy is derived from both Old and New Texas. Old Texas had an economy that depended on the production of a few raw materials—cotton, cattle, and oil. The control of manufacturing, commerce, finance, and services were left largely to out-of-state interests (Campbell 2003). The modern Texas economy in DFW at the time of refugee resettlement in 1979 had become far more diversified. While the economy still drew support from agriculture and oil, it also depended more heavily on manufacturing, commerce, and finance. It was also a time when electronics and other high-tech industries and health enterprises rose to importance. By the late 1970s, the DFW area had 4,200 factories employing 250,000 workers and produced a variety of products from electronics and transportation equipment, to oil, mining machinery, and apparel. In fact, according to the *The Dallas Morning News* (Pass 1980), the areas workforce was the largest in the South, exceeding 1.2 million.

In the late 1970s, the U.S. economy was in deep recession with double-digit inflation rates, but Texas' oil exports brought great prosperity to the state. During the span of 1973 to 1981, Texas gained more than 2.2 million jobs (a 40 percent increase), and Texan's personal income tripled (Pass 1980:445). To the delight of developers, real estate agents, and the savings and loan operators who provided the finance, Texans seemingly needed an abundant supply of new houses, apartment complexes, office buildings, and shopping malls for those from the other troubled areas of the country relocating to the Metroplex. As such, a popular slogan coined at the time became "Gone to Texas."

As Texas prosperity and growth in the midst of national economic stagnation caught the imagination of people everywhere, it created a rage of all things

Texan. Boots and jeans became fashion statements, southwestern art could be found in galleries everywhere, and Hollywood contributed with a string of popular movies and television shows, including the worldwide sensation *Dallas*. Even the Dallas Cowboys football team became larger than life, and known as America's Team. Journalist Fred Pass (1980) notes that "during this time the people of DFW took all this attention to heart. Beyond thinking that their state was special, they thought of it as invulnerable and invincible as well."

This exceptionalism added to a special identity this area already enjoyed as a part of Texas for nearly two hundred years. The "Texas mystique," as it is known, can be traced to the area's early history. According to Archie McDonald, three key historical events are attributed to formation of this attitude. They are:

> The long-term existence of the Texas Rangers and their immense popularity as figures of frontier justice; the Alamo and the titanic figures associated with it and with the creation of the Republic of Texas, men such as Davy Crockett and Sam Houston; and the cattle drives following the American Civil War, the greatest epic expression of the generic American hero, the cowboy (McDonald 1986:177).

This legacy was added to in the 20th century when Texas became the richest oil-producing state in the nation. Thus, DFW's two anchor cities became the embodiment of those icons: Fort Worth as the rancher cowboy stereotype, and Dallas as the oilman wheeler-dealer.

> From Davy Crocket and Sam Houston to J.R. Ewing and the Cowboys, the DFW Texan became transformed into an enduring national icon to those who lived outside its borders, and a state of mind for those who lived within (178).

It is within this unique historical, economic, and environmental orientation that many people in DFW draw their identity. Many are fiercely independent and proud of the fact that Texas once stood on its own as a Republic. They have thus been characterized in film and literature as having a fierce devotion to personal liberty, hard work, and rampant individualism. Author John Steinbeck made this point in 1962, when he wrote "Texas is a state of mind, but I think it is more than that. It is a mystique closely approaching a religion. Above all, Texas is a nation in every sense of the word" (Steinbeck 1961). While these generalizations obviously cannot speak to everyone in the area, I argue that they contribute to that signature assemblage of images that would envelop the Hmong who settled there.

To appreciate the Hmong's position in this area, it is important to remember America's relationship with them prior to their flight to Thai refugee camps. When the communist Pathet Lao began bombing the homes of the Hmong, they looked to the United States for help and were confused when their friends did not come to their aid. To this day, a common claim among the Hmong who worked with American troops is that the U.S. government had promised them compensation and protection in the event of military defeat by the communist forces (Office of Refugee Resettlement 1989). They don't understand why the United States left them to their "executioners." It is believed that the Hmong lost more lives from helping the United States than any other ethnic group in Laos. It is estimated that approximately 30,000 people were killed and several hundred thousand displaced (Lee 1982).

After flight to Thailand, the United States was the largest of the five countries officially taking part in Hmong resettlement. The earliest arrivals had worked closely with the U.S. military and Royal Lao Government during the Vietnam War and were a mix of some with skills and knowledge necessary to survive in a military environment, but without occupational or language skills that would translate into financial support for their families in an industrial society. This first large wave of 50,000 Hmong was admitted in 1979–1980 and equaled approximately half of the total Hmong admitted to the United States as part of the resettlement of Southeast Asian refugees, the largest refugee resettlement effort ever made by the U.S. government (Ranard 1988).

Utilizing six different NGO refugee agencies, the government found local churches and individual sponsors throughout the Dallas/Fort Worth suburbs willing to take responsibility for aiding in this resettlement. Some 250 Hmong families were originally scatter-placed among these sponsors. By the end of the first year of resettlement, influenced by the social dynamic of the extended family and clan, and the merits of the different social-service friendly states that had taken refugees, approximately two hundred of these original families had migrated out of Texas to the larger Hmong communities in California, Minnesota, and Wisconsin. By December 1980, only fifty Hmong families remained to begin a life in the DFW Metroplex in Northeast Texas.

At this point a number of obvious differences in the scale and structure of the two receiving societies of Gammertingen Germany and the DFW area of the United States is evident. As stated in the Introduction, migration theory, in general, has been drawn from "large immigrant gateway cities where researchers focus on well-established immigrant neighborhoods and ethnic institutions" (Glick Schiller 2011). As such, the diasporic connections and integration patterns have been assumed to be representative of their resettlement and incorporation practices. The vast differences in the two field site communities in this study allows us to focus on the different contexts of member-making and relations that affect processes of belonging for refugees who agencies have settled in places with distinct histories, resources, and global positioning.

The next chapter addresses refugee resettlement policies in the two field sites. I explore how these policies were derived from a combination of both national and local ideologies, as well as how their local administration affected the Hmong's perception of belonging. Appendix 1 illustrates a comparative community profile of the first generation Hmong families in the formal study sample at both field sites, the more significant pieces of which will be discussed throughout this book.[2]

---

2. Beyond the formal study sample, literally hundreds of other Hmong in the DFW field site, and all the Hmong in the Gammertingen field site were a part of my participant-observation and informal conversations that shaped the analysis of this study.

CHAPTER 3

# POLICIES, POLITICS, AND NATIONAL BELONGING

*Lu X., a Hmong refugee, arrived in DFW directly from a camp in Thailand. He was from a village where most men and teenage boys were a part of the CIA's Secret War in Laos. His father served as a shaman for their clan and when it came time for United States resettlement, he and his family were not eligible because of his father's dependence on the hallucinogens used in the shaman rituals. A few years later, his father passed and the family was admitted to America and sent directly to Fort Worth, Texas. After four years of living in the Metroplex, Mr. X. remained confused about the formalities of becoming a legal permanent resident in the United States. In 1973, during the war between the North and South Vietnam, "the American people came to the Hmong and told us that the day we agreed to fight with them, that day we became Americans. How come we come here and are not Americans when they promised us we were?" Mr. X. learned that his green card allowed him permanent resident status. Mr. X. took comfort in its durability. Then the Reagan administration enacted a policy that required them to renew their green cards every ten years. His extended family in DFW held a meeting to discuss the implications of this change in policy. "What if one year America decides to cancel our residency? I know they promised our people that we can stay, but America has not always kept their promises to us." Mr. X. called on another Hmong family in the area, who were not hill people in Laos, but had lived in the city and had an education and passport prior to fleeing the country as refugees. They gave Lu X.'s family a better explanation of the differences between and consequences of being a green card holder versus a citizen. Mr. X. finally decided that he and his family should all apply for this other thing called "citizenship." Citizenship, they were told, meant that they could stay. Almost thirty years later, Mr. X. explains what citizenship status means to him: "The citizenship country is just to say where we live as Hmong: Hmong-American, or Hmong-Lao, but we are Hmong first. One hundred percent Hmong."*

*Meanwhile, Kang Y., a resident of Gammertingen, Germany, like Lu X., has lived there since he and his family left the Thai refugee camp. "We were just looking for a place to live safely. We didn't understand anything about the conditions of our being here, just that there was a country that wanted us. There was all this paperwork, paperwork, everything with Germany is paperwork. We couldn't read any of it, so someone from the city always filled it out for us."* After living in the village for ten years, someone from the city came and asked Kang Y. and his family if they "wanted to be German." "No," Kang told the man, "We want to be Hmong." Kang did not understand that they were asking them to become German citizens, and that this was seen as an honor. The Gammertingen government explained that becoming a German citizen was in their best interest and would prevent any future revocation of their resident status. "Since we [the Hmong] were here under special circumstances, there were not tests or anything, we just had to fill out some more paperwork and we were citizens." Kang chuckled. "I still don't think that we are Germans."

\* \* \*

Anthropologist Tobias Kelly suggests that "displacement is never simply a physical movement across space, but also involves transformations in the political practices through which people are related to place" (2009:26). The stories of Lu X. and Kang Y. underscore how different experiences with nation-state formalities of citizenship and different historical relationships with the country in which a population resettles can affect a refugee's perception of belonging. While it is generally understood that resettlement policies in different localities play a fundamental role in the process of belonging among refugees, these narratives illustrate that even when the legal conditions of entry and paths to citizenship vary from country to country, the process and its many stages often mean something entirely different to the refugee on the one hand and to the host country that devised them on the other. Moreover, as federal guidelines are not implemented in the same way in different locations and do not have the same implications in every context, the local interpretations of such policies play a similarly important role in experiences of belonging. Likewise, the background of each refugee may be distinct and therefore the way refugees in the same location experience and interpret the process of belonging may also vary.

The notion of citizenship has also become the focus of political discourse and academic inquiry. Scholars across a range of disciplines have been engaged in discussions about migration and citizenship. In this chapter I will draw on political scientist Rogers Brubaker's (1992) ideas of ethno-nationalism and its critique, and Steven Castles (2002) argument that nationalization must occur before citizenship. I also draw on Ward Goodenough's (1971) theory of cognitive anthropology that locates culture in the mind, and Irene Bloemraad's recent (2006) work on comparative processes of political incorporation in the United States and Canada. It is also helpful to distinguish between legal, or state citizenship, and participatory or democratic citizenship. The former, as Angus Stewart describes it, has to do with legal status and the latter has to do with "political actors constituting political spheres" (1995:64). Both these categories are helpful in understanding how the Hmong refugees compartmentalize different forms of group membership and actions. Brettell and Reed-Danahay also suggest that ethnographic investigation of immigrants as social actors should not "ignore consideration of the ways in which the host society's policies and discourses of citizenship shape the modes of political incorporation experienced by immigrants" (2008:5). Thus, this chapter follows a local understanding of how the Hmong live the process of naturalization and political engagement and how different policy "solutions" for refugeehood engender different types of agency and understandings of belonging.

The chapter will begin with an overview of the background of the legal requirements and policies of inclusion and exclusion as it pertains to citizenship for refugees in both research sites. It will then describe how those policies were locally explained, interpreted and implemented in DFW and Gammertingen. The chapter then delves into the relationship between citizenship and belonging through the lived experiences of the refugees. Finally, the chapter assesses how citizenship status has affected Hmong identity.

## Background to U.S. Refugee Policy

The United States did not have a formal refugee policy until 1980. In 1975, Congress established a resettlement aid program called the Parole System for Vietnamese refugees and a year later, the Laotian Hmong were granted the same help. Between 1975 and 1977, the first 187,000 former French Indochinese refugees were admitted under this system that relied on the attorney general to provide special entry of refugees who had been employees of the U.S. government (CRS Report for Congress 2002:4). The Hmong who entered the country under parole status are referred to by the government as the first wave of Hmong refugees and were generally well educated leaders from Lowland Lao or high-ranking military leaders in the Lao Resistance Army that, as explained in Chapter 3, had migrated to the lowlands as a result of Touby Lyfoung's work with the French Government, and fought against the Pathet communist Lao. Not more than twenty of these people were resettled in the DFW area; however, as will be explained in a later section, only five would remain in Texas. By 1977, all paroled refugees from Southeast Asia received permanent resident status.

The second wave of Indochinese refugees admitted to the United States between 1978–1980, were generally boat (Vietnamese) and land (Hmong) refugees who fled their communist governments and spent time in Thai refugee camps. The Hmong in this group were mostly hill people who had resided near the conflict in Laos and were, for the most part, illiterate and had never participated in any formal education (Kelly 1986:141). Some Hmong learned to read a basic Hmong Romanized Popular Alphabet (RPA) script through missionaries who introduced it to the hilltribe peoples in the 1950s.[1] As the international crisis in the camps grew, so did widespread international humanitarian resettlement efforts. The United States relaxed its quota caps during this time, admitting approximately eighteen thousand refugees per month (Kelly 1986:139). However, without any formal refugee policy in place, the parole system remained a very politicized, ad hoc, and inconsistent set of processes.

The continued Indochinese crisis was the catalyst for the late Senator Edward Kennedy to propose the Refugee Act of 1980 that systemized entry into the United States and standardized the services that refugee entrants should receive. The 1980 Act, which remains in place to this day, also defined the term *refugee* to conform to the working definition used by the United Nations, and for the first time made a clear distinction between refugee and asylee status. It also established a comprehensive program for the resettlement of these newcomers, and as a country that sees itself as a nation of immigrants, concrete paths to citizenship were built within it. Its provisions gave all Indochinese refugees conditional status for one year, after which they could adjust to permanent resident status and then, as people who were no longer welcome in their last country of residence, they were expected to proceed to a naturalized citizenship status in five years, thereby establishing their loyalty to their country of refuge (Aleinikoff & Klusmeyer 2001).

This policy has also been shaped by the country's global positioning, that is, by American foreign policy considerations. For example, under the Reagan Administration, it was assumed that it was in the interest of the United States to provide an alternative for those living under cold war Communist rule, and that by pursuing this alternative, people were " 'voting with their feet' in favor

---

1. Hmong in Laos, Thailand, Burma, China, Vietnam, France (and French Guyana), Australia, Canada, Argentina and in the United States now use the Hmong RPA script as a vehicle to communicate among themselves. The Hmong media in the United States, and American public offices and hospitals use the RPA writing system for their official translations or communications, and it is now officially taught at the Central Institute of the Chinese Nationalities in Beijing and in several American public schools and universities (http://www.hmongrpa.org/aboutus.html).

of a liberal, democratic system" (Suhrke 1981:61). America's involvement in Vietnam also generated a special interest in expanded quotas for Indochinese resettlement in the United States. Senator Hayakawa (R-CA) demonstrated this link by defending the large numbers of incoming refugees as the last phase of, and a small victory in, the Vietnam War:

> By welcoming Indochinese refugees to the United States we will once and for all show up the present government of Vietnam as the totalitarian, racist tyranny that it is. Morally, we shall have won the Vietnam War (Suhrke Feb 1981:61).

America's Indochinese refugee policies and legal paths toward citizenship were based on the idea that America would become their new homeland. By enabling the Hmong to achieve permanent resident status, it automatically opened a wide range of employment opportunities for them, made them eligible for in-state tuition rates at state colleges, and made them eligible for enlistment in the U.S. armed forces. The policies were also designed to act as a symbolic commitment by the United States to those who were fleeing communism.

## Background to German Refugee Policy

Germany, like the United States, is considered a liberal state; however its policy response and self-identification to postwar immigration has been different. The United States politically endorsed immigration after World War II as compatible with its national self-description as a nation of immigrants, while during this same period of time (West) Germany's policies resisted allowing permanent citizenship to immigrants as compatible with its self-description as not being a county of immigration.

Rogers Brubaker (1992:136) has suggested that Germany's earliest 1913 informal immigration policy was an outgrowth of assumptions surrounding an ethnopolitical conflict between the German-Slav borderlands and an attempt to preserve ethnic German-ness. He asserts that Germany found it essential to adopt the principle of *jus sanguinis* (citizenship through blood ties), which would prevent the naturalization of those they wished to exclude. While Brubaker's argument of *jus sanguinis* exceptionalizing Germany as an ethnic nation is increasingly challenged (see Heisler 2000; Thränhardt 2000; Hagedorn 2001), it is the fact that Germany has a policy of citizenship through blood ties at all, not necessarily its origin, that is important to this thesis' treatment of conceptions of immigrant belonging. A more undisputed origin of racialized thinking about nations that may have informed localized ideas of who belongs in Germany, as a German, and who does not, is part of Nazi law that Germany kept after World War II.

Germany's first formal refugee act was a reversal of policy in 1966 that reinforced the idea of citizenry as a community of descent thereby allowing entrance to post-WWII East Europeans of German descent who were escaping communism. The ministerial decision that granted this right was highly influenced not only by cold war ideology meant to liberate those in the East wishing to flee communism, but by Germany's interest in return migration to the homeland. The provisions for this group were generous and granted each entrant an unlimited residence permit in West Germany without having to go through formal asylum procedures (Lavenex 2001:44). This law made citizenship accessible to emigrants and their descendants while at the same time denying it to other guest worker foreigners of non-German descent, like the Turks and Portuguese who were brought in to rebuild Germany after the war, an act that Brubaker argues "made the German Empire ideologically more German" (Brubaker (1992:114).

Due to the atrocities of the Hitler regime, written into the Basic Law of the western sector of a divided Germany was a section focused on the primacy of protecting people in need. Under this section, humanitarianism (as defined by saving people from war, other violence, and what are perceived as "the evils of communism") and the right to asylum became an integral part of a new post-War political identity. German policy had to reconcile this newfound identification as humanitarians with their long-held construction of nationhood based on ethnic ties.

In the 1970s, this translated into several groups of so called de-facto refugees which the government could grant limited residence permits. Persons eligible for this status included: Jewish emigrants from the former Soviet Union; refugees with asylum status; and a special category called "quota "or "contingent" refugees who had been received in the course of humanitarian aid (HumHAG). Entrance eligibility for this latter special category was considered by the will of the state and was first applied to groups of refugees admitted from Chile and Argentina.[2]

In response to the post-Vietnam War refugee crisis, Germany played a lead role as rescuers of the so-called "boat people" with their Cap Anamur rescue vessel that pulled more than 10,000 Vietnamese from the Southeast Asian waters. With this relief work came firsthand accounts of the dire humanitarian needs of these people. Germany deemed the Indochinese situation an "imminent

---

2. These policies remain in place to date.

threat requiring immediate action," and their post-WWII identification as a humanitarian nation catering to those in need was echoed throughout the media. One newspaper account at the time read:

> It is forgotten that these are people who are literally drowning ... and no-one, but no-one, may presume to say: this or that man must drown and this or that man is to live (Neudeck 1980).

In response to this and other similar media coverage, Germany established a revised version of the humanitarian quota policy known as the 1980 Quota Refugee Law that allowed for the speedy entry of this group avoiding the usually lengthy asylum process (Federal Law Gazette 1 1057(1980)). The five Hmong families who were settled in Gammertingen were lumped in with the Vietnamese and admitted under this status.

As quota refugees the rules of entry became far less formal and cumbersome than those for asylees, and came with an immediate work permit, permanent residence status, and one of the few direct paths to citizenship offered the foreign-born. This path to citizenship defies popular characterizations of a German ethno-national self-understanding that left immigrants outside of the realm of state-membership (Brubaker 1997), begging the question of whether the Hmong who were admitted under this program were also allowed within the self-understanding of Germany's citizenry—that is, did these circumstances expand Gammertingen residents ideas of who was entitled to Germanhood, or Gammertingenhood?

In 1999[3] Germany liberalized its naturalization procedure, allowing guest workers citizenship status after fifteen years of residency. Some scholars have suggested that this has weakened Germany's ethnonationalistic definitions of who has a right to belong and be German (Aleinikoff 2001, Heisler 2007), while others question Germany's exceptionalist portrayal altogether (Thränhardt 2000, Hagedorn 2001). However, since this policy change was not in effect until twenty years after Hmong resettlement, this research allowed for the possibility that, like in Texas, ethnonational attitudes may have existed in Gammertingen, and that its residents may have displayed "exceptional" economic, social and political characteristics that were intertwined with past patterns of immigration and racial op-

---

3. The revised German Aliens Law went into effect January 1, 2000 establishing claims to naturalization for certain groups that became full legal claims in its amended form in 1993. In 1999, Germany took the final step of introducing *jus soli* into its naturalization law, thus breaking with the ethnocultural model which had dominated nation-building since the founding of the Second Reich in 1870 (Hollifield n.d.).

pression. The empirical question I sought to flesh out was if they did, then to what extent did they impact the process of belonging?

## From Nationals to Citizens

Citizenship means different things to different people. Legal Scholar David Weissbrodt defines it as "a legal status that connotes membership in and a duty of permanent allegiance to a society which arrives with it specific rights and responsibilities" (1998: 248). Several scholars, however, have noticed a general trend of immigrant and refugee decisions to elect citizenship based more on the rights and ease of restrictions, and less, if any, on feelings of loyalty and allegiance (Schuck 1998; DeSipio 2001; Mavroudi 2007). This presumes that they have stronger feelings toward the country they left behind. On the other hand, there are other scholars like Jansen and Lofving who criticize any presumption that a "refugees' real identity, if they were allowed to be themselves, is their belonging to an ethno-national category territorialized in relation to the homeland" (2009:6). This is not to say that people have some primordial national identity, but that their identities have, in part, been forged by the nationalizing efforts of their homelands. Refugee groups, like the hill people Hmong, arrived in Germany with little previous state attachments or sense of nation-state belonging. The sentiments they did carry with them to their resettlement sites were a combination of what Peggy Levitt (2001) refers to as cultural belonging, and a dimension of diasporic ethno-belonging rooted in principles of blood ties and clan connections. This blood affiliation that binds their community, I would argue, is not too unlike the principle of *jus sanguinis* practiced by the Germans.

In the process of nation-state building, many nationalism projects incorporated kinship principles into their efforts to create similar feelings of commonality. Germany unified in the mid-19th century around the idea of a shared blood, thus promoting itself as "the Fatherland" or nation of one's father. In fact, Armstrong (1982) suggests that the principle of *jus sanguinis* originated with nomadic societies that stressed ancestry and kinship to delineate tribal membership. As tribes began to move and migrate, members were encouraged to pass on their ethnicity to generations through this priority of bloodline. Kinship-based communities that pre-dated national ones have been traditionally moved from their kin loyalties to national ones through the process of nationalism that included a combination of acculturation into a modern way of life, and nationalism defined as subjectification to the nation-state (Eriksen 2002). Scholars have found, however, that these efforts fail to create a single identity in its members, meaning, where the refugees might have initially arrived with allegiance first and foremost to the continuance of their ethnic bloodline, after some nationalizing efforts were extended to them, they could develop simultaneous identities of German, *and* Hmong, *and* Schwaben.

When refugees arrive in a new host community, it becomes the nationalistic mission of the host communities to engage them in this process with the hopes of ultimately loosening their previous loyalties in favor of their host's national ones, ultimately ending in citizenship. On this point, Stephen Castles (2000:7) suggests that before an immigrant can be made into a citizen, he must first be made into a national. What was found missing in this process or path to citizenship for the Hmong in both resettlement locations was the nationalizing, or subjectification, to the nation-state. To understand why, it is important to look at how the local nationals imagined their role in this process. Understanding this will shed light on how and why the Hmong decided to adopt citizenship and how the efforts of the locals affected their perceptions of belonging.

On closer examination, I found that any intentional nationalism was largely ignored, in part, because neither location where this research took place was prepared for the arrival of the Hmong or was given any information on their ethno-historical background. Without this knowledge, state agencies and townsmen engaged the refugees from their own cultural frameworks of having lived in a nation-state, and had no idea that the Hmong needed to be "made into nationals." Several DFW area residents told me they had worked with the Hmong as part of this process in the late 1970s with no instruction other than to "Americanize them as quickly as possible." A women working for a Washington, D.C. agency responsible for placing Hmong into the DFW community at that time recounted her experience this way:

> Initially we didn't do anything to prepare the area and greater community for their [Hmong] arrival.... We caused each other a lot of grief and pain. There was a lot of conflict ... we were woefully unprepared for this. When the first Hmong came, the people thought they were strange. We never educated the public about them, nor the volunteers who were supposed to be Americanizing them.

To the local nationals, "Americanizing them" was understood as cultural assimilation, not nationalization. Others said emphatically that introducing the Hmong to citizenship was not their responsibility. Most of the DFW local nationals I talked to operated under the assumption that the refugees already understood their legal status. As one informant put it, "We never considered that they didn't know what citizenship was!" In DFW, the responsibility of citizenship outreach at that time fell under the office of Immigration and Naturalization (INS) and has since (post-9/11) shifted to the Department of Homeland Security's Office of U.S. Citizenship and Immigration Services (ICE). At the time of Hmong resettlement in DFW, there was no official outreach campaign from INS to refugees encouraging them to apply for citizenship. In the absence of this, and operating without any understanding of how the Hmong viewed themselves vis-à-vis the state, it was left to the refugee's own ethnic community to understand the process, seek out civics classes, and to apply for citizenship.

One Hmong male informant in DFW described how he and his community worked through this process:

> Those of us who came from the lowlands of Laos, had usually been to school, had Lao passports, and understood the idea of having a legal status and rights of citizenship in a country. But the Hmong who joined us in the refugee camps from the hills had no understanding of that. They lived up in the mountains without any interaction with the government. They didn't have official birth certificates, school records, or official anything of any kind. Sometimes, if they were lucky, they got a few hours of orientation in the refugee camp before being sent to the U.S. In this orientation, someone explained about their legal status as refugees, but they had nothing to relate that to. It was just words. Usually, someone from Catholic Charities or the International Rescue Committee would try to re-explain this status to the new arrivals; but again, the explanations didn't have any meaning. When the Hmong had been in Texas for a year, the charity groups would help them readjust their status to that of Permanent Resident. But it was the Lowland Hmong who went to everyone after five years and talked to them about citizenship and what it meant. The Hmong trust each other. We count on members of our own ethnic group to keep everyone informed of what is going on. Those that have more understanding, they help those along who have less. And together we make it (personal conversation).

The issues of Hmong political belonging became even further complicated in DFW by the lack of civic outreach for their participation. Irene Bloemraad speaks of a time when "citizenship was not just an individual choice but part of a larger social and political process urged on by political parties, unions, ethnic associations, religious bodies, schools, and other institutions" (2006:247). She suggests that when political parties and civic groups do not reach out to newcomers, it moves legal belonging away from a national social process to that of personal choice. This results, she argues, in immigrants who, like the

Hmong, naturalize for practical and material reasons, such as ease of travel and fear of deportation. Eventually, most DFW Hmong were pushed to citizenship by 1990s legislation that reemphasized the legal distinctions between citizens and noncitizens. But even then, this more aggressive method was only effective when their more-educated kinsmen convinced them of its practical merits in a context they could understand; mainly, that without it they could be forced, once again, out of one space and in search of another zone of refuge.

The DFW case illustrates how issues of belonging are further complicated by the unpreparedness of receiving communities for incoming refugee populations. Because refugee resettlement is usually in response to immediate and overwhelming circumstances, good information on populations is often not available until after they have been in the host country for some time. This leaves the refugee to invest significance in their new place outside the law and within their own cultural frame of reference. In her research comparing U.S. and Canadian immigrant cases, Bloemraad asserted that leaving newcomers to themselves to make citizenship decisions has moved legal incorporation toward a devalued state of "practical and material" citizenship in the United States. However, just because citizenship is elected for a practical and material reason doesn't mean it is valued any less by those who elect it. Value is emically experienced. To the Hmong who were fleeing persecution, the status of permanence and safety were highly valued.

For the Hmong who resettled in Gammertingen, unlike the experiences of those in DFW, issues of political belonging were nurtured along by political entities and civic groups. The village hired a full-time liaison to walk the Hmong through legal changes in status. However, this process had similar results in terms of nationalizing them as were seen in DFW. The local government liaison had misconceptions about how the Hmong thought of place and therefore, administered civic advice through his own Western lens. Similarly to the DFW experience, the Hmong in Gammertingen were left to filter ideas of citizenship through their own non-nationalistic frame of reference. This process became even more complicated in Gammertingen as communication was hampered by translation problems and, unlike the DFW Hmong experience, there were no lowland Hmong who had settled with them. This meant that there were no urban or educated clansmen among them to help interpret the process. The former Mayor of Gammertingen explained the process of how citizenship was offered to the Hmong in his village:

> They arrived in our town with little more than a week's notice. We found someone who could speak French who translated our German to one Vietnamese man who also spoke French. That Vietnamese man

then translated it to a fellow Vietnamese man who spoke Laotian, who translated it in Lao to a Hmong man who spoke a little Lao, who then translated it to the rest of his group in Hmong. This was difficult as the words and meanings don't translate so nicely between languages. It was like playing that children's game of telephone where you are quite certain that the message you start off with little resembles the message at the end of the line. We were never sure that the Hmong received any correct information. We communicated the best we could with pictures, with our hands, with our bodies, and expressions, but that, of course, limited the substance of any of our conversations. We hired a special liaison to work between the Hmong and our city. All communication, what we could communicate, went through this person. He was a German. He could not speak their language, but felt for them. After a year, the Vietnamese man who spoke French moved out of our town and our liaison was just left with gestures and limited words to work with (Gammertingen Mayor, personal communication).

As the Hmong became aware of other Hmong in France, Argentina, and the United States, they wanted to visit them for fellowship and for seeking out potential spouses with Hmong blood. They were directed by the liaison that, as Lao citizens, they had to get their travel approved through the Laotian embassy; this embassy was a day's train ride away in Berlin. It was in this context that the first conversations about legal status took place. One Hmong recalls how the process was experienced from their perspective:

> They told us that as Laotians, we had to get permission to travel from the Laotian consulate. We told them "we are not Lao, we are Hmong." But I don't think they understood. Being Laotian made it very inconvenient for us to do anything. After nine years, we were told that we had the chance to become German. The man from the city government told us what a great privilege this was, and how not every immigrant gets to do this. We didn't want to be German or Laotian; we wanted to just live in Germany and be Hmong. Then he told us that our travel would be easier and that we could just go to Gammertingen's city hall for everything instead of all the way to Berlin. We were also told that as Laotians, there was always the possibility that the German government could send us back, and he knew how much we wanted to live here; so we got our German citizenship. It made travel easier and we didn't have to worry about being forced out.

It is evident from these conversations that the government liaison clearly understood that it was his responsibility to move the Hmong down the path of citizenship, albeit, with little cultural understanding of how they perceive place—that is, as a plot of land they reside on, not an entity they belong to. It is also speaks to the hill Hmong's stateless existence in that they had to be told—convinced even—that they were Lao citizens. These experiences challenge Robert Park's observations about nation-state building that suggest that new immigrant's first "cease to be provincial foreigners" (1974:157). He argues that they first unite as foreign nationals, where "Wurtemburgers and Westphalians become in America first of all Germans; Sicilians and Neapolitans become Italians and Jews become Zionists" (157). The Hmong did not become a nation, or Laotians, but saw themselves as distinctly separate from Lao, as Hmong. The reasons for this may lie in the diasporic global networked identity they developed, a subject that will be more thoroughly examined in Chapter 7.

Like in the DFW case, many Hmong families who were resettled in Gammertingen reiterated similar sentiments over how the value-added benefits of citizenship weighed in on their decision to accept it. "In Germany, a mother gets paid to stay home and take care of her baby for three years; but only if a citizen. We [Hmong] stay home with our children anyways, so this citizenship was something we could use." This offers a different trajectory to that described by Legal scholar Peter Schuck (1998) who asserts that if citizenship outreach is more hands-on, state institution-to-immigrant, the result would be a more internally nationalized form of citizenship (see also Carliner et al., 1977; Plascencia et al., 2003). The Hmong in Gammertingen, as in DFW, expressed value in their citizenship status. Moreover, the Gammertingen Hmong were clearly engaged in matters of citizenship directly by the government, yet there is no evidence that they were cognizant of, or accepted, the nationalistic loyalties the government wished to accompany the change in legal status.

What was missing in the process of citizen-making, or national belonging for both Gammertingen and DFW Hmong was the making of nationals. Absent that, and left to the group's own frame of reference to sort out meaning, the Hmong in both locations saw the choice of citizenship as a mechanism through which they could gain control over the things that immediately affected their own lives—security to live in a place as Hmong and the right to travel to be with other Hmong—in essence, the right to continue to hold their notions of cultural belonging in a world of change. This challenges sedentary notions of belonging that presume that people display a strong attachment to territory. Instead, what is imperative is an understanding that the meaning of location can take different shapes for different groups of people.

It should also be noted that not every Hmong in either area of resettlement decided to take citizenship. Things that affected their choices seemed to be the same utility-based decisions that dominated choices *for* citizenship. For instance, when one of the original Hmong in Gammertingen, who had already taken German citizenship, got married to a Hmong from another European Union country (notably France or French Guyana), the new spouse often explained that they did not "need" German citizenship because they already had the same rights to extended social benefits and ease of travel as their German Hmong counterparts. Likewise, in DFW, it was not unusual to find a married Hmong couple where one spouse, usually the man, had elected citizenship and the other spouse not, reasoning that there was no "rush" for them to adopt it because they were entitled to "all the benefits" via their spouse.

A final reason given by Hmong in both locations for not electing citizenship in the host country involved spouses from Lao or Thailand who were married after refugee resettlement, who are consequently categorized as immigrants and not refugees. In this category, ninety percent of the Hmong immigrant spouses interviewed had not taken citizenship. The barriers included the time investment in learning the language at a proficient level, the lack of language classes available, and the cost. For example, for an immigrant spouse in Gammertingen to be eligible for citizenship, they have to take get a citizen-ready certification. This certificate is given after a six-month course of study that requires an investment of 100 Euros a month and six hours a day over a six-month period of time. Most female spouses in this situation expressed that they did not have the time and/or money to invest in it. In DFW, similar barriers were cited. It was more likely in DFW than in Germany that the immigrant spouse would be working a full-time job right away and had little time, money, or available child care to invest in the lengthy process. In such circumstances, these classes were often explained to me as a "luxury," especially when the other spouse was already a citizen. Therefore, even the decision *not* to elect citizenship was based on practicalities rather than on nation state loyalties. Pragmatic citizenship is not particular to the Hmong. Immigrant scholars have noted that those taking citizenship in both the United States and Western European countries often do so for pragmatic and legal reasons while often maintaining a place-based sense of cultural belonging to their home country (Brettell 2006; see also Gilbertson & Singer 2003, Vertovec 2004). The Hmong experiences offer a different dimension to these analyses as they reveal practical reasons for adopting citizenship that coexists with an identity that is maintained in an unfixed, stateless, diasporic space of ethnic identity.

# Rights, Responsibilities, Belonging, and Location: A Complicated Relationship

Does adopting citizenship result in broader understandings of national rights and responsibilities for those who were previously stateless? How are these messages transmitted and received at the local level? And, how do they complicate the relationship between location and belonging for the Hmong? To address this question, it is useful to consider Angus Stewart's (1995) distinction between "state citizenship" and "democratic citizenship." He operationalizes state citizenship as having to do with recognized legal status as was explored in the last section, and democratic citizenship as having to do with the participation of citizens as "political actors constituting political spheres" (64). This section will investigate how the latter is experienced by those with no previous state experiences and whether the rights and responsibilities that accompany citizenship translate into alternative notions of belonging.

While not ubiquitous, in DFW, some of the Hmong suggested that citizenship was allied with notions of representation and having a voice. For example, one male hill Hmong in his fifties expressed that he became a citizen, in part, to gain this form of representation.

> I think voting here in America is very meaningful. It's why I became a citizen; it makes me feel like I have representation. We didn't have representation in Laos beyond our clan.

A similar sentiment was echoed in Gammertingen.

> I vote all the time and follow politics with great interest. In Laos, our people lived without many human rights, and here we have a chance to have a say in the things that affect our lives. That is a privilege and a responsibility we take seriously.

In both these cases, the refugees compared the duties and responsibilities of citizenship as rights and privileges, suggesting that voting became a meaningful expression of agency in regulating the changes that affect their everyday lives at a different scale than they had experienced in traditionally clan-governed units in the hills. The human rights discourse embedded in citizenship civics courses in both localities seemed to make them aware that they were missing such benefits, or at least provided an empowered articulation to previous experiences of alienation. However, when it came to exercising those rights on a local level, there was a marked difference between the Hmong living in DFW and Gammertingen.

When asked about participation in local elections in DFW, I could only find one family that voted regularly. This is not unlike the broader DFW population that traditionally has a turnout of at, or below, seven percent of eligible voters (Wimmer 2009). On the other hand, a little more than half of all eligible Hmong in Gammertingen reported voting regularly in local elections. This too, mirrors local election turnout in Gammertingen, which according to the town's website, sits at fifty-three percent (City of Gammertingen 2009). When asked why they participate in local elections, one response, typical of other German Hmong was:

> I have voted in many local elections because the decisions being decided influence my life. It's better to get involved rather than letting others make all the decisions for you. It's my duty to do it, but also I do it because I am part of the society whom these decisions affect. I feel more a part when I am participating like this.

In response to the follow-up question "A part of what?" He replied, "more like included."

Another thing that influenced the German Hmong's participation in local voting was that they were regularly courted by political parties to do so even though their ethnic group was small in numbers. As one Gammertingen Hmong male in his thirties recalls:

> I received a personal invitation to join the SPD [a German political party] from the town hall. It wasn't mandatory, only if I had interest. They asked for my participation, so I at least considered it. I went to this meeting and decided to join the party. Since then I have voted in all the elections. Doing so makes me feel like I am a part of the citizenry here in Gammertingen.

When I asked "How so?" he replied "That I am included in the decisions the people [the local community members] make." I asked how much political influence the Hmong (as a group) thought they had. One Hmong woman, a registered voter also in her thirties, told me:

> I think we have a great amount of influence. The officials work for us, we hire them. I get to vote for my perspective, and my ideas. Through voting, we all have an influence and the voting box knows no race; everyone is equal in it.

"The voting box knows no race" is a popular slogan used by the SPD in a campaign to entice eligible immigrant voters to join them. That message had effectively reached the Hmong and was echoed by another male registered voter in his fifties who went further to couple citizenship status with that influence:

> I think we have as much influence as anyone else. I don't think the fact that we came here as refugees gives us any less influence. We are citizens.

When asked if the Hmong in Germany thought the locals would elect them into a local office, the focus group participants all scoffed at the idea repeating, "We don't have any interest in politics. We leave that to the Germans." It was apparent that the Hmong who settled in Germany felt their citizenship was an entrée into the voting community of Gammertingen, a community which they thought to be free from ethnic biases, and one that also gave them the freedom to self-select out of participating at more engaged levels.

In DFW, the Hmong's experience was just the opposite, and not surprisingly, with opposite results in terms of participation. One male Hmong citizen in his forties told me:

> The Hmong in Texas don't carry much influence because our population here is too small to be recognized. In California and in Minnesota, the Hmong have politicians at every event trying to get their vote, but here, no one seems to care about our vote. I think it's because our numbers are too small. We are never approached for support by the political parties. We aren't even on their radar.

When asked if they thought they had any political influence in DFW, the Hmong man spoke hypothetically—"They should listen to us, we fought for them." When asked if they ever cashed in on this perceived clout, I was told this story about a local man threatened with deportation:

> We have some political influence as an organized group through our Hmong American Association. The government listens to them. We once all rallied together when a man from our community was going to be repatriated because of several drunk-driving tickets. Through this local organization we wrote letters to our State representative telling the story of how he was an integral part of the Secret War in Laos, and how he is now a successful businessman in Texas who employs people and brings in lots of tax money. The authorities dropped the repatriation and the community looks after this man to make sure he does not do this again. I think the local Texas representative listened to us because we were their special allies in the war.

For the DFW Hmong, it was this past status as U.S. allies that they felt gave them influence, not their present status as citizens. This idea had trickled down from U.S. political bills such as the "Hmong Veterans' Naturalization Act" proposed by the late Congressman Bruce Veneto (D-MN) to honor the Hmong people for their past contributions to the country in the Vietnam War and make it easier for them to attain U.S. citizenship. Louisa Schein suggested that such language singled the Hmong out "as entitled to membership not so much by virtue of their current participation in the United States economics and civic affairs, but rather on the basis of their clienteles 'service' to the United States in the past" (1998:180). These experiences are a form of what Rosaldo has termed "vernacular notions of citizenship" (1994:252)—where a group claims distinctive and special rights and representations different from official models of citizenship.

It was also clear that the DFW Hmong did not think this special status by the national government afforded them any political clout at the local level. In fact, their face-to-face experiences with politicians suggested just the opposite. The long-time director of the local Hmong organization expressed the limitations they felt in organizing politically. He recalled a time he attended a rally to speak along with other immigrant and refugee leaders about immigration issues. He said a politician came out to the crowd and "warned" the group sternly, saying, "Don't mess with Texas!" The Hmong leader interpreted the politician's actions to mean that getting involved in local politics was risky and might somehow jeopardize their community's right to live there. "That was the last time we tried anything like that. The Hmong here just prefer to be quiet and live in peace. We don't want to give anyone reason to ask us to leave." It was clear that the local political structures in the DFW area not only sent messages that the Hmong votes were not important, but also that they were not welcome to engage more actively in politics. The Hmong filtered these messages through their own past experiences and histories of displacement and statelessness. They were unaware of the full freedoms of expression that came with American citizenship, but could remember vividly how the Americans and Laotians acted violently toward each other in the war when one made the other angry. Their memories, coupled with the local experiences with politicians, are what alienated them from the political system. In fact, they were only willing to risk playing the "ally" card, when one of their own was in danger.

While both Hmong communities described citizenship as the right to political representation, and both communities had very small numbers, only those in Gammertingen felt compelled to exercise that right to representation at the local level. There were three crucial things that seemed to account for the differences in behavior. Firstly, the German Hmong were approached by the local parties and this made them feel like their voice was wanted, important, and counted. They were welcomed to the village by the mayor who hired a special liaison to work with them for several years as they arrived in the town. The Hmong in Germany also had no previous military or political history with the country that they were aware of or felt they needed to be afraid of. This is not to say that the Germans did not have a violent past, it is just that the Hmong were unaware of it. Politicians were visible, important, friendly, and hands-on with the Hmong from the onset of their resettlement.

By contrast, the DFW Hmong were not engaged by the local politicians or parties. They were settled somewhat anonymously into various towns and had no direct contact or relationship with any elected officials. They were also aware that politicians regularly courted the larger Hmong resettlements in the northern United States. This gave them a symbolic message of unimportance and invisibility to the local political community. The Hmong in DFW also had a history with the U.S. government where the United States did not always keep their word and they had also witnessed, and been a part of, the U.S. wrath against the Vietnamese. Bloemraad suggests that the "integrating structures of reliance" (2006:237) are on fellow immigrants and community organizations that lead their own ethnic groups into political action, and that "the ethnic community's ability to and interest in promoting political integration relies heavily on the symbolic and material support of government." This is reflected in the Hmong's experience where those who settled in DFW, with an organized ethnic association, but no political outreach or relationships with the local government or political parties, yielded lower rates of voter participation and political membership than among the Hmong who settled in Gammertingen who had no formal ethnic organization, but were openly courted by local political institutions to participate. These cases illustrate Bloemraad's argument (2006) that certain places have more supportive structures of political opportunity than others. Secondly, local voting apathy was a part of the DFW culture at large, which seemed to affect Hmong opinions, whereas voter engagement and responsibility was a part of the Gammertingen culture where their voting philosophy tells every citizen they count, and thus even a small minority feels politically empowered. Thirdly, these experiences emphasize the need to consider the political history, or lack thereof, in explaining why a group may or may not choose to engage. All these differences in voting behavior illustrate why attention to differences in where refugee groups resettle and the impact of locality on belonging merits further anthropological investigation.

The data from this study also suggests that voting made people feel a part of the political state—the territorial political unit of Germany or America—but not a part of the nation—the emotive sense of homogeneity, or psychological bond of a social group in common ideology.[4] This is significant in that political scientists have long argued that voting is a mechanism that makes people into nationals. I was further interested in whether or not citizenship status had any effect on whether the Hmong began to self-identify as "Americans" or "Germans." Do those identifications connote any sense of psychological attachment or belonging to the social group of local nationals? Brettell and Reed-Danahay (2011) found in their research on Indian and Vietnamese immigrants in the United States that after accepting citizenship, immigrants still confronted questions about what it means to be American, or ethnic, or any hyphenated identity in-between. They suggested, "these constructions of identity across boundaries and in relation to 'an other' also have important implications for how members of these two populations participate in the civic sphere and define meaningful citizenship practice."

To explore the effects of citizenship and political participation on Hmong notions of belonging, I asked respondents in both locations who had accepted citizenship and were old enough to vote a series of questions using a Likert Scale. Each response was followed with open-ended questions asking why they situated themselves in that category. Participants in each location were made of both males and females of various generations (those born in Laos, those who had been born in Laos but resettled in the West before they finished grade school, and the Western-born children of the refugees) who had adopted citizenship of the host country. These respondents were asked, on a scale of 1–5 (with 1 meaning they rarely identified and 5 meaning they commonly identified with a specific aspect of their identity), how strongly did they identify with being Hmong, Lao-Hmong, American-Hmong or German-Hmong, American or German, and Texan or Schwaben. Figure 3.1 gives an overview of the answers to that question, by displaying the mean scores of each field site.

These results demonstrate that individuals at both field sites still self-identified the strongest (4.7:5 and 4.3:5) with being Hmong—an ethnicity, and not one of the national identifiers (American 3.7:5 and German 2.6:5). As has been suggested, "To know how people refer to themselves with regard to group-labels is clearly not enough. We need to know the meaning they attach to the chosen label" (Prümm et al., 2003).

---

4. Definitions taken in part from Connor, Walker's, 2000. "A Nation is a nation, is a state, is an ethnic group, is a …", *Ethnic and Racial Studies,* 1(4):377–400.

Figure 3.1  Self-Described Hmong Identity*

|  | The Hmong of Texas | The Hmong of Gammertingen |
|---|---|---|
| Hmong | 4.7 | 4.3 |
| Lao-Hmong | 3.0 | 4.0 |
| American/German-Hmong | 4.1 | 3.8 |
| American/German | 3.7 | 2.6 |
| Texan/Schwaben | 3.5 | 1.2 |

* I initially chose to forgo a local category of DFW and Gammertingen in favor of Texan and Schwaben as I found those identities to dominate the identity perceptions of the local nationals. However, in hindsight, I should not have assumed it also dominated the perceptions of the Hmong and included those options in a separate category.

A typical Texan response to my question of why Hmong identity trumped their new nationality was:

> I feel we live in America and have U.S. citizenship but I live my life as Hmong: I participate in Hmong funerals and weddings, and the Hmong New Year and eat Hmong food and the way I raise my children is Hmong. We also use Hmong herbs from Laos for certain things.... So I feel I am Hmong first, then American. That's how I think of myself.

Likewise in Gammertingen, a typical response was:

> I gave German identification a 3 [in the middle] because we use this for paperwork when they ask our citizenship. But we are not German; we are Hmong living in Germany. We are Hmong who live in other countries. We were Hmong living in Laos, and now we are Hmong living in Germany. A nation is just a place to live as Hmong.

This particular response is interesting in that it indicates this person had actually given the term *nation* some thought and attached to it a geographic or place-based meaning. Bloemraad argues that without support for new immigrant communities to engage in the political process, new citizens are likely to become legal but not active citizens, merely "inhabitants of a physical space or carriers of a passport." In the case of the Hmong in Gammertingen, we see a much more targeted effort by political parties to engage the Hmong, who in turn, have high rates of voter participation. Yet, contrary to Bloemraad's theory, after 30 years residing in the country, they still associate nation with a space where one resides, not necessarily a community which one has group membership, a perception that comes from their stateless existence in the hills. This is similar to a condition Bowman recognized in refugee camps where refugee existence is one of "extraterritoriality," a condition he describes as being "in" but not "of" the space they physically occupy (2002:344). This ethno-geographic parallel became personified for many of the Hmong as a hyphenated identity. One DFW Hmong man explained why he used a hyphenated identification:

> We only use Lao-Hmong because other people don't know who we are or where we came from. If we say "Hmong," people say "What's that?" So we have to say Lao-Hmong so people [Americans] associate us with a place. The same when we use "Hmong-American." We live here now, but we are still Hmong. So like Lao-Hmong, we use it to explain who we are and where we live at this moment in history.

These parallel identities are then passed on to the second-generation as one such second-generation Hmong female from Germany explained:

> Growing up, our parents always made it a point to tell us we were Hmong kids and the other children in school were German kids. So I always knew I wasn't a German. Even when we got our German citizenship, our parents still saw us as Hmong. Hmong is not a nationality. We see nationality as just lawful residence, so we are Hmong residing lawfully in Germany and before that Hmong who lived lawfully in Laos. If I were to identify myself, I would say that I am a German-Hmong. If I say this to my German friends, they say, "You are German, because your citizenship is German." But my parents taught me that I am Hmong. Germany is just where I live.

Several of the Hmong interviewed in both places said that to be German or American involved changing their worldview, suggesting nationalism was more an adoption of a new state of mind. They separated the two worlds through a hyphenated identity. Here is the way one adult male in Gammertingen explained it:

> We are Hmong-German because we live here and have German citizenship. Slowly, we are adopting a German mentality. Our mentality and ways of life are very Hmong. This is how we would describe ourselves to Germans. I have lived here so long that I already think a little German. My wife has only been here a few years and has not made that leap mentally.

Another adult female asserted:

> I have German citizenship, but I wasn't born here and I don't think the way the Germans do. It comes, but slowly. I get along with them, but our way of thinking is completely different. The Hmong mentality is completely different than the Western one. I live here in Germany, but I say I am a true Hmong in my mentality and way of life. So I am at home here in Germany, but not completely.

I also heard similar responses related to state of mind in DFW from a Hmong man:

> I identify with the everyday down to earth friendships and attitudes of Americans. I like their attitudes toward technology and education and philosophy; but there is also a lot here that is bad, and I hold onto the Hmong thinking for those things; like family values and the way we take care of each other. So I say I am Hmong-American, with the Hmong first.

Or:

> Even though America is my country, I am a Hmong person, and we'll never forget that no matter where in the world we live.

It is noteworthy that the Hmong in DFW identified slightly more strongly with a hyphenated identification (4.1) than those in Gammertingen (3.8). Since their responses on how they use hyphenated identities are so similar, I posit that the small statistical difference in identification may rest more on the fact that the term "Hmong-American" has become a part of the immigrant discourse in America, whereas "German-Hmong," has not had the same impact, presumably because of their small numbers. Again, the difference is a matter of context.

These responses give us a glimpse into the way that the Hmong situate legal and cultural belonging. Their explanations reinforce Ward Goodenough's claim that "culture [is located] in the minds and hearts of men" (1971:41). Cognitive anthropology holds that culture is composed of mental structures that guide individual behavior. The Hmong in both locations express not having been able to cross that mental bridge from their worldview to that of their hosts. Hybrid identifications, in this sense, become a way to mentally separate the two. "We may live here" as one German Hmong said, "But we are not German. We're Hmong." Schneider (in Barns 1971:85) argues that even though culture may exist in a phenomenological world, because those ideations are acted upon at the individual level, actors "have some free rein to try to beat it, join it, change it, etc." These hybrid identities are manifestations of a form of cultural resistance and agency that emphasizes preserving Hmongness in the face of national subjectification. It is an example of Terence Turner's concept of culture as "the means by which a society maintains its morale and capacity for action, including both political action vis-a-vis the national society and the reproduction of its own pattern of life" (Turner 1991:304). It can also be seen as another form of resistance to state-making projects by the Hmong hill people in a long history of political and cultural refusal designed to keep state-like concentrations of power at arm's length.

Finally, I talked with Hmong participants at both locations about whether they identified themselves locally, as either Texan or Schwaben. Most respondents conceptualized a local identity in terms of its cultural particularities, and how strongly they identified with it was a matter of how well they mastered those particularities. For instance, a second-generation DFW male said he somewhat identified with being Texan because "I do love Texas and say 'y'all,' but I don't wear the big belt [buckle] or hat or ride a horse." Similarly, several first-generation respondents in Gammertingen said they did not identify with being Schwaben as "its dialect is difficult to speak and understand." Most second-generation Hmong living in Gammertingen said they "somewhat" identified as Schwaben because they were brought up "speaking the dialect like everyone else." One 21-year-old female said:

> Well I am from this area and know the dialect, and others identify me as from this region, so I guess I identify with being Schwaben a little.

One DFW Hmong man who I visited explained that he was "very proud of being Texan" while pointing to a touristic photo of himself wearing a cowboy hat, boots, sitting on a horse, and carrying a toy .53 magnum. The same was true for a German Hmong man who said he somewhat identified with being Schwaben because he recognized that when he and his wife *choose* to do German things, the kinds of choices they make (food, accent, and jokes) are indicative of this region. Contrary to choosing to "put on" a locality, they expressed that being Hmong was more intrinsic and not an accessorized choice. As one Texas Hmong man explained:

> Hmong always remain Hmong, no matter where they live, they are Hmong. I am an original Lao-Hmong, I speak fluent Lao, but I am always Hmong.

One German Hmong woman similarly expressed it this way:

> You are born Hmong. You can live here and there, but you carry Hmong with you. It's in your bones. It's in your head. It's in your hearts. It's in your past [ancestry].

In this way, none of these people found being somewhat Texan or Schwaben to be in conflict with being Hmong, because they saw "Hmongness" as something internal like "in their bones" and phenomenological as in their heads and hearts, and local identity as something external that could be put on or taken off, like a ten-gallon hat or dialect.

Because it seemed that the first-generation Hmong who did not come from a background of considering themselves subjects of a nation state and therefore had no previous experiences of nationalism, I assumed that the Western-born children of the Hmong refugees, who had been brought up in public schools that served to inculcate people into a national subjectification would have more of a nationalistic feeling about their status as citizens. I asked them what their citizenship meant to them. Not surprisingly, the DFW-born Hmong drew on Texas discourses associated with constitutional freedoms, the right to bear arms, as well as the right to chase the American Dream in their replies. On the other hand, the Gammertingen-born Hmong drew their answers from German discourses of human rights and liberties. Voting loyalty was a form of voice that they chose to express within the boundaries of citizenship; it was a status that seemed to solidify their geographic security and allow them new forms of agency, and one that ran parallel to ethnic membership. These examples serve as a reminder that ethnic and national membership is not necessarily congruent, but may, for some peoples, run along different axes.

## Reconciling Citizenship and Belonging

For Lu X. and Kang Y., whom we met at the beginning of the chapter, the process of acquiring citizenship, engaging in local politics, and becoming a German or American was filtered through Hmong kinship ideology where loyalty and attachment have traditionally been directed toward members of their kin group and not through legal incorporation into the framework of a classical state. This resulted in the Hmong's need for a new kind of ideology capable of creating cohesion between established kin relationships and new relationships with the state.

The experiences of the Hmong who arrived in Gammertingen and DFW demonstrate the struggle of refugees trying to reconcile legal citizenship status with kin-based notions of belonging where clan and lineage serve as the primary integrating mechanisms not nation or state, and vast differences in "East" vs. "West" worldviews. The refugees needed little coaching to understand the pragmatic benefits of legal citizenship and chose to accept it primarily because it secured a place for them to continue being Hmong. Participants in both field sites did not see this change in status as an identity conflict because Hmongness is not, and has never been, territorially bound but rather relies on kinship networks and face-to-face interactions for the loyalty of its members. They, therefore, compartmentalized these parallel relationships of "residing in" and "belonging to" via hyphenated identities such as Lao-Hmong, German-Hmong, and American-Hmong. This is different from other scholarship on hyphenated immigrant identities in that the hyphenated identities don't represent hybridity, but parallel relationships.

For the Hmong participants in both field sites, citizenship status also brought a cognizance of rights and responsibilities that were different and more positive than those they had enjoyed in their previous location and the agency to have a voice in a broad scale of decisions that would affect their lives through new forms of political engagement. However, whether or not they engaged politically had to do with local experiences, the amount of face-to-face relationships typical of the scale of their resettlement site, and the Hmong's previous history or experiences with the resettlement country.

This chapter also looked at whether legal status as a citizen influenced the localized identities of belonging to a place; that is being part of "the Gammertingen people" or "the DFW people." In this matter too, the Hmong in each location conceptualized local identity as being in a different compartment than being Hmong, or being a legal resident in a specific location. They expressed the supposition that local identity is embedded in cultural accessories — things you put on and take off, like an accent or a costume. How Texan or Schwaben they felt had more to do with how well they thought they adorned themselves in these cultural accessories and was not affected by citizenship or Hmong status. It is easy to see how the Hmong arrived at this position. To be a "local" one doesn't need a passport (official legal membership) or kin relations (blood membership). Notably, the social relationship to place greatly affected the Hmong's feelings of being a part of the local society. The Hmong in Gammertingen were more strongly socially incorporated as a result of the face-to-face relationships they shared with their host via the small size of the village as opposed to the relative anonymity felt by the Hmong in DFW due to their placement in a larger metropolitan area. This suggests that the direct role of scalar placement and the number of active social mediators in the host community might be strong indicators or measurements in the process of social cohesion.

If, as Eriksen has suggested, "at the identity level, nationhood is a matter of belief" (2002:104), then the experiences of the Hmong in both field sites do not demonstrate that citizenship, as a matter of status change, was accompanied by a belief in belonging to a nation. But rather, their conceptualizations of citizenship can be understood as an expression of both structure and agency—of attempts to be incorporated into independent nation-states and active resistance against it. This chapter also underscores the need to move outside the confines of the nation-state in understanding the process of migration and carefully historicize the relationship between refugees and their host countries when considering matters of citizenship and belonging. And finally, the differences in experiences of the Hmong in both locations emphasizes, once again, the need to root investigations of the unequal and differential processes by which refugees come to experience belonging in theories of locality and place.

As the particulars of Americanization and Germanization are felt at the local level, often through various agents of state and civil society, the next chapter will explore local subjectification and how it has affected Hmong paths of belonging in Gammertingen and DFW.

CHAPTER 4

# MAKING MEMBERS: INSTITUTIONAL CONSTRAINTS, AGENCY, AND LOCAL BELONGING

For immigrant newcomers, there are multiple factors that shape the process of belonging, building social capital, and becoming a member of a local community. Anthropologist Aihwa Ong (2003), in her work with Cambodian refugees, has suggested that belonging is defined in part by unofficial social meanings and criteria conveyed through relationships with official institutional structures such as NGOs, municipalities, church organizations, and community groups. Ong suggests that stakeholders use these relationships to enforce social regulations and as pressures to shape refugees into what they consider "good" members of their community (1996:738)—a process of belonging I refer to throughout this chapter as *member-making*, and from the affected refugee's perspective, I refer to it as *being made*. I differentiate between "citizen-making" that was used in the last chapter and "member-making" as used in this one, in that the former emphasizes the shaping of the more political values prevailing in a particular localized context and the latter, refers to the more socio-cultural values discussed in this chapter. Ong's position would suggest that belonging is only enabled by "being made." Renato Rosaldo and William Flores, on the other hand, put forward an alternate definition that suggests cultural citizenship is "the right to be different with respect to the norms of the dominant national community, without compromising one's right to belong" (1997:57).How then, do refugee groups transcend the forces of "being made," to claim space in a new country?

Social relationships have always been a two-way street. Scholars agree that while the people who work in member-making institutions use their positions to shape refugees, the immigrants simultaneously use these relationships to build for themselves social capital, gauge the degree to which they identify with various norms and values prevalent in the community, and through these interactions formulate ideas about their inclusion and exclusion from the host society (see Michalowski 2005; Jansen & Lofving 2009). While attention has been given to how these member-making institutions affect the process of belonging at a national level, I suggest that how stakeholders administer those responsibilities and the type of social interactions offered during this process are locally shaped, and will have different consequences in different localities. Recent attention has thus been directed to examining the localized attitudes and hierarchies embedded within these member-making relationships and their effects on the integration processes (See: Boyd 2002; Model & Lin 2002; Borjas 2003; Martin et al., 2002; and Castles 2002). Therefore, it is the position of this chapter that what is really happening to the refugee within these pluralities of experiences is less the making of *good* nationals and more the making of *good* locals, and that belonging is either enabled or transcended from a plurality of experiences at the local level. Moreover, it is expected that the expressions of being made will perform differently with different outcomes, in different locations. Jeffery Reitz suggests that theories of immigrant reception must take into account how these features are particularized and enacted in different societies, and that such theorization is "greatly aided by comparative perspectives" (2002:1007). This chapter, therefore, asks how member-making and being made are in relation to one another in a specific place that yields similar or different experiences than that of another place.

It is helpful to first identify the various stakeholders who were either officially or unofficially responsible for shaping the lives of the Hmong. As in other countries that took place in early refugee resettlement, new arrivals were nurtured through a system of private sponsors[1]. In Gammertingen and DFW, Hmong families were each assigned a sponsor. In DFW, that sponsor could be an individual, group, or church congregation whereas in Gammertingen, sponsors were all individuals. It was the sponsor's job in both locations to introduce the newcomer to the community, provide cultural orientation, informal language learning opportunities, to be a primary resource-contact for the refugee, and to provide a source of comfort, encouragement and support for the newcomers throughout the adaptation and adjustment process. In DFW, the sponsor had the added responsibilities of registering the Hmong children for school, getting them clothes, arranging doctor visits, introducing them to public transportation, enrolling the parents in a language class, and helping them find a job. On the other hand, in Gammertingen, the village mayor hired one full-time woman to oversee the daily business of arranging medical appointments and transportation, coordinating the registering of children in school, coordi-

---

1. For U.S. see Lanphier 1983; for Norway see Grnseth 2010; for Australia see Price 1986, for Canada see Dorais 1991.

nating language lessons, and then communicating resettlement "progress" and the needs of the Hmong back to the mayor. The Gammertingen model of administering the more functional aspects of resettlement was in line with the more centralized way of German social administration. A consequence of this approach was that it freed the sponsors for more informal socializing and friendship-building.

In DFW, social services (medical cards, food stamps, and any monetary help) were administered through private relief agencies that bid for contracts to administer these services on behalf of the government. The Voluntary Service Agencies (VOLAGS) active in the DFW area at the time of the first wave of Hmong resettlement were the International Rescue Committee (IRC), an earlier form of Catholic Charities, Refugee Services of Texas, World Relief, and Church World Services. By contrast, in Gammertingen, the intermediate agency dispensing these social services for the state was the local government itself. The village mayor said it was ultimately his responsibility to oversee the process and he chose to hire a full-time German man to communicate with and walk the Hmong through all legal paperwork and procedures in regards to welfare services. In both field sites, local discourses surrounding public assistance helped shape the way in which the services were administered and received. It is for this reason that I suggest that the people who create that discourse are important stakeholders in the process of member-making.

Other official stakeholders in both communities included the public schools for children and language classes for the adults, the religious organizations that were asked to help integrate the refugees, and the town folk with whom they interacted on a daily or weekly basis. The adult Hmong in Gammertingen were administered German language lessons and given clothes by the local Red Cross. The Red Cross also provided medical care for the babies and small children. The Gammertingen public schools hired a special teacher to meet with the Hmong children for part of the school day and provide extra cultural and language support. In DFW, the Red Cross provided clothes and furniture for the Hmong when they moved out of sponsor homes and into their own apartments. The public schools offered an ESL program for the children. Medical care for the adults in both locations was assigned to special physicians who monitored their first year of health. These are the official stakeholders whose relationship with the Hmong will be discussed at length in this chapter.

I begin with a story that illustrates how the basic power relations were constructed among these formal stakeholders at the local level.

* * *

*People begin to gather in the Gammertingen Catholic church sanctuary, taking a seat in a pew with excitement over what the Mayor would say about this group of "boat people" soon to arrive in their village. "I saw the advertisement in the local newspaper for volunteers," said one woman: "Those poor people ... I had to do something." Among the guests were the local school principal, the pastor and priest from the two town churches, a couple of teachers, a former missionary to China, the town newspaper editor, and several ladies that had stepped forward in response to the call for sponsors. The Mayor rose and addressed the crowd. "As you know, we have ten Vietnamese boat families coming to our town in a few days. I called this meeting as a brainstorming session on how we can best prepare for their arrival and transition them into our village. I have already secured a dormitory-style building close to the center of town where we'll house them. This will make it easy for us to get services to all of them at once. The State will compensate the city for the cost of their basic housing, food, and medical care, but as you can imagine, the needs will most likely extend far beyond that. Any ideas?" Someone rose and suggested a special account be opened at the village bank where people could make donations on the refugee's behalf. "I'll run a standing advertisement for the fund in the local paper," said the editor. The two churches agreed to host a clothing drive and solicit their congregants to help the newcomers to understand and take advantage of their services and other people-gathering events. The school agreed to set a special class for the new students. The Red Cross was enlisted to come to the dormitory and teach German classes to the adults for six hours a day, and the other volunteers were asked to act as sponsors for families whom they could teach how to shop for groceries, utilize public transportation, take care of their children, and how to "get along" in Gammertingen. The press decided to run a weekly segment on the refugees in an effort to get the town acquainted with them. The group dismissed, agreeing to meet bi-weekly over the course of the next year. "I want this group to act as a resource for one another so that we can put out any fires as they come," said the Mayor.*

*Meanwhile in DFW, VOLAG agencies were busy answering the phones. One agent yells over his cubicle to the next desk, "I got another call from the IRC in Washington. We have twenty families coming in on Friday and another ten on Wednesday that we need to place in sponsor homes. How are we doing on recruitment?" "I'm doing everything I can," replied another. "I am begging my friends, family, and every church in the city to be sponsors. Last week I was still securing sponsors as the refugees were on their way here. It's crazy." Just then an elderly woman walked in the door. "I heard you were looking for sponsors for the refugees?" They explained to the woman that she would need to meet a family at the airport, bring them back to her house and put them in an extra room or guest house for a little bit. Her main responsibilities would be to assist them in becoming "self-sufficient" and "socially adjusted" in a "short period of time," though they did not offer any* *specifics on what they meant by that. They handed her a mimeographed piece of paper that said she should get them clothes and provide food, review job skills with the family, then begin an active job search. "You might also need to explain that long-distance telephone calls cost money in your house, and explain the use and care of household furnishings and appliances that they may be unfamiliar with, particularly the use of cleansers and disinfectants." She was advised to review with them American money, banking, and credit systems, "Make sure you get down on paper what you will do for the refugees and what the refugees will do for themselves. The goal is self-sufficiency as soon as possible! They need to know this." The women contemplated the mass of responsibilities. "When will my job be over?" she asked. "When they get a job, and you move them into their own place. You might want to make yourself available to answer ongoing concerns and keep the friendship going. I think you will find the sharing of cultures one of the more valuable experiences in the sponsorship process. You'll get a check in about a month for $120.00 per refugee. This is a little something to be used toward your initial costs. If you need anything else, you know where to find us." The women left with a time and date to pick up a family at the airport and a few loose sheets of paper with scant contact information on them. As she went out the door, one of the VOLAG workers looked up at his boss, "Do you think we should contact the press and run a public awareness campaign?" "No," he replied. "We don't have time for it. We can hardly find time to get the needed sponsors! Just run another ad recruiting people. Besides, the Governor fears backlash from the public if we draw too much attention to the refugees. Our communities are already overwhelmed with so many coming at once. He just wants us to get them working. You know Texans, they are afraid that if the refugees get on the dole, they will stay there forever."*

\* \* \*

These narratives were taken from actual events and illustrate the two very different approaches to the responsibilities of resettlement and member-making taken by the two field site communities. While both locations ran ad hoc programs pre-dating formal refugee resettlement programs in the late 1970s, Gammertingen used a collective initiative that involved the whole village. This approach of building longer relationships of caring was embedded in the character and values of village-scale life. On the other hand, DFW's approach was more diffuse, and aimed at helping the Hmong quickly establish the local values of autonomy and independence that were valued in a more city-scaled area of the United States.

Anthropologists have long recognized that power in small-scale communities is most often attributed to political positions. Gammertingen's approach, via its mayor-led town meetings, gave control of localizing federal messages of belonging to the village mayor, whereas the approach in DFW, a larger metropolitan area, seemingly bypassed the local government and privileged the individual sponsor. This diffusion of power in DFW led to myriad complaints from local governments who actively lobbied for more local control and recognition as a major partner in the resettlement effort. Minutes from one such Texas meeting of politicians read:

> Miss R. spoke last, making the point that, since local governments are the primary parties affected in domestic resettlement, they have the right and responsibility to become involved in the problems, issues and solutions.... Miss R. suggested that more thought be given and concrete action taken to promoting planned placement projects, the easing of community tensions and orientation of communities before refugees arrive.[2]

We will look at how differences between the two field sites in how power was shared locally had a tremendous effect on the uniformity of messages about belonging. This will be clarified through greater exploration of the different venues that assisted the Hmong in DFW and Gammertingen.

## Sponsorship

As stated earlier, both Gammertingen and DFW used sponsors to help in Hmong resettlement. However, what *resettlement* meant was locally defined. In DFW, the Hmong arrived during a national recession and were placed into a region that, although it had better than average numbers of joblessness, held particular views of why this was the case. The ideology that every "good" citizen is self-reliant and displays the classic Texan virtues of hard work and "pulling themselves up by their bootstraps" was not lost on the DFW sponsors. Take, for example, this by a VOLAG worker.

> I was responsible for recruiting sponsors for the Hmong. I would do phone interviews with the families so that they would know what to expect. We asked them to take a family under their wings and use their contacts to get them a job. We also asked them to provide the Hmong families some cultural orientation; how to use the public transporta-

---

2. This paper was from the William P. Clements Jr. Papers, Governor's Office for Volunteer Services, Refugee Services 1979–1982, archived at the Cushing Memorial Library and Archives Texas A &M University henceforth referred to in this paper as WCP.

tion system, protocols for work here in the United States, the whole time clock thing, stuff like that. We would tell them that their job was to aid the refugee in financial and social self-sufficiency, but the government is clear in that it states that we get them financially self-sufficient as quickly as possible. That's the real goal.

As such, many DFW sponsors found jobs for their refugee families almost immediately. One sponsor relayed the following story to me with an air of pride:

> My husband talked to a friend of ours and had a job waiting for the Hmong man before he even arrived. We let him sleep a little to get over jet lag, but had him working full-time within three days and the family in their own apartment within two weeks!

Another local sponsor wrote the then-Governor of Texas, William Clements, Jr., with concerns that if the refugees didn't work right away, they would receive extended welfare benefits. The Governor wrote back saying:

> Texas refugees have the lowest welfare dependency in the country and we intend to keep it that way.... Your interest in the problems facing Texas indicates your strong Texas character (WCP Box 21).

These attitudes reflect discourses about poverty, work, and what constitutes a "worthy" citizen that began in America in the late 1950s when the meaning of the word *welfare* switched from its positive connotation of *social insurance* to a more negative one of *public assistance*—and *public assistance* came to mean Aid to Families and Dependent Children. Historian Michael Katz has described the general distaste for public assistance, which was viewed as something of a "last resort primarily for the undeserving poor," which at the time was often translated as "black single mothers with several children" and "lazy people who are dependent because of their own bad behavior or moral failing" (Katz 2001:4,341). Anthropologist Patricia Zavella (2001) found the same racial attitudes displayed against non-working immigrants receiving welfare whom whites perceived as equally lazy and a threat to their control of the state. These attitudes increasingly tied welfare to immorality, unworthiness, and being out of work. One DFW sponsor demonstrated this attitude in a conversation about the Hmong family he and his family sponsored:

> I thought it would only take a month or so to find them a job. When it took longer than that I had to call the agency and tell them I had had enough. I couldn't take it anymore. I think they were just lazy.

Another blamed the fact that "her Hmong took five months to find a job" on a welfare system that was too liberal: "Programs are giving refugees too much money. They get this attitude and come here just to save money and go back."

This profound misunderstanding of the refugee category and experience underscores the conditions into which some refugees in DFW arrived. Such misunderstandings can be directly attributed to the VOLAG agencies rush to find sponsors, lack of ongoing communication with their sponsors, their failure to adequately prepare them to host, and undervaluing the need for public awareness campaigns. As a consequence, by May of 1981, two years after the first Hmong arrived in DFW, a Memorandum for the Texas Department of Human Resources read "We recommend that orientation and preparation of sponsors should be improved" (WPC 5/28/81).

Despite the lack of preparation, I found some early sponsors gave a more sympathetic cast to their stories when talking about the same difficulties.

> Usually we had to find the Hmong a job doing something unrelated to their past experiences. There was little translation of their skills to our jobs. Culturally, I think, our work system was a great shock to them. These people were from the mountains, poor, and usually came with no conception of the way we do life. Most had never had indoor plumbing. We had to show them that the commode was not for washing things, it was for waste disposal! We found our family a job within a few days and an apartment in a week. We had to explain what a housing lease was and contractual agreements. In hindsight, I don't think they understood any of it. How could they?

These examples illustrate how sponsors communicated messages about those they deemed deserving of inclusion in their local community. The employed taxpayer was welcome in DFW while the welfare dependent would never be accepted or thought to belong. Making the refugee into a good member of the local community meant getting them to work, off of public aid, and doing things in the same manner as the locals. Some would argue that these are core values of America in general and not just indicative of DFW. However, the degree to which these values are embedded in the Texas mystique exceptionalizes their importance in this location.

In the Gammertingen context, sponsors were not tasked with helping the Hmong find employment. In fact, for the first year, no one was. The Gammertingen work system did not have a non-skilled, service sector of employment similar to that which was prevalent in DFW. Most workers in Germany receive certified craftsmen training in one profession or another, a system the country hoped would sustain their international competitiveness. Without language skills, it was nearly impossible for a refugee to get this certification. The mayor decided that since special federal funding was given to support the town's first year efforts of resettlement, the Hmong would be more successful job candidates if they had a full year of language and cultural education. The mayor informed the sponsors and others involved in their resettlement of his decision to hold off on employment efforts. At that point, he was made aware of town rumors that the Hmong (thought of at this point as Vietnamese) were unwilling, or unable to work. Aware of his community's values embedded in the Schwaben work ethic, he asked the town newspaper to run the following article:

> How are things going for the Vietnamese in Gammertingen? To counter rumors and opinions about the Vietnamese in circulation, we want to present various facts. The employment services and public wish the refugees to continue their German language course throughout the rest of the year. But our Vietnamese will not be able to continue this course if they are working; after getting a job, the funding for the training ceases. We would like to express that the Vietnamese are eager to begin employment; however, this is only permissible when the German authorities have given their consent, which we will not do until they have had sufficient time to learn the language and our customs. We are confident that they will all find jobs and benevolent inclusion in our community. The city has only a small stake in the first few months of their resettlement and I ask the population to continue to welcome a friendly partnership with and inclusion of the Vietnamese families, as was the case in their arrival (Hirschle 1980).

Here the mayor sets himself as "the German authorities" and appeals to the town's former compassion for the refugees and to their local values in hard work to justify his actions. Working directly under his jurisdiction, the sponsors became absolved of employment-related responsibilities and were free to concentrate on the task of "benevolent inclusion." One Gammertingen sponsor explained how she approached these responsibilities:

> We didn't have a written job description. It was just to do whatever was needed to help them acclimate. My husband and I were recruited as

sponsors because we had lived in China for twelve years. The mayor thought anywhere in Asia was close enough and he asked for our help. We were even shown a paper that said the Hmong spoke Chinese. So we agreed. Well, they didn't. I had to show them [the Hmong] the most basic of things: how to cook baby food, or how to prepare milk for the baby, where to buy milk for the children. It was very hard for everybody as we couldn't speak the Hmong language. When I understood a problem I had to show with my hands and feet and translate this way.

Another sponsor related:

I remember one time coming to visit and there was a lot of snow on the ground. All the children were running around outside playing with no coat and no shoes. They did not know what snow was. I had to tell them to put a coat and shoes on their children or they will get sick. This was difficult because nobody knew how to tie a shoe. I remember going over and over it every time I would visit.

In both Gammertingen and DFW, there were efforts to make the Hmong into productive members of the local community; however in one field site that was defined by becoming economically self-sufficient fast, while in the other it was about becoming economically self-sufficient over a lifetime via gaining employable language skills and holding German values. These conditions of membership were communicated through channels of sponsorship. But how were these varying messages received by the Hmong and how did they understand the role of the sponsor in each of the field sites? And what effect did it have on their understanding of belonging? We return again to the composite narratives of Lu X. and Kang Y.

\* \* \*

*Kang Y., in Gammertingen, settled his family into the large group home. They had a large room for themselves that they were free to rearrange how they wanted. They stacked the beds in the corner and slept on the floor as was their tradition. They shared the bath and kitchen with the other Hmong and Vietnamese refugee families. Someone came and took the older children off to a school and the adults were told to go down to the common room in the basement for an important meeting. Small children in tow, they made their way to the large room. Kang's family, like the others, were each introduced to a German that would be their special friend and would help them learn about their new home. Once a week the German friends would come by and take them to their homes for dinner or in their cars and drive them around town. The sponsor showed Mrs. Y. how to use the* washing machine to wash things. She was surprised when the sponsor laughed and took her dishes out of the machine—she was only trying to wash them. Kang Y. indicated that his sponsor friend took them to the market, to see the hills, on walks at night, and introduced them to ice cream. Kang Y.'s special family had a teenage daughter who came by after school and played games with all the children in the yard of the group home. Together their families shared meals, parties, and visits over the following twelve months.

Lu X., in DFW, was met at the airport by the elderly woman who had volunteered at the VOLAG the previous week. She and her husband stood waiting with a bouquet of balloons tied with colorful ribbons and a large sign with foreign writing on it that spelled "WELCOME X FAMILY!" They helped Lu and his family into their car and drove them to their home. Lu X. could not understand what his sponsors were saying, but nodded periodically out of respect. At the home, they were shown several rooms where they would be staying. Lu X. thought there would be more floor space for sleeping if those large, soft, benches which they called beds weren't taking so much room. The next morning the DFW family brought them to the basement of a church where the X. family looked through piles of clothes. The day after, his sponsor took him to a big factory. Lu X. had practiced writing his name in English in the refugee camp and was happy to use it on the papers the factory put in front of him. The next morning he went to the factory and began working. Meanwhile Mrs. X. was taken to an apartment complex to look at a place of their own. At the end of the week the sponsor family moved their bags of clothes from the church basement and their few belongings that they had brought with them from Laos into the apartment. The sponsor showed Mrs. Lu X. how to use the bus to get to the market and Lu X. how to use the bus to get to the factory. They also showed them how to use the pay phone to call them. Lu X. was confused. He did not understand anything that was being said. The next morning he rode around on the bus for hours not knowing where to get off. He was late for work and the nice man who had him sign all those papers seemed angry. He tried to call his sponsor for help but he did not remember how to use the phone. It was a couple of weeks before the X. family saw their sponsor again. Mrs. X. prepared fish for them as a gesture of hospitality. The sponsor was not pleased that she used the dishwasher to steam it. The sponsor went around the kitchen and helped the X.'s understand the proper use of each of the big machines. The sponsor handed Lu X. a piece of paper with writing on it and tried to explain that the church where they got the clothes was offering free English language lessons, but they were offered during the work day, so he was unable to go. Lu X. and his family saw the sponsors a handful of times over the next year and then not again.

\* \* \*

In contrast to the stories of the Hmong in Gammertingen who perceived the relationship of their sponsor as a "special friend," the DFW Hmong saw their relationship to the sponsors as more hierarchical (the providers of the basic needs of shelter, food, and clothes), whose approval was based on meeting certain expectations such as getting a job, getting to work on time, and working the appliances correctly. In the case of the more hierarchical relationships of DFW, there was a practical incentive for the Hmong not to disappoint their sponsors in that they feared their services might be cut off.

One example of the pressure imposed on the Hmong through living arrangements can be exemplified in the case of Hmong hospitality rules and Western bed use. Hmong traditional hospitality rules are understood as deferring to the host in matters of conduct. When the Hmong arrived in DFW, the hosts put them in rooms with Western beds; however, the Hmong traditionally sleep on the floor and found the mattresses too soft to sleep on. They tried sleeping on the floor but the host appeared insulted and insisted they use the bed. They did not want to hurt the feelings of their hosts who were providing these accommodations. To get around this, one Hmong woman said:

> Our sponsors kept pointing to the bed and telling us we were supposed to sleep on it. I could not, it hurt my back. So we would pretend to crawl into bed and then shut the door and moved to the floor. In the morning, we would mess the covers on the mattress so that they thought we were using them. We didn't want to disappoint them.

On the other hand, in Gammertingen, the Hmong were put in a group dormitory and not in the private homes of hosts, and given the liberty to rearrange the furniture as they pleased. The Germans were shocked that they did not use the beds, but as neither the beds nor the dorm rooms belonged to the sponsors, no one demanded that they use them. Not living in the homes of the sponsors allowed the Hmong a more horizontal relationship with their German sponsors whereas living in the homes of sponsors in DFW set up a more vertical relationship.

In Gammertingen, just as in DFW, there were reports of Hmong having conflicts trying to co-reside peacefully under the same roof with families of different cultures. However, in Gammertingen, the conflicts were between the Hmong and other outsiders—the Vietnamese who were also refugees. In DFW, by contrast, the Others in the house were their hosts. One Gammertingen sponsor retold one of the in-house conflicts she observed:

> The Hmong were more disadvantaged in exposure to education or the modern world than the Vietnamese who lived with them sharing

the same common spaces. As word spread around town about the Hmong's disadvantaged condition, the Vietnamese tried to distance themselves from them. They would constantly intimidate the Hmong in front of local people calling them "stupid Miao," et cetera. The Hmong were also intimidated by the Vietnamese in the dormitory. I would see it when I was there. The patience of the Vietnamese soon ran out when they realized the Hmong could not comprehend what was going on in the classroom due to their lack of any formal education. They would make faces at the Hmong or exasperated sounds and refuse to translate things for them. It was bad.

The sponsor recalled that after a year when the Vietnamese realized their efforts to distance themselves from the Hmong were futile (the local community perceived everyone in the house as the same ethnic group), they moved away to a different town.

Manifestations of the different vertical and horizontal nature of the sponsor relationships with the Hmong could also be seen in how misuses of appliances were handled. One Gammertingen Hmong recalls:

> I remember the chickens were different. In Laos, we raised our own chickens and did everything with them until they were on the table to eat. In the dormitory, they gave us these chickens with the feathers off in shiny wrappers. We understood that they were "ready-to-cook." I was making dinner for our group when our sponsor stopped by for a visit. She laughed when she saw the chicken in the boiling water and told me I had to take the shiny wrapper off of it first. Now we know, but we had never seen chicken like that back then. She also told us we didn't need to douse the stove with water to put out the heat. The next meal, the sponsor came by and cooked with us. I taught her how to make Hmong food and she taught me how to use the German food and appliances to prepare it.

This sponsor recalled to me later that it was difficult for her to comprehend the giant leap the Hmong had taken from their world to Gammertingen and that these stories were often passed around among the sponsors at their weekly support meetings and gave the locals the impression that the Hmong were not bright. However, the sponsors were encouraged by the mayor and others in the support group to handle these incidents with tact, patience, and kindness. This support trickled down to the Hmong in Gammertingen who perceived the corrective actions of their sponsors as a help, and the relationship as more symbiotic. Information flowed both ways as suggested by one sponsor who said, "I taught her how to make Hmong food and she taught me how to use the German food and appliances to prepare it." This is in contrast to the DFW experiences where the sponsors were left to themselves without ongoing support. The exasperation of the sponsors who had difficulty understanding the differences in culture was often sensed by the Hmong who told me they felt they had disappointed those placed in authority over them.

The director of the DFW local Hmong Association told me that as time went on, the few remaining more educated lowland Hmong who had remained in DFW took on the guidance roles of the community and helped the other Hmong acclimate to the area in a manner they considered less demeaning.

> Over time, we had people knowledgeable in this area or another, that we called on for questions, or help with paperwork, or when a family didn't know how to do something. We understand how the Hmong think and know where the other person is coming from.

I found this interesting because he was talking about the highland Hmong being guided by the more educated lowland Hmong, and this in itself was the formation of a new kind of co-ethnic belonging as opposed to what was experienced in Laos (this will be developed in greater detail in Chapter 6). Longstanding social divisions have held from the days that Hmong began moving down to the lowlands. The highlanders characterized those who moved as more educated and as thinking more highly of themselves, and the lowlanders, in turn, began characterizing those who stayed in the mountains as backward and slow. Overcoming these social divisions in DFW became a survival strategy. One Hmong highlander explained it this way:

> There were so few of us [Hmong] here in Texas that we had a choice. Either we get along and rely on each other, which is the real Hmong way, or hold onto some of our stereotypes and risk dying. Besides, all of us at some time had lived in the hills and everyone could still relate to each other in ways no American ever could. The Hmong are survivors, and we realized that the reason we have survived for all these centuries is that we know how to rely on each other. That's what we do best. Now, most of us don't know why there were these divisions to begin with.

This is an important difference between the two field sites. Gammertingen's first Hmong were all hill people with no education or any previous incorporation into a state. This lack of Hmong leadership and experience would prove to have consequences in the development of the German Hmong community and will be discussed in a later chapter.

Through their mutual dependence on each other, the DFW Hmong were able to find jobs and move out from under their sponsor's supervision as quickly as possible. They often spoke of perceiving themselves as intruders in their sponsor's lives and the sponsor's help as a condescending judgment of their desire to provide for themselves, a desire I argue reflects in part Texas ideology about work and welfare dependence. Further, Hmong social organization rules consider the male elder as the manager of the household. Constantly showing deference to their Texas hosts overshadowed the elder's ability to make decisions for his family, something else that factored into their desire to quickly move out of the sponsor's home. The increased knowledge and resources that came through shared cooperation within the Hmong community ultimately made that separation possible. Unfortunately, for most of the Hmong, the move out of the sponsor's house came with the unintended consequences of social separation from their American contacts.

There were notable exceptions. Two of the DFW Hmong I met spoke of a continued friendship with their sponsors. In both cases, the Hmong said the relationship changed from sponsor to friend via involvement in a church they both attended. As co-parishioners, the hierarchical relationship changed to a more horizontal one. One Hmong recalled that when the wife of his sponsor died they were the first to call on the family and did not leave their side for several days. The friendships continued as long as Hmong and sponsor were both involved in the same church or other social setting. However, for the majority of the DFW Hmong involved in this research, they had not seen nor had they had any contact with their sponsors since that first few week period of resettlement back in 1979. The Hmong agreed that this was not an intentional social separation but that they had lost contact when one of them moved away from the other. This speaks to the more mobile nature of Americans and the anonymity of city life in comparison to a village where the majority of people live sedentary lives and run into the same people on a daily basis. The scale of the village resettlement place offers one explanation for why almost all of the Hmong families in Gammertingen have kept active ties with their original sponsors, most becoming lifelong friends.

While in the field, I accompanied the German Hmong on many visits to their original sponsors. After thirty years of resettlement, they were still taking evening walks together where they would chitchat about their children, the weather, and other current events. They still had each other over for afternoon tea, birthday parties, cookouts, and other major celebrations. I found that the sponsors in Gammertingen also still played a role in helping the Hmong sort

### Figure 4.1 Evening Walks with Germans

Photo courtesy of DN/Omega Productions.

out paperwork, assisting the children with their homework, and answering questions about health care and the German law. It was the Hmong who were actively going to the sponsors for help. They explained that they feel they are still not knowledgeable about some of these things and rely on them for this kind of information. As one Hmong put it, "We trust them. They are our friends. They understand where we are coming from." Interestingly, these are the same reasons that the DFW Hmong gave for relying on the more educated lowland Hmong for this help. In the absence of lowland Hmong, relationship with the Gammertingen sponsors became their survival strategy.

Coming into relationships with these Hmong after thirty years of resettlement, I witnessed that more symbiotic friendships had developed in the host communities as opposed to the strictly hierarchical ones they spoke of in the past. On one visit, a Hmong family was considering purchasing a home and wanted the sponsor's advice on its relative worth, how to go about the paper work, and whether or not it was a "good deal." The Hmong woman told me "This couple used to give me German lessons every day after school and helped me with my homework." Now in their nineties, the elderly German couple can't drive and are in need of help themselves. That afternoon after discussing the home, I rode with this same Hmong family as they drove the elderly couple to the grocery store and back. "We do this for them every Friday," she said. Later that year, when one of the Germans was hospitalized, it was the Hmong who came over and cared for their home and cooked them meals. It was evident that they had become neighbors in the social sense of the word.

The horizontal way the mayor set up the sponsor/Hmong relationships, the nature of village life, and the lack of more educated and state-experienced compatriots, worked together to provide opportunity for the sponsors to become an important part of the Hmong's social network, and the Hmong an important part of theirs. Therefore, in the process of belonging, the Gammertingen

Figure 4.2 Dinner with Sponsors

Photo courtesy of Otto Lutz.

Hmong were more apt to see these relationships with their sponsors as reciprocal friendships and social capital rather than as being made into a certain type of acceptable member of German society. The Hmong understood these friendships as an ongoing survival tool for making it in their new environment and an important part of feeling connected to it.

The long-term effects of sponsor connections were not the same in DFW where relationships were set up vertically. As more educated Hmong in the area began to fill the leadership roles first held by sponsors, and because of the mobile nature of people in the United States and the ease of living anonymously in a city, with few exceptions, the DFW sponsors remained, in the imagination of the Hmong, distant and in the bureaucratic realm. As such, the need for ongoing association with them diminished, as did their sense of belonging together with the locals. What is noteworthy is that the horizontal set of relationships built reciprocal exchanges between the refugees and the local Gammertingers over time, and ultimately contributed to a more socially integrated population while the vertical relationships of DFW did not. Irene Bloemraad (2006) suggests that belonging is positively influenced by the social capital built through hands-on relationships between service providers and the refugee, as was the case with the Hmong in Gammertingen. What is clear from the Hmong cases is that *both* factors, co-ethnics and sponsors, became resources for survival. From this we can garner that refugee populations exercise a tremendous amount of agency in how they use these forms of capital as a resource for making it in a new environment.

## Local Discourses and Public Assistance

Another stakeholder in member-making is the local population who engage in discourse about refugee newcomers and public aid. This section looks at the kinds and types of public assistance administered to the Hmong, and how local discourses about it either enabled or prohibited the forms of local belonging. The types of help offered the Hmong in each location stem from differences in the role of the Welfare State in Germany and America broadly, and in Texas and Gammertingen more specifically. The German system of welfare as a social insurance system is based on universal coverage and generous levels of protection and developed out of compulsory social insurance in Wilhelmine Germany in 1883 (Ferrera & Rhodes 2000). According to social insurance philosophy, "the German welfare state was primarily providing wage-centered social policies for which a precondition for receiving benefits was a prior standard employment relationship" (Seeleib-Kaiser 2002:26). The system reflected the German philosophy of providing insurance to the worker who, when sick, injured, unemployed, or retired, was guaranteed to continue life at one's achieved standard of living (see Diprete & McManaus 2000; Alber 1986; Clasen 1994). Because men had been the typical primary bread winners at the time the policy was adopted, the German welfare state included family policies that relieved the financial burden of children on the breadwinner regardless of income, such as *kindergeld*, a monetary supplement paid to each family for every child living at home, and *muttersgeld*, a supplement paid to new mothers to offset the costs of a new child for the first three years of life (DiPrete & Mcmanus 2000). These benefits came from joint contributions by the employee and employer. People who do not qualify for benefits under these social insurance programs are entitled to *socialhilfe*, or social assistance, from the local town authorities to maintain a comfortable existence until their fortune turns around. The fact that everyone is entitled to social benefits in one way or another in addition to the prevalence of stay-at-home mothers and the integrated nature of village life makes it likely that anyone living in Gammertingen will at one time be or know a welfare recipient. This ties benefits to being employed or employable (having a trade certification that qualifies one for work should it come available) and uncouples it from issues of class and race.

Despite these liberal attitudes toward social benefits, the Hmong arrived in Germany with larger families than the Gammertingen norm. According to village records, in the late 1970s, the average number of children in the village per family was 2.5., down from 4.5 one generation earlier. The Hmong average upon arrival was five. This trend toward large numbers of children continued into the next generation. The local residents, who knew nothing of the Hmong culture or why their family sizes were larger, assumed that they were having multiple children to get the social benefit of *Kindergeld*. This complaint was articulated by several sponsors I talked with, and I continued to hear it articulated by local nationals in the village thirty years later. One work supervisor of some of the Hmong men said to me in an interview;

> One Hmong family has seven children, the other eight children … they have a lot of children! In Germany, we have two, at the most three children, but they have seven and eight children. A lot of children! I don't know why. Is it their culture or what? Why so many children?

I spent a few minutes explaining why some cultures have large families, after which he responded;

> I guess more children, more hands in the field. Perhaps the next generation will see that they don't need as many "hands" here in Gammertingen and that it means many mouths to feed, and costs a lot of money. We find that impossible. So many children are expensive; they need shoes, clothes, they need everything that costs money; and the Hmong don't make that much money—middle income for this town.

Similar conversations erupted spontaneously with almost any German in Gammertingen that I talked with. There was a great curiosity about the number of children they had. My discussion of the financial burden of the children with the supervisor stopped short of his tying his concerns to the village's responsibility to provide so much *Kindergled*, but others were more willing to make this connection. While not a widespread belief, some people did insinuate that the large number of children per Hmong household was directly tied to some desire to receive more social aid. It is important to note that the complaints against the Hmong receiving this social benefit was not that they weren't entitled to it, or that they hadn't earned it, but that by having more children than the Gammertingen norm, they were getting more than their fair share of the entitlement. It was the idea that the system wasn't designed to help such large families and such usage would somehow topple it.

These discourses made their way to the Hmong who in turn became self-conscious that the size of their families was not "normal." One Hmong woman introducing her family to me said, "These are my seven children. Many children yes? I know it's a lot." I asked her, what made her think it was a lot? She went on to tell me how the Hmong have trouble finding apartments in Germany with enough bedrooms to accommodate their households. She and her family had to rent two apartments—one right above the other. She showed me how they had to remove the kitchen from one apartment converting that space into four bedrooms. The spaces in the apartment below were used for cooking, eating, and entertaining. The landlord told me "What else can they do? They have *so* many children!" This woman, like other Hmong women in Gammertingen that I talked with, always appeared embarrassed when they talked about the size of their family. As in her conversation with me, they had come to anticipate that all non-Hmong would judge them negatively for it. She told me that some Germans think that they have so many children for the *Kindergeld*. She laughed,

> We didn't even know about the *Kindergeld* when we arrived. Hmong have had big families without extra financial help for centuries. This is not our incentive.

There were many articles in the German newspapers in the late 1970s and early 1980s, both locally and nationally, making the public aware of what social services newly arriving Southeast Asian refugees would receive, where the money was coming from, and what the expected role of the community would be. For example, a few days before the Hmong arrived in Gammertingen the following article was posted in the village paper by the Mayor:

> The cost of living is ensured by the state for the refugees. Nevertheless, it is desirable to launch a fund for unconventional expenses. We have therefore opened a bank account and urgently ask the residents to contribute to this important humanitarian assistance.

As the Hmong continued in Gammertingen, the mayor used the local press to stay on top of misconceptions about their use of public help, always casting it in a favorable light. As an example, I offer the following excerpt taken from a letter the village mayor posted in the newspaper six months after the Hmong arrived:

> Since the winter of 1979, ten refugee families from Laos and Vietnam left their homes to live in our city, often under dramatic circumstances. We have all seen on our televisions the gruesome fate that they fled

from, many arriving to our community only after adventurous wanderings and time in a camp squeezed with up to 3000 people in a confined space. Many lost their loved ones, and most arrived to us with great physical and mental harm. Additionally, a large number of innocent and frightened little children came to us. The city of Gammertingen, in close cooperation with volunteers of the Red Cross, maintained a zealous circle of help to provide for their immediate needs—lodging, subsistence, clothing, language and medical care. Now that many months have passed and the refugees continue to live in our city, and meet with us in offices and shops in Gammertingen, it makes sense that the District Supervisor of refugees gives some fundamental and explanatory notes of their state of the citizenry of Gammertingen. In accordance with the plans of the refugees authorities, the Vietnamese refugees after nine months should have engaged enough and be far enough along in their knowledge of German that they can obtain a job and their own apartment. Until that time, the refugees must not engage in any work, but should use all their energy to learning the German language. The Family Ministry in Bonn is responsible for covering their income expenses during this time, while the county pays for their accommodation. They also assigned a permanent teaching staff to lead them in German lessons and are reinforced in their work by other teachers in our schools. In addition, if our refugees while shopping for food often pay with large bills, then this is not because they are well off financially on government funds; it is only just because they are inexperienced in dealing with our money system. Cashiers are not right to make fools of them at the cash register—especially with the crowded lines in grocery stores—with insufficient bills given them. They have the same difficulties we do ourselves on holiday abroad with foreign money. Finally, we [the city of Gammertingen] have given in the previous months sums of money to the refugees that you may have heard that they sent to relatives in another country. This payout was primarily a unique Christmas bonus payout. Who among us could condemn this act of humanity, if, for example, a son sends several hundred Marks to pay a doctor to treat his seriously ill mother in a refugee camp on the Cambodian border? The above examples should give us pause as we ask ourselves, "Did we really have enough information to formulate those thoughts about our refugees, and were we indeed given enough correct information to pronounce a judgment on their ability to work?" If we want to integrate these families into the population of Gammertingen then it is important to treat them with dignity. Never forget; these refugees are not guest workers who are here mostly because of their possibility of their benefit to us! Refugees are homeless and have become desperate fellow humans!

This article is extraordinary in that the mayor carefully and purposely tries to regenerate sympathy for the refugee's plight by appealing to the village's sense of humanitarianism. He also tries to clear misconceptions about social services and excessive resources being spent by spelling out the necessity of the services and reiterating where the funding is coming from. He even ends with a gentle chiding to those responsible for jumping to conclusions and reiterates that these are "our" refugees, that they in essence belong to the village, inferring that the entire village has a responsibility to help them along in this process with dignity.

This article was only one of many that the mayor wrote with the same style to accomplish the same purpose. While these efforts did not, or course, stave off all rumors or negative reactions to the refugees first year in the community when they were surviving on public aid, it did go a long way in setting a top-down tone for public acceptance of their situational use of tax-payer funds.

We also see here the great efforts made by the town to move the refugees from welfare to work, as promised, after nine months. The mayor recounted that the town had a difficult time finding appropriate work for a group of people with few transferable skills. The town generously decided to create full-time maintenance positions for the five men that were respectable jobs with full benefits and guaranteed job security.

Article 1 of the Basic Law (the German constitution) guarantees people the fundamental social rights to basic health care and to enough resources in order to live in a manner compatible with human dignity. Bernd Schulte, from the Max Planck Institute for Comparative Public and International Law, has argued that employment is "the main road" toward integrating immigrants into communities because it gives them access to social welfare (2005:116). He argues that access to both work and social insurance is the ultimate manifestation of inclusion. Gammertingen's willingness to create stable jobs at a living wage for the Hmong that they could do within their own skill set guaranteed them lifelong access to social assurances and was, by Shulte's definition, "the gateway to cultural and socioeconomic integration" (Schulte 2005:116). In essence, what the mayor was intimating to his village in that article was—the Hmong have these rights *because* they belong to us.

While the jobs provided by the town removed the Hmong from the stigma of receiving what was perceived as "unearned" financial and medical social support, it did not remove them from the social stigma associated with living in public housing. The mayor told me that he was cognizant of this stigma and therefore anxious to move the Hmong out of the group dormitory and into the broader community, "like the other people of Gammertingen." The

**Figure 4.3  Hmong Homes in Gammertingen**

Photo courtesy of DN/Omega Productions.

cost and size of the units they needed, however, was not found in the village. The mayor characterized his village as "a community of home owners," and thought that the Hmong would be perceived more as members and that the town would feel like their efforts with the refugees had been "successful" if the Hmong were homeowners.

Five years after the refugees arrived, when zoning approval for a new housing development in the town was established, the mayor lobbied for the city to build into this new neighborhood several large, four-bedroom homes for the Hmong. These homes would be made available for purchase with a special one percent interest loan from the village's credit bureau. The houses were purposefully built with yards large enough for a traditional Hmong garden and chicken coop and across the street from a neighborhood park. This move was spun in the press to the village as an official sign that the Hmong had chosen to set up roots in their town. The people of Gammertingen collectively celebrated this move as the Hmong becoming, as one townsfolk put it, "real Gammertingers." The village church teamed with the press and advertised a capital campaign that successfully raised the down payment for each of their homes.

As more Hmong moved into Gammertingen from other places (more on this in another Chapter), and as the German-born children of the Hmong grew, they had the expectancy that they should also live in their own homes—that home ownership was normal. When the special building and loan program for the Hmong was over, subsequent Hmong successfully raised their own capital through savings and continued purchasing their own homes. At the time of my fieldwork, only a few Hmong were renters, and of those, two were actively looking into ownership.

During my fieldwork, informal conversations with townsfolk about the Hmong revealed an overall sense of pleasure in the fact that they had become homeowners and had stable jobs. The most recent Evangelical pastor in town who had moved to Gammertingen from a larger city, remarked;

> What is interesting to me about the Hmong is that they are all homeowners. So many Germans do not own homes and yet they have been able to accomplish this in their first generation. That is an astounding accomplishment for these refugees to own homes in so short a time as they have been here. What is also astounding to me is that they have all acquired stable employment.

Some villagers remarked about the Hmong being "good workers," by which they meant industrious—an important virtue of the Schwaben Alb. One longtime supervisor of some Hmong characterized the group this way;

> They always do whatever it is we ask them. They never tell us they will not do it or don't want to do it. They never complain. Whatever we ask them, they do it willingly and do a good job at it. There is no strife or animosity between them and the other town workers.

These Gammertingen public discourses about the Hmong and their experiences with welfare are in stark contrast to the public discourses and experiences with public aid by the Hmong who settled in DFW. The American welfare system, classified as liberal, is tied in the Texas imagination to taxation rather than to work. Although it was initially designed as a social safety net for everyone, because racial minorities were overrepresented among the poor when welfare was first introduced, the white majority of DFW was less likely to see their contributions flow back to them, and therefore, had a different perception of those who received benefits than found in Gammertingen. It has been suggested in a Brookings Institute paper on the Welfare State that since American welfare recipients were most often racial minorities, it was easy to malign their character (Alesina et al., 2001). States were initially given wide leeway on how, and to whom they gave food stamps. But "until 1964, Texas was among the states that didn't participate until a series of changes to federal rules, and the creation of new eligibility categories forced them to be less miserly with their benefits" (Guerra 2009). Thus the social welfare benefits one would receive in DFW, are by comparison to those in Gammertingen, more modest and of shorter duration. This has been attributed to Texas's historically conservative legislative mentality, and underlying assumptions that protect the rights of landowners and hold those on welfare with contempt (Hancock 2004). Those who rose from poverty, or in the case of Texans, had "pulled themselves up by their bootstraps," were likely to think everyone should (Alesina et al., 2001). Texans resented what they perceived as the transfer of their wealth to the needy, and the needy, as stated previously, were associated with blacks and being lazy. As one Texas welfare reform blog post puts it:

> Why, when I go to the grocery store and see some fat cow buying cakes, cookies, and sodas with their Lone Star [Food Stamp] Card, should I not get angry? Forget them ... they can starve for all I care. I should *NOT* have to take care of people other than my own family! (Guerra 2009).

And another;

> Why work when the state will pay you to sit at home and have babies. If these people had to work forty hours a week like everyone else they may see how embarrassing it is to use those cards, instead showing everyone that they can stand on their own two feet. It's not fair that they have a bunch of kids, never work a day in their lives, but have all the taxpayers paying their way.

The specific benefits received by the Hmong in Texas admitted under the Parole program were indeed sparse and administered under this air of suspicion that refugees would remain on "the dole" for long periods of time. Initial compensation in DFW, therefore, was given directly to the DFW church or family who hosted them and not to the refugee. The Hmong only received a security deposit for their apartment and medical care for the first year. While Food Stamps were available, as most Hmong in DFW went to work within a few days of arrival, they were not eligible to receive them. Cash Aid to Families of Dependent Children (AFDC) and Food Stamps were not an entitlement to refugee families until after the 1980 Refugee Act was signed. Many of the original Hmong who were settled in DFW, upon hearing of other clan members in Wisconsin, Minnesota, or California, and who were not able to find work right away, moved north to pool resources with those living in the more liberal welfare states. The roughly two hundred and fifty Hmong left in DFW after this large migration, were those who had found jobs right away and did not need to depend on public assistance. One local national I had talked to concerning the story of the Hmong thought the 250 who remained where "the ones that were supposed to be here," the "true Texans," claiming that Texas's paltry social benefits were their way of "sifting out the riff raff." Those who belonged were the ones who could fend for themselves.

Something that could have curtailed this attitude was that there was no central figure, like the mayor in Gammertingen, charged to launch a public awareness campaign concerning the Hmong, the reason for the social benefits extended to them, or to dispel rumors. Left to themselves, the local newspapers ran articles that both fed into the misconceptions of the DFW public about the refugee's dependence on aid and distanced them from it. For example, when a refugee resettlement report was given to Congress in early 1981, it listed national Southeast Asian refugee dependency rates to be upwards of sixty seven percent. Even though Texas state levels were sharply lower at roughly twelve percent, the sixty seven percent figure was picked up by the press as an easily cited, and quoted, headline maker. Susan Forbes, of the Refugee Policy Group in Washington, D.C., blamed the publicizing of that figure without any context as having "paved the way for a public view of the refugees as a group that is reliant on public assistance."

Likewise, when Southeast Asian refugees first started arriving into DFW, the *Dallas Morning News* (Henderson 1977) ran a piece in their Letters to the Editor titled "New Immigrants a Tax Burden" that argued against the area taking more Indochinese refugees. Occasionally, the *Dallas Morning News* ran news articles meant to put some of these rumors into context. One such article quoting a report from the Senate Refugee Subcommittee chairman read:

> Of the 38,707 refugees receiving cash assistance through state welfare agencies, "a considerable percentage were fully or partially employed," although not earning as much as the welfare standard. Thus, their incomes were supplemented by public assistance, not exclusively supported by it.

Another local newspaper intending to disconnect Indochinese refugees from negative images of "living on the dole" highlighted core Texan values—hard work and taxpaying—in an article titled "Refugees prefer to turn welfare around and fare well" (Mallison 1980).

> About 5,000 Indochinese refugees have settled in Tarrant County, say workers at Catholic Charities of the Fort Worth Diocese, the agency that found sponsors for most of them. "Within three to five years," Simon said, "the average immigrant family earns as much as the average native family. After that, they tend to earn more, so they pay more taxes. They're a heck of an economic benefit." He said. "The image of immigrants on the dole, on food stamps and welfare, using up all our money, just doesn't hold water." And it appears that their main mechanism for getting ahead is just real hard work. Mrs. X. has lived in America for just one year and saved $10,000. "Many of our American friends do not understand," Mrs. X. said. "They say, 'How can you do it? We've been here all our lives and can afford nothing. But you have a nice car; you have a nice house.' The answer is that in our country, it was very hard to make a living. So we try very hard here to be self-sufficient." Catholic Charities often has difficulty persuading a newly arrived refugee family to take food stamps or welfare until jobs are found. Kermit Shotts, a program specialist with the U.S. Office of Refugee Affairs in Dallas, said Texas has 40,000 Indochinese refugees. "Texas' warm weather is one attraction and the other is the booming economy, and there is ample evidence that most refugees quickly contribute to, not drain, that boom."

Despite these favorable articles, data from my local newspaper content analysis for the first five years after the Hmong arrived show that negative stigmatizing of the population and images of the Indochinese dependence on welfare outnumbered articles on self-supporting Hmong by 4:1. One example of is this comment from a DFW man, who commented to a news reporter about the Hmong:

> Upon recommendation of Secretary of State Vance, President Carter is approving 15,000 more Indochinese refugees to be admitted into our country. This makes a total of 165,000. I think the taxpayer has been most charitable in acceptance of legal and illegal aliens in the past few years, but the day of reckoning is approaching and collapse of our country is inevitable. I suggest President Carter put half on his peanut farm and let Congress take the other half. The taxpayer has had enough (Henderson 1977).

National newspapers, also widely read by the DFW population, reported negatively on the Hmong's dependence on welfare by 6:1. These reports essentialized all Hmong communities in the United States, including those in Texas, despite the fact that they were doing exceptionally well. As recently as 2009, in an interview I had with the Director of Division of Community Resettlement at the ORR in Washington DC, he remembered his work with the Hmong thirty years ago, saying:

> Strategically, when we [the Government] gave the Hmong three years [on welfare assistance to get their footing] they took all three years. They wouldn't begin to work until twenty-four to twenty-five months after arrival. They went on AFDC and were totally forgotten and there was no end of their dependency. The frustration I had, was that I would track the outcomes from every single community and we weren't getting results. Nobody was taking jobs. They would go through vocational training as a Plumber and say "alright, that was nice. Let me try something else." Because there was no stick to the carrot and everybody was becoming a vegetarian. There were large public housing projects that were very nice and comfortable, so the Hmong took them over and there was no progress, no integration going on.

To him, integration meant working, out of public housing, and self-sufficient. When I asked him to explain the relative success of the Hmong in DFW, he shrugged, saying "these are just general statements."

With their limited English skills, the Hmong were not likely to read or be influenced by the disproportionally negative newspaper articles during their first few years in DFW. However, they were influenced by the exclusionary attitudes that such remarks generated. For example, in 2009 one Texan wrote in a blog about immigrants and welfare that he "would eat out of a garbage can before applying for welfare. But that's just me, a proud American who will one day obtain his dream." Likewise, in one initial household survey interview, I asked a Hmong man what, if any, kinds of financial help his family received when they first arrived. The Hmong man proudly answered, "I'm a good Texan! I didn't accept any money from the government." Another explained:

> No Hmong wants the government assistance. Some have no choice, but when we buy food with food stamps we feel ashamed ... so most people get off assistance as soon as they can. We don't lose time (from work) for having a lot of fun or to have parties. We don't spend money on fancy clothes. We don't go off on luxury vacations ... we just work and work. My family, we want to stand on our own feet. We don't want to live on help from the government. We don't make very much money for such a large family but I am very proud that we take care of ourselves. We're Texans!

Like in Gammertingen, there was also a certain shame associated with living in public housing in DFW. People living in these communities were stigmatized as "poor" and assumed to be on welfare because the apartments were subsidized by taxes. Since the Texas resettlement emphasis was to get refugees out of the sponsor's home and into something affordable as soon as possible, and because refugee work was often paid at minimum wage, "something affordable" often meant moving into these less than desirable neighborhoods. In Dallas, in particular, an entire low-income housing complex became the preferable placement for Southeast Asian refugees and was given the nickname "little Asia." A salient difference between Gammertingen and DFW resettlement is that there was no concerted effort to move the refugees out of these housing complexes and into less stigmatized homes. As far as the sponsors and the government were concerned, their job was finished when the refugee was working and able to afford *any* apartment.

Interestingly enough, when I asked a high-level U.S. government refugee resettlement director what he would be noting when he thinks of a "successfully" resettled refugee, his answer was not much different than that given by the mayor of Gammertingen. He said:

> If I see a Hmong whose got a house, he's got a mortgage that he pays, his kids are in school, he has a job that he goes to where he speaks English, he speaks his own ethnic language in the home ... basically living the American Dream.... I include home ownership because in a lot of places, that is the way membership in society is measured.

What was different from the Gammertingen situation is that the DFW resettlement program made no efforts to ensure this level of success for the refugees, no clear path to this "measurable" form of membership. Maja Korac suggests that "the level and character of these forms of assistance depend on the character of the welfare system of the receiving society, which tends to influence policies of integration" (2009:13). Thus the different approaches to refugee integration are spillovers from the fundamental differences in philosophy between the two countries. The United States is a country that sees itself as a one of immigrants and welcomes everyone, albeit with the caveat that "real Americans" make it on their own. On the other hand Germany, a welfare state, has seen immigrants as guests who have the right to be taken care of within their post-WWII definition of humanity. While attitudes in Germany toward immigrants have significantly changed since the early 1980s, some localities, like Gammertingen, continued with "migrant friendly" policies. Thus, DFW agents and sponsors helped the refugees get their first apartment; however, unlike in Gammertingen where people helped them move into nicer areas, the DFW Hmong were left to figure out how to become "real Americans" for themselves.

Indeed, the DFW Hmong quickly became aware that the apartments they were placed in were not the acceptable norm:

> I remember they gave us some furniture. We would leave during the day for work, and the kids to school, and come home and everything in our house was gone! Someone had to show us that we must lock the doors. The door had several of these locks on them. Sometimes, even when locked, our things were stolen. I remember hearing gunshots and ambulance or police sirens in the night. There were many fights. We thought to ourselves, "What is this? We have fled one war zone just to be placed in another!" We did not feel safe at all. The Hmong just want what everyone wants; a nice, safe place to live where our children can go to a good school. We realized that would be a place out of the city. We also wanted permanence. We had lived in temporary houses and huts for a long time. We were anxious to stay put. We decided to save every penny we had and purchase a home.

One DFW refugee VOLAG Director explained that having this epiphany is an important and expected step in the process of becoming a Texan:

> If someone is content with living in the conditions of the refugee camp housing situation they may think the cheap ghetto housing here is an upgrade, and become content with it. But the Texas expectation of success would be that they do better than that; that at some point they realize where they are at and move up and out.

He then went on to talk about what he characterized as a "failed" group of refugees who have "remained content" with living in their first housing projects since they arrived twenty-five years ago.

Michael Alexander, (2004) of the Amsterdam Study Centre for the Metropolitan Environment, in his comparative research on local migration found that housing and urban development policies significantly affect migrants at the local level. He suggests that implicit or explicit spatial policies may encourage migrant enclaves to congregate or disperse, may affect access to services and employment and because of the symbolic nature of space, may include or exclude immigrant populations in the cities' imaginations. In essence, local policies could actually ease refugee social isolation and stigmatization. These cases demonstrate how the local integration workers understood the spatial domain as a part of member-making and how housing was used as a tool for managing the degree to which its newcomers belong. But how did the DFW Hmong fare in terms of moving out of the projects without the hands-on support and low-interest housing loans offered by Gammertingen?

Even without this support, within five years of arrival, eighty percent of the Hmong who remained in DFW had become homeowners in middleclass neighborhoods in the Metroplex suburbs and only twenty percent of total Hmong households were renters. This was lower than the Texas average as a whole where twenty-nine percent of total households were renters, and lower than the national average where 25.5 percent were renters (WPC 4/15/1982). Which suburb they chose to live in was determined by proximity to their jobs and not by clan, a trend that continues to this day. As of the time of this research, ninety-eight percent of all Hmong families in the DFW Metroplex live in owner-occupied housing units with only two percent living in renter-occupied housing.

> We are all homeowners. Nice homes too! When a new Hmong family moves into our area, we encourage them to save and get a home within five years.

The Hmong community leader told me that this was one thing that distinguishes them from the larger Hmong settlements in other parts of the United States. This perception is indeed correct as the 2008 American Community Survey demographic profile for the Hmong lists national Hmong owner-occupied housing levels at less than fifty percent (U.S. Census Bureau 2008).

> The most important thing to the Hmong in Texas is home ownership. We don't want to live in somebody else's home; it's a sign of failure, or not achieving economic self-sufficiency. When we meet Hmong who have lived here for more than five years and are still renting we question them. It is an embarrassment for them. They will sacrifice and make this one of their first priorities and scrimp and save to achieve this.

Another difference in the public assistance discourse between Gammertingen and DFW was that the newspapers in DFW were noticeably absent of information on where the support money for the refugees was coming from. This often resulted in public misunderstandings. For instance, Mrs. X. in the newspaper cited above said she was often asked how they could save so much money. Having saved money or pooling and saving money to purchase a household car was often the impetus for rumors that suggested the Hmong were getting so much social aid that they were able to buy fancy cars and stash money. Even though Mrs. X told her own story in the newspaper it had a more dismissive effect on the public than when the mayor of Gammertingen addressed the town on the refugee's behalf. This was evidenced by a letter sent from the Texas Conference of Churches who worked with the Hmong sent to the Assistant Commissioner for Coordination of Refugees in Texas (1980). In discussing their position against a proposed Texas-wide placement policy, the letter read:

> ... Added to this should certainly be education of the U.S. citizenry in cultural sensitivity to the refugee.... Further concern is that the policy is discriminating. The criteria for determining an area [to settle refugees] are included "Community attitude toward refugees" and "the number of refugees and their ethnic composition in the community." Are we admitting that we are going to do nothing about developing an educational program to do something about these attitudes?

A letter sent to the Governor of Texas by a confused Texan illustrates these "attitudes":

> I think that the people of Congress and the President are taking advantage of the state of Texas ... I realize that the Cuban and Viet-

namese refugees are an important matter to the United States, however, I do not understand why Texas should have to give these refugees jobs and advantages just because they may be treated a different way in their home county. I also feel that these refugees must come into this country knowing some kind of definite trade and not come into this country and receive immediate welfare payments and a job right off hand. I am a proud native Texan and I would like to know what I and my peers can do to help our state of Texas remain as strong as it already is? (WAP June 10, 1982).

Instead of using this opportunity to educate the Texan on the plight of refugees and social inclusion, the Governor chose to respond in a way that reiterated Texas's exceptionalist position and reinforced the idea that welfare defenders have no place in their state:

> Texas refugees have the lowest welfare dependency in the county and we intend to keep it that way. The influx of Indochinese into the United States has slowed in the past year and will continue to diminish in the future. Your interest in the problems facing Texas indicates your strong Texas character.

There were also notable differences between the types of jobs that the Hmong in DFW and those in Gammertingen acquired. The Hmong in DFW were forced to work right away without the benefit of any language training or an education in cultural competence. The farming skills they came with did little good in the Metroplex. Even for those with education, they could not speak English and had to start at entry-level jobs like everyone else. Of all the Hmong interviewed, only one DFW man worked for the same company that he had started with 30 years ago. Although the jobs given the Hmong in Gammertingen were described as "simple" jobs, any government position in Germany guarantees a living wage that will keep with the cost of living, offers full benefits, a generous retirement pension, and the guarantee that you will never be laid off. On the other hand, jobs found for the Hmong in DFW, though also described as "simple work," were typically minimum wage, unskilled labor positions without any benefits, little security, and little room for advancement. Some would argue that these jobs just transferred the refugees from one stigmatized position (on the dole) to another (the underclass) (Portes & Zhou 1993).

William Clark suggests that as immigrants funnel into lower wage jobs it is "the acquisition of human capital, which is perhaps as important as eliminating discrimination, that will slowly, if painfully, integrate society and overcome patterns of inequality" (2003:52). The DFW path started the Hmong in a position of disadvantage, both socially and economically, while the Gammertingen one started the Hmong with enough resources to live, as their basic law interprets "with dignity." These differences stem from the different ideologies that in America everyone is welcome but one must struggle to move up the social and economic ladder (Lieberson & Waters 1988) or as personified in Texas ideology, that one must "pull him/herself up by their bootstraps," thereby proving their right to belong. The German ideology is such that dignity is a fundamental social right and should be afforded everyone upon arrival. Despite these stark differences, and without the extra initial support of the Government that the Hmong in Gammertingen had, the Hmong in Texas quickly reached the same level of economic self-sufficiency. They attribute their success to working hard and using the social capital of the more educated Hmong and pooling resources among them. However, we cannot discount the myriad job and housing opportunities available in a city that made these choices possible. If there are no jobs and there are no houses, all the effort in the world will not make them appear. Because of the opportunities afforded in a city coupled with their own ingenuity and resourcefulness, the DFW Hmong were able to move into better paying positions and jobs with benefits, and become home owners in middle-class neighborhoods within the same five-year period as the Hmong in Gammertingen.

This is where the Hmong case study departs from the position of Irene Bloemraad's (2006) research on refugee integration. She compares Canadian immigrant groups who were given more hands-on help by the community and service providers to that of groups settling in the United States with its more hands-off approach, arguing that those with more status nurturing fared better. But the two cases of the Hmong seemingly refute that, as both did equally well in securing a position in the middle class. So, if not the hands-on integration plan, then what in the process accounts for the similar results?

## Ingenuity and Agency

The data in this chapter suggests that the answer may lay not just in the analysis of the social, political, and historical construction of the two spaces, but also in its scale—that is, the recourses available to the refugees who settled within that space, and the ingenuity of the refugees to manipulate those resources. These perspectives were illustrated when I asked the mayor of Gammertingen and the Hmong to reflect on why they thought they were able to obtain the level of "success" they had. The mayor replied:

> I think it was a combination of placing the right amount of people in the right size town. Although our village is small, it had the right number of doctors, dentists, schools, churches, housing, club programs, transportation, jobs, able volunteers, et cetera, to adequately help the ten families [five Vietnamese and five Hmong] that came here. I don't think this town could have absorbed more people. With, say fifty families, the outcome would have been different.

When I posed that same question to the German Hmong, one man said:

> The Hmong are survivors. We wanted to survive here. We did what we had to do to survive. Is that so different than what anybody else does?

While the town thought they were setting the Hmong up for inclusion, the Hmong were simultaneously orchestrating their own forms of social capital and utilizing their traditional forms of kinship and reciprocity to negotiate success both in terms of Hmong and Gammertingen values. It was a combination of structure and agency that ultimately facilitated a space where the Hmong could fit in. The situation was not dissimilar in DFW. While some Texans have claimed that the Hmong's success is a result of the state forcing them to "sink or swim," it was equally a matter of the Hmong taking advantage of their environment, both economically and in terms of the housing market, and using their own social capital of educated Hmong to negotiate the values of the receiving society. It was a combination of structure and agency that facilitated their social inclusion and staked their claim to the right to belong.

This chapter has also demonstrated how a refugee is sent messages from the moment they arrive in their resettlement location by member-making institutional structures, such as sponsors, NGOs, municipalities, and politicians, of who belongs and who is an acceptable member of the local community. These messages are often embedded in unofficial social meanings imparted through relationships between newcomers and official member-makers, through local public assistance discourse, and through the spatial domains of resettlement neighborhoods. These differences resulted in different outcomes in the types of social interaction offered, access to language classes, access to enhanced employment opportunities, and the ability to participate in local decision-making. Despite the myriad differences and varying paths traveled as a consequence thereof, both groups of Hmong made significant leaps to the middle class in terms of housing neighborhoods, job stability and benefits offered. They read the member-maker's messages concerning who belonged and why, then used the resources available to them to progress into those "acceptable" categories.

The refugee's agency in the process of "being made" is often overlooked and lost in top-down policy approaches aimed at getting the refugee to do more. The Hmong needed little incentive to make it. Gammertingen and DFW represent contrasting types of policy approaches to reception and integration of the Hmong, yet it took ingenuity and agency to read local messages of belonging and orchestrate their own forms of social capital needed to achieve this end. Ironically, the effects of member-making programs and policies often facilitate, rather than discourage, long-term dependency, social isolation and stigmatism. It takes structure and agency; that is, belonging to a new locality requires a certain ingenuity to make it while being made. This is an area where raw statistics on quantifiable modes of incorporation can be misleading. Housing and labor market figures are two often-cited domains in measuring successful integration. However, anthropological analyses on the localized forces that shape the policies and how refugees respond to them help give meaning to figures and a more thorough understanding of why the more managed style of integration shown in Gammertingen realized the same ultimate results in terms of home ownership and employment stability as the more laissez faire approach of DFW.

CHAPTER 5

# Religious Institutions: Intervening Mechanisms of Belonging

Anthropologists know that belief systems serve as an integral part of any cultural framework and that immigrant populations bring them along on their resettlement journey as an important mechanism in coping with their transition to a new land. Much has been written in the area of how the religious organizations that newcomers construct for themselves offer needed social services and serve as a form of emotional support. We also understand their role as arenas for civic engagement, solidarity, and cultural continuum.[1] Less is known about the role of religious institution in the receiving area where refugees are resettled and what way they served as intervening mechanisms of belonging.

What has been written about the relationship between religious institutions and refugees within the larger framework of resettlement has mostly emphasized Christianity's encroaching ideology on refugee faiths in general[2] and as an agent of citizen-making in particular (Ong 2003). Gozdziak and Shandy remind us that beyond this one-way relationship, religion can "operate in compelling, competing, and contradictory ways" that serve as "a source of resiliency as it both facilitates and impedes the integration process" (2002: 131). Dianna Shandy in particular, explored the socio-political role of Christianity in the forced migration experiences of the Nuer in America where she found an im-

---

1. For social services and emotional support see Warner & Winter 1998; Ebaugh & Chafetz 2000; for the role of religious institutions as arenas for civic engagement see Stepick, Rey & Mahler 2009; for the way these institutions perpetuate ties to the homeland culture see Chou 1991; Levitt 2007; to national identity see Tiryakian 10=991; Ahmary 1998, and to interactions in transnational social fields see Vertovec 2001; Vertovec & Castles 1999; Levitt 2003. For observations on the role of religious institutions established by refugees post resettlement see Stepick 1998; Portes & Rumbaut 1996; and Godziak & Shandy 2002.

2. See Comaroff & Camoroff 1986; Peterson & Allman 1999; Godziak and Shandy 2002.

portant "flexibility and improvisation" (2002:219), in their beliefs that helped them transform their religious practices in a way that made sense to both their homeland identity and the faith traditions of their new hosts. I find this framework helpful in explaining a similar malleability of belief witnessed in the small-sized Gammertingen and DFW Hmong resettlements. We will see how they intersected with and negotiated the local religious institutions that were charged to aid in their resettlement.

This chapter builds on these discussions. It first looks at the traditional Hmong beliefs held before resettlement and then at the role DFW and Gammertingen religious institutions played in member-making and local belonging. Reflecting on how the Hmong in each field site negotiated the local cultural constructions of religious ideology embedded in the resettlement approaches, we will examine how they uniquely adapted their belief system in a way that made sense to both their own identity and to the local environment.

## Hmong Traditional Religion

Traditional Hmong religion is animistic, sometimes called pantheistic (see Tapp 1989), and characterized by diverse spirits and elements of ritual practices. Hmong cosmology has been strongly linked by scholars to the Chinese Otherworld:

> The Hmong world of *yeeb ceeb* parallels the Chinese world of *yin,* the dark world of the spirits: the Hmong world of *yaj ceeb* parallels the Chinese world of *yang,* the bright world of men and women, of material objects and nature (Tapp 1989:59).

Besides two fearful lords of the Hmong Otherworld, there exists a host of spirits and supernatural forces known to the Hmong that are associated with everything from vocations, such as hunting and herbalism, to seasons and biological functions (61). Indeed, every life crisis event in Hmong society is marked by rituals of sanctification and protection from bad spirits, as are the major turning points of the agricultural year, after the harvests, and at the New Year. In this way, Hmong traditional religion permeates every aspect of life including much of what is glossed over in literature as "customs." Because spirits and the Otherworld cannot be seen by human eyes, a shaman is an important community member who is believed to have the power to enter it unharmed and make contact with the spirit world and negotiate on behalf of Hmong. The life of a traditional Hmong culminates at death in the most complex and in-depth ritual of all—the funeral. This religious practice has as its "ultimate aim the safe dispatch of the soul of the deceased to the otherworld and its reincarnation as a member of the same clan" (81). In order to be reunited with the right ancestors, each subclan follows its own unique funeral rituals and types of grave used in burial (Leepreecha 2001:167). Because of its ubiquitous nature and particular mortuary rites, Hmong traditional religion has not only been considered an essential element of Hmong identity, but an important marker of subclan identity.

As such, Hmong traditional religion has served many important functions in their society. For instance, gender roles are established and reinforced as the elder males have the dominant role in conducting all ritual ceremonies, and are assigned this role for their experience, seniority, and knowledge of how to perform them (Moua 1995). Kinship solidarity is also reinforced, as important spiritual decisions for the family are made at the subclan level and rituals are performed in the household where extended family and other kin come together to engage in them. The role of shaman as healer serves the communal function of "physician, psychiatrist, and religious mediator" (Moua 1995). As shamans are the only ones with access to the spirits, they carry great status and further reinforce hierarchical roles within the community. In these ways the natural environment and social order of the Hmong are closely entwined with the supernatural world, shamanistic ritual, and domestic worship.

Scholars have explained why Hmong convert to or resist Christianity in terms of the deeper philosophical role and meaning of religion to the Hmong. Anthropologist Tam Ngo (2009) explains this instrumental function inherent in their traditional religion is embedded in the Hmong word, *Kevcai*. This refers to "ways" in the sense of "roads or paths" and is thought of predominantly in terms of proper daily behavior in the many rituals that are a part of everyday life, principles of lineage, affinal responsibilities, "marriage and death, but also including those of the New Year celebrations, and more widely of birth, subsistence, litigation and dispute" (20). He suggests that it is this "medium of these ways" that are what is important to the Hmong and which must be transposed in a way that makes sense when negotiating conversion to Christianity or other belief systems. We see how this transposition occurred when Christianity first entered the Laotian hill areas.

Descriptions of missionary visits to the hill people were first described in William Hudspeth's 1937 work on the Hmong of Southeast Asia. He links their conversion to the fact that the Hmong "mistakenly" associated the written form of the Bible with their legend of long lost Miao writings from China:

> Long ago the Miao lived on the north side of the Yellow River, but the conquering Chinese came and drove them from their lands and

homes. Coming to the river and possessing no boats they debated what should be done with the books, and in the end they strapped them to their shoulders and swam across, but the waters ran so swiftly and the river was so wide, that the books were washed away and fishes swallowed them.

This was the story when the British and Foreign Bible Society sent the first Gospels. As these were distributed the legend grew—the once upon a time lost books had been found, found in the white man's country, and they told the incomparable story that Jesus loved the Miao. Only the imagination can conceive what this meant to these hills-men, some of whom travelled for days to view the books (Hudspeth 1937:32). Likewise, anthropologist Nicholas Tapp speculates that other prominent legends of the Hmong being led by Kings became identified with indigenous Messianic conceptions of a returning King (1989:78). These myths flourished during the Vietnam War. One story circulated that Christ was about to return wearing American clothes in a jeep and distributing rifles (Garrett 1974; Tapp 1989).

Of the five original Hmong families who came to Gammertingen, one of the older men had been converted by missionaries under these circumstances back in Laos in 1962. These examples demonstrate that as a result of contact, long before refugee resettlement to the West, the Hmong had been adapting their own beliefs to that of the "other" and trying to control missionization by internalizing Christian ideology in a way that made sense of their present circumstances and important past traditions. Let us consider next how the two field sites used Christianity as part of their member-making efforts, first beginning in Gammertingen.

## Gammertingen and Religious Member-Making

According to the mayor of Gammertingen, the recruitment of the village churches at the outset of resettlement was to "… help socialize the newcomers into the town." He explained how the two centrally located churches were the hub of social activities and that most residents of the village in the late 1970s attended either the Catholic or *Evangelische* (the southern German equivalent to a Protestant) Church. "If we could get them [the Hmong] coming to the church dinners and other social activities," said the mayor "then they would meet and interact with their neighbors in a social setting."

The Gammertingen Evangelisch pastor at that time explained how he saw his church's position in this process:

> The church plays an important role ... because I think it's important that people find a community to which they can share their lives and hopes and beliefs; and it is important for integration because everyone needs a place to belong. I believe the city recognizes this role as well in that the mayor often comes to us pastors when a new population comes to town and asks us to make special efforts to make them feel a welcome part of this community.

When I asked him to explain how they fulfilled this request, he said:

> Several of the sponsors were church members and would be the liaisons between the church and the Hmong. They would pick the children up every Sunday and bring them to Sunday school. The parents were encouraged to come along, but many didn't. I don't think they understood the sermon but we hoped they understood our hearts. Our church did some welcome dinners for them, and had the children involved in plays. But mostly we tried to communicate that we were there for them—whatever they needed. We cared.

The Pastor went on to explain their "caring" less in terms of evangelism and more in terms of Schwäbisch ideologies of social justice, peace, and social help. In a historic missionary conference in 1901, German mission theorist Gundemann (Gunning 1901:305) advocated that the goal of missions work ought to be to establish folk churches with the dual approach of moving people toward conversion and establishing community. This idea of Christendom as community led the 20th-century German Evangelisch church toward medical care, education, irrigation and other development projects. The engagement of social services, while only indirectly evangelical, became the rationale for the Schwaben long-term goal of community-forming through social service. From the perspective of the Gammertingen Evangelische church, the inclusion of the Hmong was their social responsibility, which they understood to be their primary spiritual responsibility. This social responsibility played out in recruiting sponsors from the church, the church raising money for the Hmong's resettlement needs, and eventually in raising the down payments for their first houses. The "community" aspect of the church's philosophy came by planning Christmas parties, dinners, and social events where the Hmong could showcase their culture while interacting with villagers.

At first it was not known what the Hmong's spiritual beliefs were, but because word had spread around town that they were holding some sort of religious service in their homes, it was widely assumed that it was pagan. As one villager told me, the Gammertingen people had never thought to ask what they believed, but assumed their religious practices were "primitive" and "exotic" because the refugees were "oriental" and had exhibited a "severe lack of technological understanding." One informant said:

> Many in our town believed that people were committing sin if they didn't go the Protestant or Catholic Church. I believe this caused some Germans to reject the Hmong's [house] religion outright.

The Hmong had no idea that this was the perception of them until nearly six years after their arrival when, for the first time, one local German realized that a group of Hmong were practicing what appeared to be a form of Christianity in their homes (their transition from animism to Christianity will be discussed later in this chapter). She recalled that afternoon when she was visiting an elderly Hmong man who was having particular difficulty learning the German language:

> I came to their house to take the children to Sunday school. I saw their father reading what looked like a Bible in another language. My heart jumped. I went to him and asked if he believed in God. I did this by pointing to his Bible, then to his heart and then to the sky. I clasped my hands in prayer and then looked up hoping he understood. He just lit. He smiled this big smile and nodded his head. I then made the same motions this time pointing to my own heart and told him that I did too. Somehow we connected. We understood each other. We both started crying. I think it was at that moment that we both felt that maybe, we aren't so different after all. He then pointed to the other Hmong in the house who were gathering for their service making the same motions and shaking his head "yes." This whole time we both had assumed that each other practiced a strange belief, when all along we were really the same. That morning I stood in our church and told everyone about this special visit and what I had learned. Soon, everyone in the village knew. We started inviting the adults to our services and sporadically picked them up and brought them to our church. We learned that they were Baptists. We don't have this religion in Germany, but we understood it was some type of Christian.

While the locals rejoiced that they were, as one local man put it, "really one of our own," the Hmong families described their visits to the town church as cordial, overwhelming, and mostly unintelligible. They recognized some of their rituals, for instance, they knew they were praying when they collectively bowed their heads, and knew some of the melodies of a few hymns, and recognized that the pastor of the church was the one speaking at length from behind the pulpit, but they were frustrated that after six years their language skills weren't good enough to understand the nuances of the religious vocabulary or relate to the cultural stories that were a part of the liturgy.

Despite these obstacles, the village pastor's wife perceived the efforts of their church as facilitating the integration process and planned a big event in an effort to concretely connect the two:

> We arranged for the church to sponsor this celebration for these Baptist Hmong who had come to visit our church services and we had a big exhibition on Hmong culture for the town's people. We displayed their Hmong Bibles, Hymn books, food, clothing, and handicrafts for the others to see. We asked the Hmong to bring their traditional food and costumes, and the children put on a play for us. I think that day was important for us Germans and the Hmong. It was a nice event. Naturally, some of the church people were a little stratified [by which she meant segregated] and didn't go directly up to the Hmong and engage them. But for the greater majority they were comfortable talking with them, and were genuinely happy to celebrate with them. Another thing that was very nice is that as part of the celebration we showed a film in the church about the Hmong in the Thai refugee camps. Us showing this was like a public service education to the community on these foreigners who lived among them, some of whom still carried citizenship from this land. And the people in the church who saw this film had a connection to the Hmong and could all of a sudden imagine all the troubles they had adjusting to life here in Gammertingen. And I think this celebration was important for both the Hmong and the villagers as a bridge for the two to get to know each other, where they came from, and why they did some of the things they did. It helped the process of integration along. I think the Hmong experienced a feeling of camaraderie with the Germans here, and the Germans saw a story and humanity beyond the strange Asian faces who lived on the hill that needed help with learning German and doing homework. They became real people with a real story. I remember everyone had such a great time. Matter of fact, the next Christmas, the Hmong invited the villagers from our church to celebrate with them in their home church to what had previously been their private Christmas fest. I think this church experience allowed us all to be open to each other's world, to appreciate each other at a different level, and thereby become not strangers but friends. Then we all started talking more to each other in the village.

Figure 5.1 Evangelisch Hmong Celebration

Photo courtesy of Pastor Kerst (Germany).

The Hmong expressed that they enjoyed the friendliness of the people and began attending this church on a regular basis while continuing to hold services that they could more thoroughly understand in their house on Sunday evenings.

A month after this joint celebration the pastor and wife were surprised by a phone call from the Hmong family that was holding church in their house saying they wanted to join the Evangelische church. "When we came to talk with this one family we were surprised to find the whole clan waiting!" They were even more surprised the next Sunday when the entire Hmong community showed up to be included in formal membership.

> We were so happy and excited! Not because we didn't think they were Christians outside of this membership, but because, to us, this membership signified a milestone in social integration and that they wanted to be among us and not stay to themselves.

In essence, the pastor's wife thought it was an outward sign that the Hmong wanted to belong to their group. When I asked the Gammertingen Hmong how they perceived these events they said:

**Figure 5.2 Membership Service at Evangelisch Church**

Photo courtesy of Pastor Kerst (Germany).

Everyone in town looked like they were a part of these churches, and we wanted to show that we were a part of the town too. We had been reluctant to join these groups before because we did not know what they believed. When we learned that we believed the same thing, membership was our way of saying, "Yes, we are one and the same." Our Hmong community gave this church a gift. It is a very large *Pa Ndau* [a traditional hand embroidered fabric depicting Hmong history and their values]. We hoped the story could communicate what we could not. They were very happy to receive this gift and hung it in the church entryway. It still hangs there today.

These experiences substantiate previous observations about religion as a coalescing force, especially when there is a perception of a shared faith between the refugees and their host.[3] It was this perception that facilitated a sense of belonging in the village. Indeed, prior to the initial epiphanic encounter between the refugee and host there is no evidence of any overt evangelical efforts by the townsfolk to convert the Hmong over to their faith. They were content to think of them as exotic others to whom they were obligated to pour out good will. Once they thought of each other as fellows in the same ship, they were able to open up to each other at a different level.

---

3. See Monica Eldestein 2002.

Figure 5.3  Pa Ndau Hanging in Evangelisch Church

Photo courtesy of DN/Omega Productions.

This relationship, mostly unspoken, remained in effect while the Gammertingen church made great efforts to accommodate the Hmong's language barriers. A church member recalls:

> We continued to read the scripture in German and then have one of the Hmong stand and read it in Hmong from their Bible. We would sing a Hymn we both knew alternating verses between English and Hmong.

Stories about the Hmong's parish involvement were reported in the monthly church newsletter for the first year and a half after they joined the congregation. I counted nine such stories in the eighteen newsletters that covered this period of time that particularly emphasized the church's integrative gestures. For example, one article was about a church confirmation service and celebration for Sunday school children featuring several photographs of the event: Anglo children riding scooters, children's art work, people under tents in the church courtyard eating on picnic tables, and one of a Hmong women serving food behind a table. The caption under the photo read: "A stand where the Hmong toiled giving out tastes of authentic spring rolls." Another parish news article was written by a young Hmong teen who reported how he likes eating certain Gammertingen potato dishes, that he had found many local friends at the church, and that he "likes it here." With regard to the potential impact of these articles, church records indicate that upwards of 2,500 villagers received this newsletter in the mail and ninety-one percent of all respondents who attended the church said they read it from cover-to-cover when it came and considered it a reliable source for local news.[4] Gammertingen's mayor was one who regularly received and read this newsletter. When he read about the Hmong's church membership, he used it in appeals to the religiosity of his villagers in requests to continue treating their newcomers with patience and to contribute to the special account set up for their aid. One article he wrote in the local newspaper, in part, read;

> Roughly half the Vietnamese families [referring to the Hmong] are Christians and like to attend the services of the Evangelisch Church. For them, as for all families, they have been through a lot and I invoke the words of Christ on their behalf: "Whatever you do for the least of these, you have done unto me." Please continue to support the important ministry of the refugee working group and inclusion of these families and further donate to the special account set up on their behalf.

Within a year and a half, however, the Hmong grew weary of having two church services and said they felt "more free" to express themselves and "be Hmong" in their own services. The village pastor's wife recalls this time:

> We began to notice that only a few Hmong were still attending. Without the language skills, Sundays boiled down to just a time of fellowship with other Germans for them and we realized they weren't really getting fed here—spiritually. So we encouraged them to continue the Hmong services in their home but to continue coming to our big events for integration purposes. We gave them our blessing, so to say, to do their own thing without judgment. And the Germans in the church here understood this.

Since that time, the Hmong house church and the town's Evangelisch church have remained separate, but notably the Hmong and the villagers both speak of each other as being "members of the same church" and coffee visits, parties, events, and lasting friendships still exist between the two. In fact, a section of the 2008 *Bishops Report* on the village Evangelisch church reads:

> From the beginning, global initiatives such as asylum work and the integration of the Hmong families have been very closely connected

---

4. Figures are from the Bishops report on the State of the Gammertingen Church in 2000.

### Figure 5.4 German Hmong House Church

Photo courtesy of the Lo family.

with the parish. This parish's active involvement in this work occurred under the guiding concept of "peace, justice and integrity for all of creation" (*Evangelische Kirchengemeinde Gammertingen* 2008).

As we will see in the next section, this was different from how the DFW churches saw their role in the resettlement and its very different implications for the process of belonging.

## DFW and Religious Member-Making

Of the four major refugee agencies contracted by the United States to handle resettlement in DFW, three of them were faith-based—one Catholic and two Protestant. Few Hmong were resettled by the Catholic program that ended up working mostly with Vietnamese; therefore in this section I will focus on the role of the Protestant resettlement agencies in the area. While their mission as per their government contract, was to help all refugees with rebuilding their lives indiscriminately, a videotaped interview with a director of World Relief in the Indochinese resettlement efforts entitled "Replanting Lives" (World Relief 1988) reveals a different agenda.

> God has called all of us to witness to His good news, even to the ends of the earth ... the world is coming to us. This is significant for our missionary cause. We at World Relief believe that God has specifically brought these people from all over the world to the United States in order for His church to minister to them.... Because their lives have been turned upside down and they are experiencing culture shock and feel vulnerable and strange in a new environment, many immigrants are more open to God. Mission's experts tell us that immigrants during their first few years in a new country are the second most receptive group to the gospel after children.... We have an incredible opportunity to meet both physical needs and to offer a place of friendship and belonging—a place where they can meet God.

Recruiting brochures from this time asking churches to engage in refugee sponsorship likewise emphasized the "biblical command to welcome the stranger" and suggest that doing so is the answer to "balancing the call to social action and evangelism" (Gazley n.d). In one section the brochure emphasizes sponsorship as fulfilling the "need of a theology that balances the unconditional love and compassion of Christ with the truth of proclaiming fallen man's need for a savior to all the nations" (Gazley n.d). A local Baptist pastor in DFW told me how they would meet with members who had taken refugees into their homes to strategize on ways to "win them over to Christianity." This evangelical focus was particularly strong in DFW where, according to its website, *Time* magazine opined that "If Texans had a state religion, it would probably be Baptist." Claiming that "more than any other group of Christians, the general conditions in Texas, both good and evil, can be laid at the door of the Baptists of Texas." The implication of these comments was that proselytizing the newcomer was to become a leading rationale for many churchgoers engaging in refugee resettlement. This was fundamentally different from how the evangelical church in Gammertingen saw their role. In Gammertingen, social belonging was the priority. Church members felt this was the fulfillment of their obligation to God. In DFW, by contrast, where an ideology of evangelism permeates the area, church members saw proselytizing the exotic foreigner as their main mission, and social integration as a tool to be used in that process. These differing perspectives had unique consequences for the Hmong as they developed their sense of belonging.

Many of the DFW Hmong who were not already Christians when they came to America spoke of their first encounters with Christianity through their sponsors. Most indicated a sense of obligation they felt to attend church with them while living in their homes and to engage in their Christian rituals without really understanding what they were doing. They also felt free to abandon their host's religion once they moved out of their homes.

To accommodate the few Hmong who arrived in the United States as Christians, organized Hmong churches sprang up across America, particularly in the larger resettlement areas of California and Minnesota. Upon word that the Texas community had a few Christians, pastors were sent to DFW to train leaders and institutionalize Hmong language churches for them. The Baptists were among the first to organize there. Those who trained the Hmong leaders in this religion quickly encouraged them to move their services out of the houses suggesting that, rather, they share a church space with an already established "white" church of the same denomination. One Hmong pastor said doing so "looks more legitimate to the locals." Revisiting the experience, one DFW Hmong man who had been converted to Christianity by missionaries back in Lao and then had been re-trained as a pastor in the Baptist tradition while in Texas, said that there was a Baptist Church in the Metroplex that he heard had helped ethnic churches in the past. He approached them requesting to share space. The "white" church director tells the story from his perspective:

> Our understanding was that they were meeting somewhere in Fort Worth but had Hmong coming from all over the Metroplex, from as far away as Plano [roughly forty miles]. They were looking for something bigger and a little more central. We had just organized this African congregation who was using one of our spaces upstairs into their own congregation and building so we had some extra space and invited them to come here. We had lots of space in this building that we weren't utilizing so it wasn't uncommon for us to lend it out to ethnic groups.

When asked what led them to share with the Hmong, he said:

> It is the command of Jesus to go and preach the gospel and tell folks about how their lives can be changed. We assume that all ethnic groups need to know the gospel. Which is the reality. A lot of those folks don't have the financial wherewithal to go out and buy a piece of land and build a building, so this gives them a place to meet. We see the Hmong as a mission, an extension of our church, these people are members of our church who just don't happen to speak English as well as some of us do and want to hear a sermon in their own native tongue.

Similar to the World Relief refugee resettlement literature, the Anglo pastor said he "sold" this arrangement to his congregation by saying the congregants didn't have to go around the world to do mission work; they could do it right upstairs in their own facility.

> When people started complaining about the new smells or sounds coming from the space I would respond, "Look at all the people that we are reaching out to who are different from us and who are getting to hear the gospel in their own native tongue. They are able to eat together with other people from Laos! Isn't that a positive thing?"

Thinking back on the situation in Gammertingen, I asked the pastor if his church felt it was their "mission" or responsibility to help them integrate into the broader community or even the larger congregation. He said:

> I don't think it was ever our mission to incorporate them into our traditions. I know it used to be the goal of missionaries to make English-speaking Americans out of everyone but we aren't interested in making them into a congregation or people just like us. Our goal is to give them the space to practice Christianity while being themselves. Let them worship as they see fit. I go back to the African church with their incense burning and such. I'm sure there were people in our church who wanted us to go upstairs and tell them, you know, "You got to stop burning the incense!" And we just tell them it was never our idea to do that. We want them to have their own traditions and be themselves and feel like they can worship as they please.... So maybe in a sense, we are not really thinking about assimilating them into our congregation or town, but just providing a spot for them to act out Christianity.

An unintended consequence of that philosophy is that his congregation and the Hmong have little interaction. Looking back over the past twenty years he could remember only one socially integrative event, a Thanksgiving dinner in the 1990s. He remarked that the preschool children continue to have Sunday school together "because we have all the puppets and things," but admitted that he has only had one or two conversations with the Hmong himself over the years. "Do they even speak English?" he asked in our conversation. To illustrate the distance, when I visited the church for observation I had to ask nine different Anglo attendees where the Hmong service in their own building was only to be met by blank stares and responses in the line of, "The who?" We finally encountered an elderly man who said, "I think there is some sort of ethnic gathering going on way up in the attic." The white Pastor was remorseful when I told him this story saying, "It makes it a little bit strange that we would send a team of folks to Mongolia and the Sudan when we neglect to send our people up the steps to the group on our own property." He went on to say that "integrating" the two churches for events would be hard because "they don't speak English" and were Laotians. I asked if it would surprise him to know that at the time of our conversation in 2009, except for one elderly couple, all the Hmong "up there" spoke English; that the youth didn't even speak Hmong; that 90 percent of the congregation were U.S. citizens, and that the Hmong pastor, who had earned a college degree after arriving in the states had, over the past 25 years, worked his way from an entry-level engineer assistant up to an executive for Texas Instruments; and that his wife, with a similar degree from a local college had, after twenty-one years, become the Senior Human Resource manager for a large American firm. He appeared at a loss. "I had no idea…. Maybe we ought to consider taking them out of the category of Foreign Missions."

It is noteworthy to add that conversations with the Hmong pastor revealed that they were OK with this distal arrangement. They wanted a space to practice their religion without the constraints of forced interaction with the host church. The Hmong pastor thought this arrangement, while void of intermingling, gave them more autonomy and a space where they felt they were, in the words of the Hmong pastor, "in charge" of their own actions. "We could push for more interaction," he said, "but we don't." To the Hmong, keeping that separation was an act of empowerment that allowed them to maintain the boundaries of their cultural identity within a space that was socially approved by their hosts. While it is a credit that the DFW Baptist church gave space to the Hmong without further cultural impositions, it has had, unbeknownst to both of them, the negative consequence of reinforcing the idea of the Hmong as exotic Others, foreigners, and not Americans. Keeping the Hmong in this position served the evangelical ideology of the host church and allowed them to say that they were engaged in foreign missions without really engaging in face-to-face relationships. In this way, both churches were more interested in including each other in their institutional idea of religion than into their communities; whereas the opposite objective characterized the Evangelisch church in Gammertingen.

## Flexibility and Improvisations

Because the Gammertingen church did not see their mission as overtly evangelical, the Hmong expressed that they never felt any direct pressure to convert from the town church. They did say, however, that they felt this pressure from one Hmong family that had arrived as Christian. A Hmong observed that since their traditional beliefs entailed their entire way of life, asking them to convert to Christianity was tantamount to asking them to cease being Hmong. At some point, however, the Hmong families in Gammertingen realized that their new environment was not conducive to being Hmong as they knew it. Eventually all the initial refugee settlers converted, acknowledging western religion was a better "fit" for their new life. One man recounts how his family came to that decision and the Gammertingen Hmong became, what he refers to, as a "Christian community":

> He [the Hmong Christian] would talk to us all the time about God. We would listen. We had many questions. Most of us had heard about this religion or that white missionaries were bringing it to the Hmong, but didn't know details about it. The man started holding church services in his home and invited us. Some of the Hmong started going, soon we all were going. It was initially a way for our small community to come together every week. We would have these big meals after and it reminded us of the way we lived back home. One by one, the Hmong families became Christians. It was just easier. It was very hard for us to practice our traditional beliefs. We didn't have a shaman to perform the needed rituals and we had little knowledge of how to perform them correctly ourselves. We thought, "What happens to us when we die? There are none of our elder relatives here to perform the Hmong funeral rights that will reunite us with our ancestors and our souls will wander forever." Christianity, we were told, offered another, easier way to die in peace and be reunited with our families afterward. This became clear to us when the Christian family had a baby that died. We all attended the town church for the burial. It was very different then what we had practiced in Laos. There were no animal sacrifices and it only lasted an hour or so. Our Hmong funerals last for days and require lots of animals and a shaman and things that we could never find or afford here in Germany. We saw the practicality of his way for our life here. We thought, "That's why the Germans do this and not our way; because they can't." I think it was this that convinced us that if we were going to live in Gammertingen, we needed to follow a way that would work here. Our way seemed old fashioned and this way was more modern. Christianity fit.... One by one the other Hmong started to follow too. It helped us stay together as a group. It was the right thing to do. That's how we all became Christians.

The fact that he kept referring to the Western religion as a "way" is indicative of how the Hmong translated old conceptions into their new experiences. When I asked participants what was meant by a "better fit," I was told that the Christian religion was "more modern—like Germany." The appeal of Christianity was not based so much upon its particular characteristics, but rather on the characteristics of their traditional religious practices and beliefs. Animal offerings were no longer plausible and knowledge of how to perform rituals properly was lost. Anthropologist Tam Ngo asserted that post-resettlement, Hmong converts to Christianity around the globe started to refer to Christianity as "*kevcia tshiab*" or "new way," and "*kevcia qub*" or "old way" used to refer to their traditional religious beliefs and practices (2009:20). At some point there was an acknowledgment that alternative modes of doing things, or *kevcia*, were needed. Anthropologist Cornelia Kammerer (1997) witnessed similar reasons for conversion among the Akha Highlanders of Thailand who, in the face of encroaching modernization, chose to replace their old religion with one that made sense in the West. As Chen has noted, salvation, like forced migration, "embodies the dialectical forces of dying and birthing, destructing and reconstructing" (2008:10). In this way, the German Hmong's choice to convert to Christianity could be seen as an act of agency, of embracing the new, of fitting in or belonging in the Gammertingen environment.

Anthropologist Nicholas Tapp has noted that when the Hmong change religions they generally do it in groups, suggesting "the tradition of whole village conversion continues, often the male household heads following the example of a village leader or important shaman in his conversion to Christianity" (1989:83). It was this kind of community conversion that happened in Gammertingen. In this way, important communal and kinship practices that were a part of Hmongness in Laos could be re-created in the rituals and experiences surrounding church life. For example, meeting extended family at church every Sunday and partaking in communion and praying for good fortune together all took the place of kin gatherings in the home for animistic rituals that reinforced the same values. With their own extended families dispersed in resettlement, church members came to rely upon one another for emotional and material support in the same way they would have their subclan back in Laos.

One Hmong man who moved into the Gammertingen community ten years ago has chosen not to convert. He spoke of how this decision ostracizes him from the rest of the Hmong and, he feels, the villagers of Gammertingen:

> They [the Christian Hmong] used to come by my house all the time and try to get me to be a Christian. They would keep at me to come to their house church on Sundays. I would see all the other Hmong out my window coming to the house with their food and I could hear them singing and then watch them as they ate outside afterward. My wife and I just wanted to be with the other Hmong but it seemed like all their gatherings were church related. So we started to go. I didn't

believe in that, I still don't. I just wanted to be included in whatever was going on. Now we only go to the events at the Hmong church but we are not one of them. We are Hmong [traditional] religion. The Germans don't know what that is. When I try to explain it, they look at me like I am crazy then they don't want anything to do with me. None of them do.

In Gammertingen recreation, friendship, and social belonging were transformed from Laotian village life to community church life. Both immigrant needs and institutional outreach strategies drove the community's religious conversion. As a result, conversion became a source of belonging for the Hmong to both to the people of Gammertingen and to the local Hmong community.

The Hmong in DFW talk of their conversion to Christianity in much the same terms as the Hmong in Gammertingen. When the majority of the first-settled Hmong left Texas for the larger Hmong communities elsewhere in the United States, the few families that were left found themselves without the elders, livestock, extended family members, and the shamans they depended on to continue in the traditional Hmong system. "We couldn't afford the expensive offerings for the funerals. We didn't know what would happen to us when we died." They were left in a situation similar to that of the Hmong in Gammertingen. According to the Hmong Planning and Development Corporation of DFW, a few families found the religion of their hosts a viable option and chose to convert. The new Christians quickly convinced others to convert in much the same manner as happened in Germany. Like those in Gammertingen, the DFW Hmong also used the words "more modern" when describing Christianity, saying of the Hmong who remain traditional, they "need to get with the times."

As Hmong conversions grew in DFW, two major churches developed, the Southern Baptists and a Hmong Christian Missionary Alliance congregation. According to the Christian Missionary Alliance website, they have been active in the Laotian highlands since 1949 and had been the source of many pre-resettlement conversions among the Hmong. Many refugees who were a part of this organization in Laos gravitated toward this organization as it set up Hmong churches in the United States. A Minnesota man, Rev. Joshua Vang, is credited as the first Hmong leader appointed by the Baptist Home Mission Board as Ethnic Missionary for the Indochina refugees in the United States. As of July 5th, 2010, the Hmong Baptist National Association listed on its website, Rev. Vang was the one who coordinated the joining of Lao and Hmong with the Southern Baptist in 1976. In 1982, a large effort was made by the

Southern Baptists to establish Hmong churches across America, this included the one in Texas.

These congregations soon became gathering places where the geographically isolated Hmong could come together for activities, a sense of solidarity, and networking not unlike the communal experiences they had left in Laos. In terms of proselytizing, one Hmong pastor who was a Christian before resettlement tells how he convinces Hmong to forgo the "old ways" using their established cultural hierarchy from the past:

> First you must approach the oldest male of the family as all decisions are made through him. I would explain the case for Christianity then wait. You cannot push, you just have to wait until he gets back to you, and it may be some time. When he returns to you he may say "no" or may invite me to speak to their family. In this case the oldest male will call all family members together for my presentation, after they would openly debate its merits among them. The authority figure listens to all sides and then decides for the family. Either they all come, or they all don't. The influence of the family is strong. Rarely will one cross it.

For the Hmong, religious conversion is a daunting decision. It signifies not only a conversion from their own belief traditions but could also be seen as an abandonment of loyalties from one's family. "Protestant Christianity" suggests Chen, "is particularly threatening to the family because it prohibits the practice of ancestral veneration" (2008:69). For this reason religious conversions are not taken lightly and require more serious deliberation. As churches recognize this as an obstacle, Chen suggests they begin to "cultivate a culture where conversion is normalized and encouraged" and do this by "exerting explicit and implicit pressure to convert" (66). When I asked what the Hmong pastor would say to try to persuade a family he said, "We tell them that there are no religious specialists down here in Texas, and when they die they will not be able to be buried in the traditional way that will join them with their ancestors." As in Gammertingen, the Christian burial process is quicker, cheaper, and easier to execute in Texas. Resettled in a locality where independence and Evangelicalism mixes with Bible-belt euphemisms such as "God helps those who help themselves," it is easy to understand why many Hmong found what they refer to as "Texas's religion" a more acceptable fit for their new life. With the emphasis on funeral rights and communal living, those in Texas, as in Gammertingen, found Christianity a viable way to relate spiritual beliefs from the past to their new local religious environment.

Depending on whom one asks, the actual number of DFW converts ranges anywhere from 60 to 80 percent of the total local Hmong community. Because of the unavailability of shamans and ritual knowledge, remaining "traditional" is difficult and results in a life that challenges conventional Hmongness. Those living outside of a church-family and without extended family are subject to a much looser social organization that leaves authority and decision making essentially to household heads. For example, of the nine clans represented in DFW, there are only three families living in the area that belong to one of the smaller clans. I asked them, absent of a family pastor, if they had someone in the area who they considered a clan elder. When he said no, I asked how then, with such fragmentation, family decisions were made. He said "We [our clan] make our decisions American-style," which he explained as at the autonomous household level, rather than at the subclan level. For larger, more important Hmong family rituals that also function as important DFW Hmong community social gatherings, such as weddings and funerals, the non-converts pool money from the entire community to fly in a religious specialist from a larger community. Because the activity serves as an important social event and such events are far and few between, even the Christians contribute and attend, being careful, as they told me, not to take part in what they consider the "bad" parts involving "false gods or spirits." In these acts, those who are Christian can still maintain a sense of collectivity with those who are not while still adhering to their new faith. As I noted in a previous study (Nibbs 2006) that compared the Texas Hmong to other larger Hmong communities in the North that have more elaborate cultural gatekeeping systems in place, what has emerged in Texas is a less dependent, more individualistic, more self-reliant, and more self-assertive community than their more modernized Hmong Christian contemporaries of the same generation in other larger resettled areas of the U.S. (Nibbs 2006).

Unlike in Germany, the DFW Hmong practicing both the "old ways" and "new ways" does not cause great social division within the community. This is something significantly different between the two field sites. As one informant put it;

> We have all just learned to get along down here. I mean, at one time there was so few of us that we really couldn't afford to hold grudges. We all needed each other, so we learned to modify our behavior [religious traditions] around each other not to offend.

For example, everyone in the DFW Hmong community I spoke with told me that the Christians don't eat meat or blood used in animist sacrifices. Since animal sacrifices, especially chickens, are such an intrinsic part of traditional life, such meat is commonly served at Hmong gatherings hosted by animists. In order to continue operating as a joint community and not exclude the converted Hmong, two different meats are served. I witnessed an interesting blend of these two styles of worship at a Hmong wedding (traditionally steeped in ritual and sacrifice) I attended between a Christian bride and her animist husband. The formalities alternated between prayers by the Christian pastor offering thanks to the Christian God and an animist offering prayers to the bride's supernatural entities, the waving of chicken feet by the animist followed by the sign of the cross. They served food that had been offered as a sacrifice and food that had not. The "strong drink," usually hard liquor that is drunk by the groom and wedding participants throughout the ceremony, was toned down to light beer, I was told, "for the sake of the Christians."

This is a unique feature by comparison to Germany and the larger U.S. Hmong resettlement communities. The religious malleability of ritual has become part of its identity, even to the point of drawing other Hmong to the area. One DFW informant recounted her experience with Christian conversion as a reason why she moved to Texas from California:

> When my father became a Christian [in California] he was excommunicated from his family. His own family would not talk to him saying he wasn't Hmong anymore. The church had to become his entire life, but that was hard because the Hmong community is so interconnected. We had to move to get away from feeling all the time like outcasts. So we moved to Texas. We don't feel like that here. You can believe what you want and still be Hmong.

Nicolas Tapp has suggested that since group conversions are often out of respect for the authority of leaders, people do not necessarily "jettison all faith in such traditional aspects of their culture" and that common traditional practices need to be incorporated into religious beliefs "in order to have harmony" (1989: 83). In this last section, I will examine more closely the local expressions of Hmong Christianity that developed in both field sites for evidence of how Hmong identity is reproduced and expressed through their new localized faith practices.

## Localized Identity in Expressions of Faith

In Germany, there were no organized Baptist or Hmong Alliance denominations to give oversight or training to the new pastor. In DFW, even though they were a part of a larger denomination, the Hmong pastors were hastily trained by other Hmong pastors in a short visit to Texas. Occasional national training conference were meant, albeit unsuccessfully, to standardize ritual practices. This left Hmong churches with autonomy to reinvent their Hmong traditional ways in a Western Christian context, specifically a Gammertingen or DFW-friendly one.

One example can be seen when a Hmong becomes ill. Traditionally, herbal medicines are used in conjunction with shamanic curing rights. When one converted Hmong became ill in Gammertingen, the Hmong pastor would pray over the sick while they were receiving Western medicines in a similar manner as they had seen among the Christians of Gammertingen. When asked about this practice, the Hmong said they associated the medications with healing the body and the prayers with healing their soul—a substitute that made sense in relation to their traditional, bifurcated conception of body and soul. Likewise in DFW, Hmong Christians who were ill often said a prayer while tying strings around their wrists. When I asked a Hmong woman what her strings meant she said, "They remind me that God is holding my spirit together" and likened it to a local advertisement she had seen advocating Texans to tie a string around their finger to remind them about using a seat belt. In actuality, the string ritual in the Hmong church is a holdover from an animistic practice where the shaman would tie strings around a sick person's wrist to signify the binding and holding intact of the soul that had fallen out of equilibrium. By giving the seat belt explanation to me and other locals, this research participant was putting the practice into a less exotic, more DFW-friendly context.

During one church celebration of communion that I witnessed, the German Hmong administered wine to the parishioners in shot glasses collected from the local wine festival; one was even decorated with playing cards and sensually posed female silhouettes. When I asked the pastor about the cups he told me that in the German church communion service, they used small glasses and these were the smallest he could find. In Texas, the Hmong used Big Red carbonated soda rather than wine in their communion ritual. The pastor's wife told me that "Southern Baptists don't really use wine and this was an inexpensive red-looking substitute." Both substitutes made sense in light of their local context.

In both field sites members of the churches used Hmong hymnals decorated with Hmong traditional embroidery patterns. The hymnals were filled with Western hymns translated into the Hmong language. They also had Bibles translated in the Hmong language. The liturgy in the German and one of the DFW Hmong churches was done exclusively in the Hmong language. The other DFW church celebrated the service in both Hmong and English because, as the pastor said, "Many of our youth don't understand Hmong anymore."

### Figure 5.5 Hmong Cultural Church Items

Photo courtesy of DN/Omega Productions.

The frequent fellowship meals in both field sites centered on traditional Hmong food accompanied by local food. In Germany, for example, they would add German cakes, a popular soda pop that was a mixture of orange soda and cola, German beer, sausages, and *wurst* salad to their church buffets. In DFW the Hmong food was served with Dr. Pepper, potato chips, finger sandwiches, and banana pudding. A deacon gave announcements at both churches and this weekly event served as a time to share news from across the diaspora. In the DFW church, a deacon, or someone with a similar position, also read weekly newsletters to the congregation on the state of Hmong oppression in Laos or Thailand, or about Hmong events in other parts of the United States that had been downloaded from the Internet. In Gammertingen mention was made of upcoming visitors to the community from other parts of the world. Churches in both field sites also had what they called "dress-up days" where parishioners would come wearing their indigenous clothes to pose for pictures that they proudly mounted on their church website and parishioners took home to mount on their walls. In the background played music CDs with Hmong Christian lyrics sung to traditional-sounding music.

The sermons delivered in both countries used scripture to teach against the spiritual realm of their traditional animistic lifestyle, offering instead the substitute of faith in Jesus to fulfill the same needs. The pastor in DFW told me that animism is an intrinsic part of every aspect of Hmong life, and that "many people don't even know when they are doing something wrong." He felt his job was to expose the parts of their traditional culture that were "bad" and offer a Christian alternative that was "good."

Hmong lineage was a common theme preached in churches. Traditional Hmong clans follow their own household and ancestor spirits through life and into the afterlife where they are reunited. Anthropologist Leepreecha found that "departure from these practices generates a breakdown of both ritual and kin ties between lineage and subclan members" (2001:167). The Hmong fear that their conversion to Christianity potentially severs them from their lineage and its members still following animism in other parts of the world. In response to these concerns the Hmong pastors at both field sites often remind their congregants how resettlement has left them cut off from their extended families and that God provided this new way for the Hmong to come together as a family for one another. This merging of fractured clans to form one large extended clan was emphasized using text from the Bible that refers to the church as "one body," and "the family of God." As such, members are free to continue to address each other in the Hmong custom of brother and sister, aunt, uncle, et cetera. In this way the church elders become substitute clan elders making community decisions that were traditionally made by the subclan leaders, and kinship solidarity is reinforced through a new family—the Hmong Church.

All these adaptations suggest that important traditional functions of Hmong religion continued through ritual in the Christian church in both field sites. Where the shaman was used for healing and played the role of physician, psychiatrist, and religious mediator, the Christian pastor now performs this role through laying his hands on the sick and praying for their recovery, offering spiritual guidance, and mediating family and marital disputes. The pastor, in the place of a shaman, enters the spirit world on the group's behalf. Whereas the pastors, church elders, deacons, song leaders, and ushers continue to be men, the age set and gender roles established in animism are continued through Christianity.

## Making It or Being Made?

The DFW and Gammertingen case studies are valuable in the questions they raise about the role of religion in forced migration. In her work on Cambodian refugees, Aihwa Ong suggests that because of their ubiquitous involvement religious institutions exert great influence in shaping the lives of refugees and therefore become "vital agents in converting immigrants into acceptable citizens" (1996:745). However, thirty years after resettlement, despite the different uses of an ideology permeating religious institutions as an integrating mechanism, both the DFW and Gammertingen Hmong have congregations that remain apart from the local "mainstream" population and steeped in ritual that emulates their pre-settlement lives. The findings here suggest that while Western Christianity is used in resettlement efforts as a form of member-making, it is simultaneously used by refugees as a transformative space for making it. It is neither a blanket encroaching force for being made as Ong argues, nor a benign institution manipulated by newcomers. It is importantly both.

Moreover, this chapter illustrates the impact of specific local contexts and scale on the ways in which Christianity is deployed as a mechanism of local belonging. Gammertingen's social focus drove their efforts away from proselytizing and toward offering the Hmong a sense of Gammertingen-ness. This approach produced a great deal of social capital for the Hmong and provided opportunities for their membership in the broader community. The character of face-to-face relationships in the village aided these relationships as members ran into each other on a daily basis in the process of participating in everyday life. On the other hand, the charge to churches in DFW to act as integrators for the refugees became overshadowed by an evangelical ideology that sought to proselytize the newcomers. Once the Hmong became Christians, these churches felt they had fulfilled their mission and had no further need for purposeful social contact. While autonomy is favored and an accepted facet of life in the city, this approach did little to change the perception of the Hmong as exotic others, or them build social capital among the broader population.

From the Hmong's perspective, conversion in these two field sites was negotiated as a response to their new environment, modernization, economic plight, and a loss of traditional knowledge. In breaking away from mainstream Western churches and having services over which they could hold creative control, the Hmong found ways to adapt Christian beliefs and practices to *kevcai,* or Hmongness. Significantly, the converts did not simply become Christians in either place; they become Hmong Christians. Those who choose to remain animist in Gammertingen risk ostracization from the larger group, and as it is essentially impossible to practice traditional animism by oneself, they also risk losing their ethnic identity. By contrast, the Hmong in DFW who have not converted have found new local forms of *kevcai* to continue to practice animism while still maintaining communal ties to the larger group. Chen suggests that religious conversion for immigrants can therefore serve a duality where "the process of belonging to the community and adopting Christian meanings mutually reinforces one another" (2008:61). We see this in both field sites where Christian conversion became a flexible sight of improvisation for the Hmong to re-create, and to some degree redefine their ethnic identity to one that they felt "fit" in their new environment, thereby creating a space where they could belong.

CHAPTER 6

# Growing Pains: Negotiating Co-Ethnic Belonging

*Even though Lu X. didn't know all the Hmong his family was resettled with in Gammertingen, he was glad that the agency placed them together. This almost wasn't the case. He and the other Hmong families pleaded with the German government to put them together rather than splitting them into different cities so that they could have some semblance of familiarity around them in their new homes. The first thing Lu X. did was find all the other X. families in the group. He knew that as a clan they would have certain family rights and obligations to each other that they could rely on in this new world of uncertainty. While the few families formed a strong bond, one of the things Lu X. and his kinsmen longed for was the large communal feel of having lots of family and clan members living around them. They wished for other Hmong to come and settle there too. They soon got their wish, but didn't anticipate the affects that this shift in dynamics would have on their identity and ideas of Hmongness.*

*Similar identity transformations were happening in DFW where Kang Y.'s family had been resettled. Many Hmong who hadn't found a job or missed the larger pooling of resources that occurred among mass kinsmen were moving out of Texas to live near family in other parts of the country. Kang Y. had to make family out of those who remained, stretching long-held ideas of Hmongness into new forms. Soon, other Hmong were drawn to the area where Kang Y. and his "kin" schooled them into what had slowly become a distinctively Texas-Hmong way of doing things. Two newcomers to the area scoffed at how non-traditional these ways had become, questioning their desire to be Hmong. In defense Kang Y. said, "We have had to make a Hmong life out of what we have with who we have here in Texas. What you see isn't our efforts to abandon it, but to preserve it." One family had trouble not reconciling the two and moved back to their larger Hmong community in another state, but other families found the new forms a better fit for their Hmong-American lifestyle and joined the Texas community. While Kang Y. wel-*

*comed the new arrivals, he wondered what long-term potential his community had for growth under these circumstances.*

\* \* \*

The previous chapters focused on the social and political bonds between the Hmong and their host communities and how these have been instrumental in developing their strategies for different forms of belonging to a foreign place. However, this research does not assume that the Hmong communities of Gammertingen and DFW have in any way been a homogeneous movement between a point of origin and a point of destination. Rather, the social spaces of their communities, like most migrant communities, are not static. They have changed over time and are divided along at least as many divisions as any local community. Sawyer (2008:242) cautions that "unquestioningly grouping [a] diverse population of people under the banner 'migrant' can imply that coherence or 'essence' exists in what is a culturally, ethnically and nationally diverse group of people." It has been argued that notions of origin transcend territory and allow people to move in and out of their physical environment without altering their adherence and belonging to their people group (Ottino 1998). However, with the markedly different local identifications that groups assume, I question Ottino's position. As the demographics of the Hmong communities in Gammertingen and DFW change over time, with co-ethnics from multiple social and geographic locations moving in or out from diverse places and for myriad reasons, I expect their own claims about "natural" membership into their group to be challenged. As Michael Fischer (1986) has suggested, ethnicity itself is a continual reinvention. How diverse groups negotiate intracultural belonging over time after mass displacement is therefore worthy of serious consideration.

Kenneth Karst (1986) has described two distinct paths that foreigners follow to satisfy their need to belong: turning inward to group solidarity, or outward toward the mainstream community. Existing research on negotiating group solidarity and collective identities in migrant communities has mainly focused on its usefulness as a starting point for a collective resistance to injustice (Gamson 1992; Castles 1997; Barker 1999; Sawyer 2008). I contend that the same complicated negotiations and translations of personalized identities involved in forming a collective resistance exist in welcoming newcomers of myriad backgrounds into the dynamics of an established refugee enclave. With each shift in population, belonging isn't just negotiated in relation to the society to which one migrates, but also renegotiated within one's own culture group. In this way, it may be useful to think of a migrant's need to belong not in terms of an insider/outsider either/or, but as a demonstration of a combination of both. This chapter explores how individual and collective Hmong identities are contested and negotiated by changing demographics in the two field sites. It investigates who has power to define who can belong and under what conditions. How do localized forms of identity and ideology adopted by the originally placed refugees contribute to this process? And finally, how do the new community members negotiate a place for themselves without transgressing their own version of ethnic identity?

We begin by looking at the demographic changes in Gammertingen's Hmong population, including those added as a result of the fall of the Berlin Wall, those added or subtracted through marriage exchanges, and those who self-selected to move in or out of the community. It then turns to the DFW comparison and examines how demographic shifts in their population were brought about through secondary migration, a targeted recruitment program, and marriage exchanges. I analyze throughout how intracultural belonging was challenged and negotiated within each community of co-ethnics and how the strategies used in the respective field sites was a response to local forces.

## Gammertingen

As discussed in Chapter 3, the Gammertingen Hmong community began with just five families and twenty-three people. Population changes over the past thirty years have come through two main venues; the first was a result of the fall of the Berlin wall in 1989. Between 1976 and 1986, the Lao communist government sent top students and sons of high ranking officials to be trained in military science and socialist government in the GDR where, among other things, they were required to enroll in a three-year Marxist Leninist curriculum core (Bryson 1989:64). The lowland Hmong, who followed Faydang and therefore backed the Pathet Lao, had remained in Laos when those who backed the Royal Army were forced to flee. The Laotian school system educated these lowland Hmong and the brightest were sent to the GDR. In 1989, at the time of German reunification, approximately five[1] promising urban Hmong attended the University of Humboldt in the former East Germany on this privileged exchange program. One of those men remembers how the fall of the Berlin wall changed the trajectory of their lives:

> Six months before we were to graduate the wall came down. Within a few months our program at the university was discontinued; there

---

1. Precise numbers are unknown. These figures came from eyewitness accounts at the University of Rostock at the time of reunification.

was no need to continue having a program on socialist economics as the west operated under a different system. The foreign students were returned to the country from which they came because there was no more East German exchange support for this program. Two of the Hmong went back to Laos. The others, including myself, went to the West German government and asked for asylum, because we didn't want to return to communist Laos. We were put in a refugee camp [asylum house] in the former West Berlin where we, and all the other guest workers and students who came to the East from communist countries and wanted to remain, waited to hear our fate. It was quite a stir in the German government. They didn't know what to do with us, whether to repatriate us, or let us stay. After a few months I was granted the right to stay and was put through the asylum program. Shortly after, I went for a visit back to Laos and married my wife. When she moved to Germany, she was lonely living in the German world. She didn't speak German and was used to the communal life of the Hmong. She was not happy living isolated from other Hmong. She said to me, "I want to live around my own people." I had heard from a Laotian acquaintance that there were a small group of Hmong living here in Gammertingen. I found them, made contact and said that we wanted to move there. That is how we ended up in Gammertingen.

Recounting this time, one of the original Gammertingen Hmong said "We had already been here for ten years by ourselves and were so happy just to have more people join our small Hmong community. We eagerly welcomed them." German reunification brought a total of two single men and two Hmong couples into the Gammertingen community. Unlike the original Hmong refugees, the asylees' presence was marked in the village with no fanfare. Other than the local Hmong and the district asylum offices, no townsmen were alerted to their presence. This meant the newcomers would need to rely more heavily on the support network within their culture group. It was within this environment that both the newcomers and the original Hmong were confronted with intracultural variability that questioned assumptions of shared experiences between them.

The first Hmong in Gammertingen had local Germans act as sponsors, had a wide array of community resources available to them, and the general sympathy and patience of the broader village. These asylees were un-sponsored, leaving the original Hmong to fill this role. They had to provide housing, meals, help the men find work, and school the newcomers in what they perceived to be the Gammertingen way of life. This kind of help was not new to the Hmong. As one described, such mutual support is part of a long history of hospitality and reciprocity obligated to Hmong members of the same clan.

> We don't have a big house, just three bedrooms and already had six people living in it at the time, but it is our tradition for them to live with us until they can get a good start. We cleared out a bedroom and all worked together to make them feel welcome and taught them how things go here in Gammertingen.

Those who joined the community from East Germany had financial support from the federal government until they found work. They pooled their resources and shared what they had. While the asylees might not have needed monetary support, the other support they received from the local Hmong was just as important. A former Hmong East German student explained it this way:

> We initially stayed with them so that they could orient us to the town. Then they found us this apartment next to their house and [a member of] my wife's clan found me a job at his place of work. All the Hmong here from every clan brought us food and things for the apartment and helped us move in.

Scholars have long recognized that ethnic sponsorship is advantageous, particularly in the case of groups with strong kin ties (Portes & Rumbaut 1996; Grigoleit 2006; Blake 1990). On the other hand, scholars have also noted limitations to the kinds of help that such sponsorship can offer as it is restrained by the sponsors' own social and socioeconomic position (Grigoleit 2006; Portes & Rumbaut 1996). They offer examples of co-ethnic sponsors with limited language skills that are stuck in an economic underclass not being able to offer the same kinds of financial help to newcomers as local natives with more status. These kinds of limitations made for awkward moments between those coming from East Germany into Gammertingen, as the newcomers had a higher human capital (better language skills, a higher education, and more exposure to modern technology) than those of their own group who were sponsoring them. One of the former GDR Hmong recounts:

> We could see right away that these Hmong were farmers and hadn't ever been to school. I knew that I could lead them to a more modern way of thinking, but that it needed to be done the Hmong way.

He explained the "Hmong way" as one that involved deference to the elders and hosts. As newcomers, they would have to tactfully and selectively suggest things to the other Hmong until they had earned respect. Having the same clan name as several of the Gammertingen families, this particular man knew he was under prescribed obligations of respect and reciprocity. But it was more than an obligation to respect kin traditions and preserve face. The asylees also counted on the local Hmong for social support and recognized that these Hmong hosts possessed something equally valuable for helping them reestablish themselves: an important local knowledge about the village, its people, its intricacies, how to negotiate it, and interpret it, something I will refer to as *local capital*.

Whereas the incoming asylees needed the local capital of the Hmong who had a very different political past then they did, I was interested in how they negotiated a supportive relationship in light of their obvious differences.

One of the former East German Hmong said:

> When we called here to ask my family [kin] if we could join their community, we introduced ourselves as asylum seekers who had just been through the refugee camp process [asylum house]. We had to explain to them in this way so that they could see that a political asylee was the same thing as a refugee, the same as them. We all wanted out of communism. We all wanted freedom. We tried to focus on this common point. We didn't talk about the past.

I found it interesting that he framed this discussion to the Gammertingen Hmong in terms of fleeing from communism. This is telling of the lowland Hmong's former urban position in Laos where they had been incorporated into the state. For the sake of living communally, the new Hmong chose to focus on the shared experiences of rebellion and flight and shared value of freedom to be self-governed, despite the fact that their experiences of flight and incorporatedness were lived from completely different subjective positions. Having more Hmong was the only way to re-create the familiar communal way of life that served as a social safety net for the hundreds of years they had existed outside of state-sponsored social welfare systems. This level of support and cooperation was more important to continued survival at that moment than ideological differences, so they had a strong incentive to overcome any political variability. Every time I asked about these differences, the Hmong always shrugged the question off, saying, "we are all Hmong." I don't think that they were implying any primordial assumption that, beyond surface distinctions, all Hmong were innately the same or occupied some imagined "territory without terrain" (Dufoix 2008:73). Rather, their response connoted a survival coping mechanism, or a survivalist adaptation to their new environment and an example of their nested identities. This is not to say that they weren't aware of differences between them, or that they forever banished these differences from their minds, just that they first downplayed them for the sake of creating a mutually beneficial community of co-ethnics. As this local community began to establish more ties with the global Hmong community, some of these differences would become important in negotiating diasporic belonging, a subject that will be more closely examined in Chapter 7.

The circumstance surrounding the fall of the Berlin Wall brought a demographic shift to the Hmong of Gammertingen and the recognition of intracultural variability and vast inequalities between them. This shift brought those who had fled under persecution of the Pathet Lao face-to-face with co-ethnics who, by their loyal support of the Pathet Loa, had never experienced that trauma; those who were previously incorporated into a state system were brought together with those who had not; those who had the benefit of a full education where brought together with those who had not; and those who had been raised in large lowland metropolitan centers with access to technology were now in communion with those who had been swidden agriculturist from highland villages. This placed the incoming asylees in a position of deference to the existing Hmong community in the traditional Hmong environment of reception. Since those with higher human capital were dependent on those with a greater local capital these inequalities were somewhat offset.

Claudia Briones has suggested that migrants construct different "maps of meaning" to make sense of regional differences within their people group, and that these maps "promote different strategic installations and affective investments of belonging" (2007:101). I would suggest that the precarious economic circumstances of the Hmong moving into Gammertingen from the East and the unpredictability of their future caused them to give a priority to traditions of lineage reciprocity. The imbued meaning of this shared tradition, which "despite our backgrounds we are all from the same lineage and obligated to help each other" was the "map" that led to the development of strategies that neutralized the intracultural variability between them. In other words, lineage reciprocity became the signifier of their Hmongness; it was the medium that neutralized their diverse backgrounds and multiple identifications. To the extent that they were able to re-create their social networks and imaginings of a community connected by kinship, the Hmong were able to maintain a distinctive identity.

These strategies continued in negotiating demographic changes brought about by the second major population shift that occurred among the Hmong in Gammertingen as a result of marriage. As previously stated, the Hmong traditionally practice exogamous marriage with partners outside their clan. The small population that had resettled in Germany offered a very small pool of eligible suitors within this tradition. The close relationships forged between those who were available, in their words, made "the thought of marrying one of them unsettling—like marrying a sibling." Another said, "It's the same like marrying a brother or sister, even though we know that they are not."

Edmund Leach identified this same kind of pseudo-kin extension in the Trobriand clans that resulted in an incest taboo among anyone with who they grew up in close proximity. Their word *luta,* meant "alien children resident in one's own subclan hamlet" (2004:160) with whom sexual relations were prohibited. While there is not an explicit incest prohibition among members of the Gammertingen Hmong community, or single Hmong or German term that embodies this concept (like *luta*), the same feelings of impropriety in marrying a Hmong from their own small community is nevertheless expressed. In this sense, I would suggest they continue Hmong tradition by practicing exogamy between clans, but because of their distinctly local positionality a new rule of exogamy has developed in relation to co-ethnics living in the same community. The German local population is excluded from this rule; therefore, before ties to other Hmong around the diaspora had been forged, first marriage partners were sought from within the Gammertingen population of German nationals.

One of the asylum seekers was the first to marry a German woman, and while she was not Hmong, the relationship was accepted by the community at first as a viable option as long as the outsider was willing to live in the Hmong ways. The couple ran into difficulties which they both describe as a result of intercultural miscommunications. The Hmong man in particular, and the Hmong community as a whole, grew to "regret" that decision, and he dissolved the relationship. The former husband explains the difficulties of an outsider "living as Hmong" as he perceived them:

> I had not been in Germany that long [four years] and even though I spoke good German, I was still very much Hmong. That meant my life revolved around family in a way that became uncomfortable for my wife. She was used to living for herself and resented the Hmong way of life which she said was a "constant invasion of privacy." She tried to be involved in our Hmong community but didn't speak the language and felt like an outsider all the time. She just didn't understand me or why I did certain things. I had the same problems with not understanding her ways. I think we were just of two different mind sets: I thought like an Asian, and she like a German. We didn't know enough about each other's worlds to make it work. The Hmong here saw my sorrow and convinced me that a Hmong wife would be more suitable. As we learned that there were Hmong in France, we started making visits back and forth. In one of these visits I was introduced to a Hmong

woman who really understood me. We were naturally more comfortable with each other. So I got a divorce and married her. Because my wife was German and didn't follow Hmong ways, she kept the children. The children have now grown up German. They are not Hmong at all. See, this is the problem with marrying a German. They don't understand that in Hmong culture the children belong to me; to my family group [clan]. But they live by different laws and while here we need to obey them. But when Hmong marry Hmong, we don't have these problems. We all understand the way things should be and respect by the Hmong traditions.

This man's divorce and remarriage, something uncommon in their lives back in Laos, convinced the Gammertingen Hmong that marrying a German would only cause sorrow, divorce, and tear children away from their clan. German inter-ethnic marriage became frowned upon, and even explicitly forbidden by many of the Gammertingen Hmong families. For those looking for a spouse who "thought like them," and who did not want to marry someone they grew up with and who wanted to save face within their local community, were left with no alternative but to look for a spouse outside of Germany. This meant connecting with and looking to the many pre-war Hmong settlements in Southeast Asia and post-war Hmong resettlements around the globe. As of 2010, the Gammertingen community had been joined by Hmong spouses drawn from Argentina, France, French Guiana, America, Laos, and Thailand.

Traditionally, the Hmong practice patrivirilocality where a new couple moves in with the husband's family. In Southeast Asia this served to situate the new family and any subsequent children firmly within the clan structure of the husband. Open spaces in the hillside villages of Southeast Asia offered plenty of room for structural expansion to accommodate new brides. It is the men who seek spouses and often find them through relatives in other villages who suggest suitable partners. While the giving and taking of spouses occurred irrespective of national boundaries, the couple always practiced patrivirilocality (Tapp 2004). It is important to note that this is still practiced in Gammertingen when the husband and wife both come from a developed country with economic opportunity. Since all the Gammertingen marriages cross national boundaries, over the past thirty years since resettlement, this practice has resulted in a loss of daughters to husbands in America, French Guyana, Thailand, Laos, and France. On the other hand, marriage migration has also brought in new Hmong wives from these same countries.

The cross-national marriages that occured were faced with issues of varying citizenship and reunification laws, unequal access to wealth, and varying sizes of Hmong community. These factors challenged traditional Hmong residence rules. Decisions of where a couple would reside after marriage became dependent on several things. The first consideration was the relative wealth of the country of each partner's residence. Jack Goody demonstrated how a woman in a patrilineal situation can have "magnetic powers" over resident decisions in cases of an extreme differential distribution of wealth (1969:114). Such influence has turned German virilocal decisions into uxorilocal ones. This is not to say that the Gammertingen Hmong families themselves were wealthy by German standards, but the economic position of Germany in general, and Gammertingen in particular, was seen as more desirable than that of Southeast Asian countries, particularly in terms of social benefits. This differential gave female marriage partners from Gammertingen power to convince their husbands to resettle in their German community. This is not unlike other immigrant communities to the West whose status has offered co-ethnics from lower-status countries a path out via marriage (see Rapaport 1987). This situational pattern of post-marital residence, where a married couple may choose to reside with either the kin of the bride or of the groom depending upon their relative position, became common in Gammertingen in cases where a spouse came from Southeast Asia. One Hmong woman from Germany who married a man from Thailand explained how this perception of her relative wealth played out in her husband's decision to live near her family in Gammertingen:

> My husband, who lived in Thailand at the time, had a cousin [meaning of the same clan and age-set, not his father's brother's child] who lived here in Gammertingen. My cousin would talk to him about me and then my husband asked him to send a picture of me in a letter. This man must have liked what he saw because he wrote me back and sent a photo of himself. About three months later my cousin here in Gammertingen arranged for him to come for a visit to meet me and my family. He stayed for a week. During this time he asked me to marry him. Three weeks later he came back here to Germany for the wedding. After that he decided that we would be much better off living here than in Thailand. Things were more modern here and he had the opportunity to make more money. The German laws allowed him to come after just a little waiting. His family had no problem with the decision because his success is better for them if they ever need help. If someone in the family is doing well, then everyone benefits.

However, in early 2000, when the German economy took a downturn, her husband was laid off of work and, in over a year of searching, had not been able to find another job. His family in Thailand, partially dependent on his support, told him of job openings back home. For economic reasons the entire family relocated to Thailand. With the turn of events, the husband's home in Thailand was seen as more prosperous.

Four years later, when the economy in Gammertingen turned around, they all moved back to Germany.

> Even though there were more Hmong there and we could live more traditionally than here in Gammertingen, it was less modern and the education for the children was not as good.

They were able to move back and forth because the wife purposefully kept her German citizenship and the husband his Thai. This is another example of how a minority group can use multiple citizenship status as a strategic resource for survival.

The determinants of Hmong residence, however, are not limited to perceived economic opportunity. Another factor of consideration is the relative ability of a community to offer Hmong communal life, or as they often put it, the opportunity to "be Hmong." Residence decision making is considered the responsibility of the husband; therefore, his perception of optimum communal life matters most. This mental image of a "good place to be Hmong" is colored by his age set and where he was raised. For example, a first-generation Hmong man who was born or brought up in Gammertingen's comparatively small Hmong community is more likely to feel more comfortable living there than in the larger Hmong communities of, say, parts of France or the United States. This is how he knows Hmong life to be. On the other hand, a man who was brought up in the larger communal life of the Lao Hmong communities may feel like Gammertingen's Hmong population is uncomfortably small, and stifles his ability to "be Hmong" as he has experienced it. Let me demonstrate how matters of relative wealth and perceived opportunity to live as Hmong all influence decisions regarding post-marital residence.

Chua (a pseudonym), a first-generation German Hmong who had been brought up in a Lao Hmong community in the urban center of Vientiane, was a part of the East German group that resettled in Gammertingen and was single when he arrived. He met and married his wife on a visit back to the city in Laos. Because of the greater economic opportunities and social support offered in Germany, they chose to reside there. But four years later, they contemplated moving to join a larger Hmong community in France.

> We have lived here for years. We like Gammertingen. There is a lot of opportunity for us here. My boss, he was so upset when I told him I was leaving. He said "I wish all my employees worked as you do." My

> son's teacher is also sad because he is an "A" student and she doesn't want to lose him. But there are not enough Hmong here. You can't really live Hmong ... I mean spend all our time with other Hmong people where there are always meals and parties and weddings and celebrations where we can really live in our traditions.

When asked if they had ever considered moving back to Laos where his wife is from, he replied:

> We also don't want to live without the modern things we have here, or have to farm for a living with no health or retirement pay. Laos is very poor. I have a relative [clan member] in France who has been talking to me about moving there. He said there are a thousand Hmong in his town and there is also plenty of work. Because we have German citizenship it would be no problem for us to live or work there. I want my children to grow up around other Hmong and learn our traditions. All these Hmong [in Gammertingen] are Christian and they don't do the Hmong things anymore. My wife too, she misses all those things. We want to live where there are more Hmong. We leave on Tuesday.

Gammertingen's small group's inability to offer the communal traditions at a level at which he was comfortable, was reason enough to leave, even if it meant having to learn French.

A similar decision process was used by another Gammertingen couple. The man was from a large Hmong community in French Guyana (approximately sixteen hundred Hmong per resettlement site) and married a Hmong woman who was born in Gammertingen whom he had met at a New Year's celebration in France. The husband decided that they would live around the wife's relatives in Germany because it was "more modern" and had "better economic opportunities." But shortly after the move, the husband became depressed constantly complaining that "life here is boring. There are no Hmong and nothing to do," referring to the lack of communal activity the small Gammertingen Hmong group had to offer. He began to weigh all the legal options available to them within their citizenship status (French and German). He eventually decided he would move his family to France, even though neither of them had ever lived there. Not only did their EU citizenship status allow this option, but, in his own words,

> I can find work that is physically easier than the farming I did in French Guyana, still live with the modern conveniences of Germany,

but also live around a larger group of Hmong where I can continue in our traditions.

Since he was a converted Christian, I asked him what specific Hmong traditions he missed in Germany. He spoke of living around a lot of Hmong and sharing big meals, reciprocity which he expressed as "taking care of each other." Issues of varying citizenship, reunification laws, unequal access to wealth, and the relative small size of Gammertingen's Hmong community. These all played important roles in decisions of where a couple resides after marriage. In this way, marriage ceremonies and negotiations can operate as a type of "third space" of diasporic gathering where different understandings of Hmongness must be negotiated within the changing context of westernization and resettlement.

One final factor that affected demographic changes in the Gammertingen community that I want to address, is loss of face. This often results in a self-imposed exile away from the Hmong. Face in Asian cultures is akin to the Chinese concept of *lien,* which "represents the confidence of society in the integrity of ego's moral character, the loss of which makes it impossible for him to function properly within the community" (Ho 1976:867). Goffman defines face as "the positive social value a person effectively claims for himself by the line others assume he has taken during a particular contact" and as an "image of self-delineated in terms of approved social attributes" (1955:213). Face is lost when confidence in the expected moral character of a member is diminished, usually due to some public behavior deemed to be outside the precepts of the localized version of culture (Ho 1976). Therefore, the boundaries of what is approved moral character vary from community to community, may change over time, and can only be measured by "the extent to which a particular person's social functioning is adversely affected" (Ho 1976:872). The repercussions of losing face can be so demoralizing that face-protecting maneuvers are practiced in public at all times by communities that uphold this worldview. I find this concept useful to an analysis of why some Gammertingen Hmong have self-selected to move out of the village.

As stated previously, marriage with Germans became frowned upon, and even forbidden by many of the Gammertingen Hmong families. Once this community-wide taboo had been instituted the male heads of each family enacted defensive face-saving measures to ensure that their sons and daughters did not engage in this behavior. Traditionally, it is the Hmong male who initiates courtship. Gammertingen men were encouraged to travel to other countries to find a Hmong wife whereas women, somewhat at a disadvantage, had to wait to be found. As the second-generation in Gammertingen grew to marrying age, many young women expressed their powerlessness to attract a male suitor from outside of Germany, saying, "They don't even know we are here." At the same time that these women were "waiting" they were also spending hours a day in school with German youth with whom they felt less of a cultural divide than their parent's generation had. Even though many Hmong women in Gammertingen expressed a desire to date, live with, or marry the German nationals, as in many Asian cultures, their actions were directed away from their own desires and toward the necessity of meeting the expectations of their respective families.

Despite family pressures, three women and one man eventually decided to, in their words, "go against their family" and made the choice to marry or just co-reside with Germans. They spoke of their decisions in terms of a loss of face that resulted in being ostracized from the rest of the local Hmong community. One man, calling himself "the lost son," shared his story:

> I was born in Germany and I left my family and the Hmong community when I was twenty-two years old. Until then I lived a life in two cultures—the Hmong culture and the German. On the one hand, my parents told me and my brothers and sisters to live in the strict Hmong way and on the other hand we were told to find our way around in the German environment. So no one could tell me to which I really belonged. Eventually the German life "outside" the Hmong world became a big part in my life, too: I had German friends, went to German parties, completed a German school career and found a German girlfriend. I decided to leave the Hmong community for the German life. If I had decided for the other way I would have had to break the relationship with my girlfriend who has become my life partner; because to be with anyone who is not Hmong would not be the real Hmong way to live—or so say our parents' Hmong laws.

In another conversation he went as far as blaming his decision to live with a German girl as the reason his parents relocated to America.

> I guess one of the main reasons why they went to USA was also the disappointment of my "German conversion." Maybe they wanted to prevent my brothers and my sister from the same by bringing them together with a larger Hmong community in America where my parents think Hmong life is led like they always wanted it to.... I think they were just embarrassed.

In another example I traveled an hour away to talk with a Hmong woman who had decided to marry a German man. During the engagement, the German man made it clear that he would not pay any bride wealth for her saying,

"I will not purchase her as if she were some sort of property." This publicly shamed the woman's family adding insult to injury. The woman said her family was so offended that they told her that if she married him she would belong to him and forever be cut off from her family's provision and good wishes. "I knew what he was saying," she recalled, "He meant that I would be out of their lives. To a Hmong, that means cut off from everything Hmong." She chose to proceed with the marriage anyway hoping things would change, but the reception to her and her new husband by the Hmong community was cold. She recalls their decision to finally move away:

> We had shamed them and they would have nothing to do with us. My husband was not welcome in their home and neither was I. We didn't know what to do. The Hmong live among their families all the time. We are always eating together or just hanging out with each other. Without their constant presence in my life, I felt off. I was sad all the time. My husband said that we needed to move and start over fresh somewhere where we felt we belonged. So we moved to another town without Hmong.

Loss of face is not necessarily permanent and can be regained (Ho 1976; Brown 1977; Goffman 1955). Shedding shameful behavior considered outside the accepted bounds of Gammertingen Hmongness also affected decisions to move back into the local community. Take for example, one Hmong woman who had also married a German and had been ostracized from the community. She eventually divorced her husband. That prompted her move back to "her people" to what she characterized as a more "welcome" environment.

As a result of asylum, marriage migration, and attitudes surrounding what constitutes a proper marriage partner, this local Hmong community experienced shifts in their population that brought a more acute awareness of their intracultural diversity. The original refugees spoke of Laos being their homeland but have, with the inclusion of Thai marriages partners, had to also consider broader places of origin. All these differences forced the community to reshuffle and expand their localized identity to a more expansive one. This was best illustrated when I posed the question, "What makes you Hmong?" The original refugees revealed that their self-perception as rural shifting cultivators who shared an expulsion experience from Laos had given way to an acceptance that they were really a part of a larger network of Hmong of varying backgrounds who were united by a kinship system of lineage reciprocity, a love for the freedom to "be Hmong," and a growing historical memory of displaced, stateless, and subordinated people. These answers were the newly imagined boundary markers of their community. From the context of a community so small in numbers this perception convinced them that they all shared an obligation to hold those boundaries through a preference that Hmong should only marry Hmong and reproduce cultural Hmong.

Throughout the past century, scholars have credited marriages between culturally diverse Hmong groups across long distances, such as those that happen regularly in Gammertingen, for a certain noticeable homogeneity of Hmong society across borders (see Savina 1924; Geddes 1976, Lemoine 1972). I suggest rather that the Gammertingen experiences demonstrate how wide-ranging marriage patterns bring about a constant shift of boundaries and a reimagining of what constitutes the cultural glue that holds a people group together. Moreover, the particulars of these experiences illustrate how such shifts contribute to localized versions of group identity as opposed to globally homogeneous ones, thus affirming the complexity of ethnic categorization and what it means to belong to a particular group.

## Dallas/Fort Worth

Dallas/Fort Worth never experienced any group of unplanned asylees as did the Gammertingen community after the fall of the Berlin Wall. On the contrary, they experienced a large secondary migration of Hmong *out* of their area will be discussed, any Hmong who moved into DFW thereafter were specifically targeted to fit a particular local profile.

As stated previously the DFW Hmong settlement began with 200 families constituting roughly one thousand people. Population changes in their group over the past thirty years have come through five main venues that will be explored in this section. The first was a mass secondary migration out of DFW to the larger, northern U.S. Hmong communities that was discussed in Chapter 3. This left only forty-five Hmong families to begin a new life in the distinctive context of North Texas. Those who remained found jobs, were law abiding, and had become economically self-sufficient with little government social support, a factor that contributed to a particular DFW notion of Hmongness outlined earlier. As in Gammertingen, these first forms of social identity developed out of a combination of the Hmong's own historical memories and the highly localized identity of their resettlement site. Where the two field sites differ is that the localized version of Hmongness that developed in DFW was not as challenged when newcomers entered their group, but rather it was reified and cast onto all newcomers. There are several factors that led to this difference. The first can be attributed to how the demographics changed. Whereas the Gammertingen community acquired its first wave of newcomers through an asylee program from the former East Germany, the majority of newcomers to the DFW Hmong community came through a federally sponsored targeted recruitment effort.

In early 1982, America was in the midst of a deepening economic recession and the labor market was characterized by extreme competition for the kinds of entry-level jobs taken by most refugees. People in the large Hmong communities had trouble competing with experienced Americans with fluent language skills for jobs. High unemployment rates were typical in these already overpopulated areas of unskilled labor. At that time in San Diego, for example, 95 percent of Hmong adults were on welfare, and 77 percent were unemployed (Scott 1986). In all of California, where, by some accounts, the world's largest Hmong population lived, 80 to 90 percent were still unemployed seven years after the first refugees arrived (Viviano 1986). And, in Minneapolis, Minnesota, which had the most services available to Southeast Asian refugees, a forty percent rate of unemployment lasted through 1991 (Duchon 1997). The Office of Refugee Resettlement (ORR) was compelled to address these circumstances in areas affected by mass Hmong migration.

In early 1982, the ORR received twenty million dollars from the federal government for a new, targeted assistance grant. It bypassed the states and provided funds directly to Mutual Assistance Agencies (MAA) and refugee self-help associations to recruit Hmong from economically depressed states into places where self-sufficiency was more likely to be achieved. At the same time, the ORR noticed that the Hmong in Texas, although a relatively small community, had achieved these results. In 1985, the ORR recruited a very educated Hmong, who we will call Mr. Lue, whose family in the highlands of Laos had sent him to live with lowlanders to go to school under French occupation. He was resettled in France after the war and went to a French university for a master's degree, after which he moved to the United States. He had been working at the University of Houston in a small business development center when the ORR invited him to come to Fort Worth and take part in their resettlement operation. Its intent was to recruit and relocate Hmong refugees from the high public assistance states of California, Minnesota, and Wisconsin to the DFW area. Even though Mr. Lue was Hmong, similar to the reasoning of the more educated Hmong moving into Gammertingen from East Germany, he knew that Hmong leadership and respect had to be earned over time.

> I would not do it at first because I knew how the Hmong are. You can't just go into a community and set yourself as a leader. They would not accept me or my help. They would be suspect of my motives and it would work against the idea of a successful development corporation.

But the government kept after him. Mr. Lue tested the possibility by first traveling to the two known key Hmong communities in the United States at that time, Fresno, California, and St. Paul, Minnesota. There he sought the advice and asked for the blessing of their community leaders. They encouraged Mr. Lue to pursue it and paved the way for his success by sending word along to those in the DFW community that they should accept him and his help. Mr. Lue said that even though he had the community's approval to come to DFW he was still under "watch" for five years. He remembers this time as "difficult years" having to prove that his business dealings and intentions were honorable, and had to prove that he was there to humbly help and not lord over the existing community. "They looked at me as an outsider—like an American."

These sentiments are similar to the ones expressed by the asylum Hmong from East Germany who joined the Gammertingen community. The education of the German asylum seekers and Mr. Lue, and their knowledge of technology or business, did not automatically afford them status in their new communities. Status was garnered through preservation of face and respect for elders, something that takes time to establish and maintain. Cashdan (1983:48), in her work observed that the nomadic Bushman exhibited a similar flexible territorial behavior in order to ensure possible future access to resources. Extending her definition of territorial environment to include co-ethnics living in the same community, I suggest when the Hmong move from one community into another they have a similar incentive to adapt their behavior to the accepted norms of the localized group in order to gain access to valuable resources that come through lineage reciprocity.

Since the success of Mr. Lue's relocation efforts depended on the amount of trust and respect he garnered from the communities from which he would be recruiting, he also had to spend time establishing relationships with key elders in each of his target locations. Mr. Lue said that at first clan elders were reluctant to let people move out of their communities to Texas, and often issued the threat that they would not attend their funeral if they moved. "This," insists one Hmong who had trouble getting permission to relocate to DFW "is the highest insult for us." However, the attitude of elders in these large communities began to change as the economic situation in the larger Hmong communities worsened. Mr. Lue said elders began to realize that without stability and economic self-sufficiency there would be no one to take care of their aging population.

> This kind of progress wasn't happening where large numbers of Hmong were unemployed. The leaders want their old people to be taken care

of so they started to give their blessing to families who wanted to move to Texas.

Mr. Lue, under the auspice of his newly established Texas Hmong-American Planning and Development Corporation (MAPDC), spoke of selling favorable aspects of DFW to select groups of people carefully chosen by the St. Paul or Fresno elders people thought to be a "good fit" for the unique Texas Hmong profile. Targeted recruits were generally young families less dependent on traditionalisms (such as shamans who were not readily available in DFW), somewhat independent relying less on clan leaders and large extended family (also absent in Texas), did not have large families (it was determined that families with four or more children would be adversely affected by the lack of social services in DFW), and had been unemployed for some time (two or more years).

This was distinctively different from the forces that shaped the demographic shifts in Gammertingen. The Hmong asylees in Berlin self-selected to join Gammertingen; it was not an ongoing federal targeted recruitment process. The German Hmong were operating under the assumption that all their co-ethnics share a certain base level of cultural homogeneity which includes valued resources accessed through communal living and rules of reciprocity, and therefore it was better to be with some Hmong than none at all. The move in Germany threw people together who had very different backgrounds and ideas of Hmongness and forced an impromptu reshuffling of local identity. On the other hand, the recruitment to DFW, although paid for by the government, was conducted by the Hmong, who acknowledged that there was a certain type of people (although they wouldn't call it that) who were more likely a match for the DFW profile. This brought Hmong into the community who already shared certain similarities, who knew beforehand the kind of community they were joining, that it was somewhat different than the one they formerly belonged to, and that they would be expected to fit into it. This enabled the original DFW Hmong the space to establish a certain localized version of their identity and then socialize newcomers into it. This became the context for a less expansive localized identity than was experienced in Gammertingen.

MAPDC records indicate that they recruited an average of twenty-five families a year between 1985 and 2009, slowly building the community to its present size of over 250 Hmong families. Families were frugal and saved their money to invest in homeownership. Within five years, an astonishing 60 percent of the families had purchased their own homes. They worked hard and took advantage of the many U.S. government programs that opened for the poor, such as the Comprehensive Employment and Training Act (CETA), that offered one or two years of technical skill training and a GED. Soon the Hmong began moving up in the workforce out of minimum wage jobs and even exploring entrepreneurial ventures. After an average of two months, 95 percent of the employable recruited adults were off public assistance and working in full-time jobs with fringe benefits. The government deemed the Hmong resettlement program a success. As of 2011, nearly a quarter of the Hmong in DFW were small business owners. For example, my informants included the owner of a donut shop, a restaurateur, and proprietors of a dry cleaning business, a tax consulting firm, and owners of an apartment complex. "It's inspiring," I was told by a Hmong who had recently relocated there from Kansas. "Living here puts you in a whole different mindset. We don't have to settle for a life of poverty. We can really make something here." She talked of the community's support for her to attend college as a nontraditional adult student in the near future. This environment where economic success and self-sufficiency are becoming the norm is also the context in which uncharacteristic ideas of individualism and collectivism thrive and into which newcomers are quickly socialized.

The idea that one must prove oneself to earn a position of respect was a shared cultural norm found in both field sites. However, what actions were considered respectful was somewhat locally determined. Mr. Lue said that he does little active recruiting anymore, because "Texas has raised up some very educated and capable people as role models for self-sufficiency and success who are able to make those convincing arguments directly to relatives in other parts of the country." In talking with Mr. Lue, I could see how the Texas environment had influenced his worldview in that its economic ideology had become a part of his own. An example of this is seen in his response to why he thought DFW had been an attractive relocation choice for so many Hmong.

> Texas is not a welfare state. Statistics rank Texas as the 45th or 39th state in public assistance. But there is a lot of employment opportunity for blue collar, white collar, and entry level jobs that really don't require good English skills. It helps that Texas is not a welfare state. Historically, the Hmong have never known a government welfare system. In Lao, they had to work for their very subsistence. If you didn't grow and harvest the crop, you didn't eat. We survived on our own. We didn't depend on any local or state government to help us become self-sufficient. We fought against the nature of having someone do something for us; we fought against this for thousands and thousands of years without ever knowing that the state had any kind of welfare system to help us out. Even before the Hmong came to the United States, we didn't know of or understand the U.S. welfare system. It was the re-

> settlement agencies that told us about the welfare system, so the Hmong applied for it because of their lack of language skills, industrialized technical skills, and so on. But in doing so, they know that they don't have the freedom to do what they love to do [be self-sufficient]. Texas is not an ideal place, but in providing limited assistance, it becomes a first step for the Hmong to fight for their own future, and to start a fresh life.

This answer is embedded in the Texas "pull yourself up by your bootstraps" ideology, which he had appropriated onto his understanding of Hmong ideology. Nicholas Tapp, describing the power of place-making for the Hmong in China, wrote that "the waters and soil of a place inscribe social identities as much as particular histories are remembered through their being inscribed in particular places" (2004:146). The attitudes of Mr. Lue are an example of the way that rememberances of the past are refashioned through interactions with local peoples and their social forces.

Mr. Lue talked about how the Texas Hmong collectively socialized those recruited to DFW into this ideology and pressured them to work hard and become economically self-sufficient. Newcomers spoke of being admonished by local Hmong to get a job right away and to stay at it no matter what until they were stable. These statements echoed those told to the original Hmong settlers by their Texas sponsors. More evidence of how this ideology had worked itself into forms of Hmongness was found in answers given by Mr. Lue when asked about the consequences for those unable to achieve those community-imposed standards.

> If they don't, the authorities will punish them in that they will have no public assistance to help them out. The burden of their existence will then fall on their clan relatives. So, on a lesser scale, those who are not successful will be condemned by the Hmong community and elders. There is tremendous social pressure to have your family live above shame. Living above shame is very important in the Hmong community, it always has been in the past and that is something that stays with us. Any Hmong who cannot care for himself, shows disrespect, and is lazy. This becomes a shame for his whole family and even to some extent, his extended relatives living in Texas. It is a big shame. This pressure we bring with us here to the states is also the thing that drives the Hmong here to self-sufficiency. No family wants to be a shame.

As in Gammertingen, the drive to preserve face drove newcomers to adapt to localized versions of moral character that were portrayed in terms of Hmongness. An interesting byproduct of attaining this self-sufficiency is a decreased need for the resources and social safety net that extended family and clan leadership have traditionally provided. This, in turn, has led to socializing the Hmong away from traditional forms of Hmongness that in Laos, had been expressed in terms of reciprocity, toward a new version of Hmongness that is expressed in terms of self-sufficiency. One DFW elder put it this way:

> We teach everyone who comes to Texas how to fish for themselves. The Hmong love that. We tell them not to let the newcomers, even extended family, depend on you too much. If they depend on you, and you don't help them in the future, they become sensitive to that and say "oh, he turned against me and doesn't like me anymore." So we let them struggle for their own good and teach them all the while to fish. It is the Texas way.

The DFW Hmong were able to project a more fixed identity on the newcomers because, in part, they held both the human capital (skill, command of language, and economic advantage) and local capital over the incoming Hmong. In contrast, Gammertingen's more expansive identity was, in part, a response to an equalizing of status that occurred when the newcomers with the higher levels of skill capital nevertheless deferred to the local Hmong who had higher local capital.

Nadia Lovell has observed that "who 'we' are depends on context, on historical shifts and reconstructions, and on contextual differentiations which arise as a result of dynamics and shifts in meaning" (1998:53). Applying these ideas to an analysis of the Hmong suggests that in both locations they represent their identity as a localized version of some common understanding of themselves. In this way we can see how the economic ideology of Texas had become a constitutive part of who the DFW Hmong are, and by extension, who they perceive the Hmong more broadly to be. In like manner, the distinct positionality of the Gammertingen Hmong led to new forms of kinship that extends traditional rules of exogamy to co-ethnics living in the same community.

As in Gammertingen, another source of population shift in DFW came as a result of spouses (mostly women) brought in through marriage. The original Hmong settlers sought marriage partners from outside their small, local community, and similar to Germany's extended rules of exogamy, expressed feelings of impropriety when considering a local partner. However, in contrast to Gammertingen, there were other Hmong settlements within the same country; therefore American Hmong became the largest pool for their potential spouses. After marriage, because couples did not have to choose between countries of residence, they continued the tradition of patrivirilocality bringing new brides into DFW and exchanging young women out to live with their new husband's family. Like those who relocate to DFW for economic reasons, the wives are socialized into a localized Hmong identity. While American Hmong are by far the most common source of marriage partners, international Hmong events, the Internet, and ease of travel have made it increasingly common for DFW-area Hmong to take partners from the broader international diaspora. For example, one woman I talked with met her husband at an international Hmong religious conference in France, another couple met on a church mission trip to Vietnam, and yet another met at a Hmong New Year celebration in Thailand. In all cases, the couples chose to live in the United States because of its "economic advantages" and "more modern conveniences." Like in Germany, this highlights the dynamics of how scale and economic advantage can shape specific immigrant communities.

A third reason for DFW Hmong to seek marriage partners outside the United States is part of a growing trend of specifically older, first-generation, divorced men motivated to find what they call "traditional Hmong wives" who "know how to cook and respect their husbands." To this end, some DFW Hmong are traveling to Laos, Thailand, and China, reestablishing or developing ties with kin of the same clan name, and bringing back "more traditional" partners. Like in Gammertingen, this trend introduces different constructs of Hmong identity into the community. However in their case, it serves to contest the authenticity of localized versions of female Hmongness. Because there are far fewer of these marriages than in Gammertingen, these challenges have had less impact on the broader DFW community. One Texas Hmong man in a conversation about this trend said, "These men are still living in the old ways. They blame their inability to adjust on their wives." This statement implies a moral failing on the part of the DFW men who look for wives in Southeast Asia, and that by doing so, they are directly contradicting locally held expectations of adjustment and modernity. It is yet to be seen if this failing results in enough loss of face to reverse the trend.

By contrast with Gammertingen, there are no longer social sanctions against marrying a non-Hmong in the DFW area. That does not mean that this form of cultural preservation did not ever exist. One elder told me that the DFW Hmong used to discourage their children from marrying "Americans" as they feared it would weaken alliances and break the social safety enjoyed in lineage reciprocity. However, unlike Gammertingen, those who did were never ostracized from the community. One elder told me:

> Several of these marriages happened early on and they are still married today. The husbands were good to our women and respected our traditions and allowed their wives to continue living as Hmong. We saw that maybe this wasn't such a bad thing.

One American Hmong who recently visited those in Gammertingen said she was stunned when she was sat down by her host and shamed for over a half hour for having married a white man.

> We don't understand why all the smart, educated Hmong women think they need to marry white men! What is wrong with Hmong men! How could you have done this to us? Your children aren't even Hmong!

The difference in Gammertingen and DFW attitudes toward outsiders was in their respective perceptions of how much tradition should be respected and in locally understood boundaries of Hmongness. The Anglo-Americans that I met who had married Hmong were a part of the Hmong community and not, as in Gammertingen cases, peripheral to it. They participated in valued traditions such as the bride wealth, Hmong marriage ceremony customs, deference to elders, New Year celebrations, and, most importantly, in lineage forms of reciprocity. Saying they "took care of" their wives, suggested that the Anglo partners were seen as responsible providers and, by extension, an important economic resource for the clan. On the other hand, the first Anglo marriages in Gammertingen were to women who, in the tradition of the Swabian Alb, did not work so were not an economic benefit to the clan. And, by virtue of them being able to take the children away in divorce, were actually seen as threat to their scant resources. Whether or not their attitudes toward outsiders would have developed differently had the first non-Hmong partners been German men, who they perceived as contributing to the community, will remain unknown.

As time went on, the acceptance of Anglo-spouses became appropriated into the DFW Hmong localized identity, one that was already more individually, as opposed to elder-governed, and one where few of the DFW born children speak Hmong.[2] An informant summed up this perception:

> The Hmong here are more than happy to allow their children to marry non-Hmongs. It is no longer perceived as breaking or weakening the

---

2. Further investigation needs to be done to tease out if and how the German Hmong marriage problems or Anglo-Hmong marriages were affected by class differences between the spouses. Unfortunately, this was something I did not consider looking at during the course of this research but can see how it would have added more depth to the analyses.

alliances between clans. That kind of thinking was for a while here in Dallas and is still very prevalent in other U.S. cities. That kind of thinking by clan elders is just a way of controlling the preservation of the language.

## A Doubleness of Similarity

When immigration scholars talk about belonging, it is often thought of as a homogeneous group of people trying to fit within a foreign environment. The Hmong experiences in this chapter draw attention to the fact that belonging is complex and multifaceted and that what constitutes Hmong behavior and culture can differ greatly between groups depending on local and national context. To make sense of the distinctness of the two locations I find Stuart Hall's (1990) discussion of identities helpful. He describes diasporic identities as a "doubleness" of similarity and difference suggesting that they are framed by two simultaneously operating tracks. On the one hand, they reflect a similarity and continuity of a shared past, and on the other, a difference and rupture that reflects their dispersion to different localities. Deterritorialized people who move from one cultural community to another must first reconcile this situated doubleness with that of their co-ethnics and in doing so, negotiate belonging within their own diverse local ethnic community. Thus, I argue that the group identity of the Hmong in each field site needs to be analyzed as convergences of people, place, and perception of a shared past and local positioning, of structure and agency, of intersections and scale.

When I look at how the lives of the Hmong has changed over time as a result of demographic shifts, the most significant marker in both field sites is how they, as a community, conceptually imagine the Hmong world and their place in it. Out of the experiences in Gammertingen, the group was able to plot their divergent experiences into a single, history-oriented narrative of Hmongness. For newcomers, this meant forgoing cartographical or political perceptions of belonging in favor of a more expansive and historic one. This meant remaining loyal to categories of blood, kin, and reciprocity while at the same time embodying them into their distinctly local position. This was demonstrated in their extended forms of exogamy, or their locally influenced decision making process for post-marital residence. By contrast, in DFW, the state of Texas' master narrative of self-sufficiency was repeated in the original refugees own anecdotes of prosperity which was then appropriated onto previously held narratives of Hmongness. The economic scale of their city contributed to their success and gave them the power to selectively recruit members into their community, thereby protecting their localized form of Hmongness. In this case, belonging and loyalty to the Hmong community meant abiding by these principles.

These changes call attention to the complexity of negotiating between the "multipolarity—a presence in several countries (or communities)—and interpolarity, the existence of links between the poles" (Dufoix 2008:63) that is the reality of a diasporic people. It also calls attention to a more complicated process of localized identification. It has been argued that notions of origin transcend territory, and allow for people to move in their physical environment without altering their adherence and belonging to their origin group (Ottino 1998). However, the experiences of the Hmong offer an alternative point of view. Secondary migration patterns into the two Hmong communities served as sites for reimagining relations between self and others. They were places to contest formerly taken-for-granted boundaries and relations to them. This suggests that cultural group belonging is a phenomenon of locality that fuses, molds, and reflects perceived ideas surrounding underlying principles of a cultural group with a particular place; that people are first and foremost members of local communities where notions of origin are transmuted from the local onto once accepted versions of history. This means that cultural solidarity may require dislocated migrants to embrace uncharacteristic localized understandings of what it means to be of a particular group. Therefore, the experiences of the Hmong further our understanding of how transient, sometimes unclear relationships can contribute to an individual's position vis-à-vis a collective identity. It also helps explain how scale, or different capital flows, influence experiences of belonging for migrant communities who reside in particular localities.

I have covered how belonging is negotiated within the host environment and within the local Hmong community. In the next chapter we look at how the Hmong negotiate those intersecting forms of belonging within the broader diaspora.

CHAPTER 7

# Mapping Hmong Networks: Diasporic Belonging

*People from the Vue clan started arriving at Lu X.'s house. As his wife took their coats, she ushered the women into the kitchen to set down their pans of food. The men went into the living room. Some found room on the couch, others on folding chairs brought out of the closet. The women eventually joined the circle of people gathered around a speakerphone in the center of the room. They were waiting for a clan-wide conference call that would connect them to other kin around the world. There weren't very many Vue in Texas, so they looked forward to this monthly event. In the corner of the room, some teenagers gathered around a desktop computer connecting to other Hmong youth beyond their small town. Others pulled out their cell phones and began texting their Hmong friends. Into the room walked a deacon from the Hmong Baptist church. He handed Lu X. an international church newsletter that he received in his e-mail containing news stories of politically oppressed Hmong in Burma. One of the stories mentioned a man who shared the same clan name as the group. "We'll be sure to share this information on the call," said Lu X.*

*The phone eventually rang and the event lasted for hours. The group sat patiently staring at and speaking into the little box as clan members from around the diaspora shared news, talked about job prospects, the state of the Hmong in the world, and concerns about the cultural preservation of their customs.*

*Meanwhile in Gammertingen, Kang Y. and his family helped their Hmong friends from France unload their luggage from the car and showed them into the house. They had traveled the two hours from Strasbourg to stay the weekend with the Gammertingen Hmong in anticipation of this special event. A distant relative from the U.S. had sent their college-age daughter for a visit and the entire Hmong community was bustling with preparations to celebrate their visitor. Kang Y. set up a video recorder so people could tape messages that would travel back with the young lady to the Hmong community in the U.S. Joining the party were a couple of Hmong U.S. army soldiers stationed a few hours away, and the parents of another Hmong family visiting from French Guyana. A German-Hmong teenager pulled out his laptop and Skyped his older sister who had recently moved to France so she wouldn't miss the occasion. The American visitor was happy she brought her camera with her and snapped pictures, it seemed, nonstop, often looking down at its digital screen, smiling, and saying, "This one's going on Facebook!" Finally, it was time to eat. The festivities began with the Hmong from France and Germany exchanging gifts with their U.S. guest. Kang Y. stood and formally welcomed his distant niece to Germany. Soon, however, his speech turned to tears. "While it is wonderful to see us all gathered together, this occasion is a somber reminder that our people have been scattered all over the earth."*

\* \* \*

The concept of diaspora originally referred to the dispersal of the Jews from their historic homeland (Tölöyan 1991:4). Today it is often used to describe groups which have an experience of displacement and population dispersal that have resulted in multiple communities that maintain a sense of collectivity—like the overseas Chinese, the Armenians in exile, the Roma, or the African diaspora.[1] Most definitions of diaspora regard it as a social form, a type of consciousness, a mode of cultural production, or community that connects dispersed populations and cultures across many geographic regions (Vertovec 1998). Thus diaspora can be seen as a form of social organization—in fact, Cohen (1995, 1997) explicitly uses the term *social organization* in his description of the term. The concept of social networks is often used to capture the most common form of social organization that emerges through or within diasporas and hence, scholars write about diasporic social networks. Through these networks, actors mediate the experiences of separation entangled with processes of integrating into receiving societies and the maintenance of links with their homeland as well as with co-ethnics settled in other localities. In this regard, I find the concept of diasporic networks more precise, and therefore will use it to refer to the communal linkages among Hmong peoples at different nodes of a global network.

Through the impact of growing international mobility and communication, the opportunities for forming these networks of relations between deteritorialized groups has rapidly increased. Sheffer argues that migrants choose to join modern diasporas because, even in displacement, they "consciously maintain their ethnonational identity" (2003:9). However, as Cohen argues, for some ethnic groups, these diasporic forms of social organization may "have pre-dated the nation-state, live within it and now may, in significant respects, transcend and succeed it" (1995:16). I find this to be the case with the Hmong,

---

1. See Clifford 1994; Cohen 1997.

who as argued in Chapter 1, have historically lived relatively stateless lives irrespective of national borders. This problematizes the current trend in studying diasporas that defines the diasporic subject in notions of homeland. Glick Schiller (2010) suggests such trends are unable to take into consideration disaggregated identities, thus, concealing how the transnational movements of ethnic identification striate diaspora in a specific locality.

Lok Siu has suggested that *being* diasporic is "living at the intersection of different cultural-national formations" and is experienced as an "ongoing formation of a consciousness, a positioning, and a subjective expression" (2005:4). This chapter argues that being diasporic is living at the intersection of *cultural-local* formations. One way of looking at meta-group belonging is as a "constellation of forces." Siu suggests that the varied geopolitical positions of global members with strong political, economic, or social clout present a "constellation of forces" that can influence a sense of belonging on other members that is contingent on buying into their vision. Under this framework, membership is not so much contested in diasporic spaces, as much as it is subjugated, similar to the kind of member-making discussed in Chapter 4 that is imposed by the State on refugees when they arrive. However, as I have argued in the context of state subjectification, refugees demonstrate a great deal of agency at different times for different reasons that turn their position from "being made" by others into strategies for "making it" in their new environment. Likewise, the character of how diasporic social networks are utilized is not only shaped by the outside influences imposed through diasporic citizenship, but also by differences in the structural forces and conditions provided by different locations. In other words, there is more than subjectification going on in diasporic networks. Localized communities are, at the same time, "making it" as they are "being made."

The material in this chapter examines these "third spaces" where Hmong across the diaspora meet. It will add to our understanding of the global process of belonging that is manifested in the diaspora by examining the various tensions that present themselves in these diasporic spaces and how they are worked out in the context of the DFW and Gammertingen Hmong communities. What are the ways in which these community members decide to use diasporic modes of engagement as a source for making it in their host societies? How do they balance their need to belong and their localized identifications with those of the intersecting cultural-political-economic forces and understandings that emerge within global networks? How is cultural authenticity negotiated within and between them? And, to what extent do children of Hmong refugees find diasporic networks useful? The chapter begins with a look at the historical development of Hmong diasporic contacts, and then attempts to answer these questions by examining three types of physical and virtual diasporic modes through which the Hmong at the two field sites engage; specifically through political activism, media and technology, and wedding rituals.

## The Hmong Diaspora

Hmong culture was traditionally passed down to successive generations orally though stories and myths. Prasit Leepreecha, for example, recalled how parents told these stories to their children "over and over again before bedtime, men shared other stories at night at funerals, and ritual specialist performed them as songs or hymns during ceremonies" (2008:89). As I have argued throughout this book, the previously held worldview of the Hmong has been altered and adapted to fit the various localities where the Hmong have resettled. Localized variations of these stories and their associated ideas of Hmongness went relatively unchallenged in the past as those who followed vastly different migration trajectories lived separately and rarely met (Tapp 2004).

When the Hmong refugees from Laos were dispersed to Western countries, common to other victims of forced displacement, they made efforts to reach out and connect to the diaspora to maintain their identities and nurture a sense of belonging. This has been facilitated over the past three decades by new communication technologies, a proliferation of print and video media, and the ease of transportation available in the West. Through these efforts, awareness about the diaspora has grown, and stronger interconnections through exchanges of material culture and the organization of diasporic events have minimized the distance between individuals and groups creating proximity in spite of physical distance. This has led to an increasing number of intracultural marriages and business ventures that have united Hmong groups formally separated by geographic space (Tapp 2004). It is also in these spaces that the Hmong are confronted with the various localized adaptations of their worldview, and are faced with the reality that the Hmong homogeneity they have been taught and on which they have relied, is an illusion. Robbed of homeland, the U.S displaced Hmong led efforts to reunite the myriad factions around the world through various discourses of belonging and Hmongness transmitted primarily through diasporic participation.

## Political Activism in the Diaspora

Scholars agree that in many ways refugees continue to be oriented toward their country of origin after arrival.[2] Politics is one area where this is manifest. Hmong political activism in the diaspora takes on many forms because, as pointed out in the last chapter, the country of origin is not ubiquitously shared. These different positions have resulted in two types of political activism that have affected the Gammertingen and DFW Hmong populations.

The first of the two is similar to Dufoix's formulation of diaspora as an "exile polity." Exile polity takes place in a "political space" formed by "groups who refuse to recognize the legitimacy of the current regime in their country of origin, or who consider the country to be under foreign occupation" (2008:63). Dufoix argues that the goal of those operating within this space is to liberate their country of origin and unite diasporic members to that end. The Hmong in DFW talked about this kind of diasporic activity initiated by those they described as "older men" residing in the more largely populated states of California, Minnesota, and Wisconsin, who had held positions of high status during their work with the U.S. military, or with the French or Laotian governments in Laos. Unable to cope with the loss of status, they use the diaspora to regain it. They organize efforts to "take back Laos for the Hmong people," with the goal of setting themselves as leaders in a new regime. These men often display strong emotional and financial support for the so-called Hmong "freedom fighters" left in the hills of Laos after the Vietnam War still fighting the Laotian military today. They hope through their efforts to regain a portion of that country, and their status as leaders. As one DFW Hmong put it:

> When we came here to America, they lost that status. They have never gotten over it. They have been looking to regain it for a long time. Those people keep their eye on returning to Laos as conquerors, establishing a Hmong land, and ruling over it. I have heard that they promise people who give large amounts of money to their effort positions in the new regime. It attracts other people without status to the cause.

General Vang Poa, who was the first and only Hmong in the Royal Laotian Army to achieve the rank of General, led the Hmong in helping the U.S. Central Intelligence Agency in its fight against the Communists in the 1960s and 1970s. He became the unofficial leader of the Hmong refugees in the United

---

2. See Lovel 1998; Barnes 2001; Dufoix 2008; Casteneda 2003; Delanty et al., 2008.

States until his death in 2011. Many Hmong who had served, or who had family that had served under his generalship, continued to look to him for leadership. He has been publically associated with political efforts, such as in the well-publicized sting led by the U.S. Department of Alcohol, Tobacco and Firearms in June of 2007. The United States government accused him and his followers of conspiring to purchase large stockpiles of weapons, including Stinger missiles, to supply Hmong resistance fighters in Laos and aid them in launching an alleged "massive" attack on the Lao government (Warner 2007). According to U.S. newspaper reports, money was collected from sympathetic Hmong around the United States who wanted to filter weapons through bands of "freedom fighters" in the Laotian hills who talk on satellite phones with their Hmong-American relatives "almost every day" (Warner 2007). While news coming out of the U.S. Hmong television and newspapers emphasized Vang Pao's innocence, the arrest caused collateral damage in other areas of the diaspora. The Laotian and Thai governments, for example, both used this news to label Vang Pao and the Hmong Freedom Fighters as terrorists, and quickly ended the tradition of sanctuary for Hmong refugees in Thailand. Forced repatriations of Hmong refugees in Thai camps began almost immediately. Lisa Vang, a journalist for Hmong Lao Radio in Southeast Asia reported on the effects this arrest:

> Some radical Hmong groups based in the United States are spreading rumors concerning claims of unrealistic goals of the creation of an independent country for the Hmong, causing great confusion on the actual situation of our people which are hiding in remote mountain areas inside of Laos and are not seeking independence, but try[ing] to survive (Kinchen 2007).

These political actions also had a direct effect on the Hmong in DFW. I was in the throes of my fieldwork at this time, and immediately, any family with the same surname as the General opted out. One elder from another clan explained that they were "shamed and scared" by the event. His arrest caused a great loss of face for the entire extended family and others wondered if clan ties would cause the Department of ATF to knock on their door. One informant of mine with a different surname confessed that he had an older brother who was still a part of the resistance in the hills of Laos. He wondered what this news meant for him.

I asked the director of a DFW Hmong association how closely his area's members could relate with these groups' political ambitions. He said that some are pressured by clan leaders in the larger communities to contribute money to a "united Hmong" fund, but didn't think people were aware that their contributions might be directly funding a resistance. He added that the DFW Hmong were younger and were "doing well," insinuating they were not motivated by the same lack of status suffered by others in the North. "The Texans have little desire to go back to Laos. They have accepted that Texas is their home now."

I left for my fieldwork in Germany six months later. I found the Hmong families there had satellite TV and access to a Thai-Hmong station. The news of General Vang Pao's arrest and subsequent refugee repatriations to Laos were aired over that station to France and Germany. However, the news coming out of Thailand was slanted toward the General's guilt. The Hmong in Germany who were talking about this event had divided opinions. Some had heard from relatives in America that the U.S. government had set up the Hmong. As a result of these rumors one particular family with strong ties to the United States opted out of my research saying:

> You are an American and we cannot trust you. We don't know if you will take our private information and sell it to the American government, or what. You are welcome to come by the house for coffee, but we will not answer any of your questions.

Other Hmong, mainly those without strong ties in America, or who had never been part of the war effort, tended to believe the Thai news reports. I couldn't find anyone in Germany who had given money to a United Hmong fund, or even knew what it was. This group had reluctantly come to accept their future in the West saying that such a return to Laos or creation of a Hmong Land, while wistful, was unlikely to ever happen. When I asked one man if he wanted to return to their own country, should one be created, he replied:

> What would we go back to? Our homes and villages were destroyed? We are here now and this is the future of our children.

This differs from the mindset of the Hmong who were involved in the upper echelons of U.S. military efforts who suggest that their exile is only temporary. For them, political engagement in the diaspora helps fulfill their complex need for continuity relating to the emotional and status aspects of their pre-resettlement identity. They look forward to the day when they can return "home" and everything becomes "normal" again. Because of this they have a vested interest in portraying Hmongness as a Lao, geographically-based phenomena, and thus, belonging is experienced in more nationalistic terms. The localized economic situation of the DFW Hmong distances them from this form of political activism. However, clan ties and obligations of lineage reciprocity may, at least peripherally, keep them financially obligated to it. Likewise in Gammertingen, while the Hmong did not identify with these efforts or have close enough relations to be asked to contribute financially, clan affiliation, and the psychological concept of defensiveness embedded in face behavior, tied them to the politics of these actions. The lack of a consolidated homeland and various narratives of displacement and emplacement that have emerged in the diaspora are causing the Hmong in both localities to juggle identities. They balance lightly the needs of their localized identifications and that of the intersecting political forces that emerge in the diaspora on the one hand, with cultural values of kin obligations and face maintenance on the other.

Another way that Hmong people in both field sites participate in diasporic political activism has arisen in relation to the treatment of current Hmong refugees who cross the borders of Burma or Laos into Thailand. Since the closure of the last impromptu Thai refugee camp in 2005, some 8,000 Hmong have gathered in makeshift roadside camps, such as at Ban Huay Nam Khao, a northern province of Thailand (*The Nation* 2007). Most of the refugees claim ties to the U.S. CIA forces that battled the Pathet Lao during its fall to communism before 1975, or that they fled from the insurgent fighting still going on in the hills. The Thai government, exhausted from playing host to Hmong refugees for thirty years, now considers the group "merely illegal migrants who entered Thailand with the hope of being resettled and eventually enjoying a better life abroad" (*The Nation* 2007). Categorized as "illegal migrants," the Thai government sought to repatriate them. However, human rights groups such as Amnesty International, Human Rights Watch, and Society for Threatened Peoples International condemned these plans, saying, "Laos has an ugly record of persecuting groups of jungle Hmong and the refugees should be screened by UN officials so that those with legitimate fears don't suffer a traumatic forced return" (*The Nation* 2007). Other reports of repatriated Hmong "mysteriously disappearing," or being shot upon reentry to Laos were widely circulated around the globe by way of newspapers, Internet, short wave radio, and satellite TV.

Hmong who had been resettled in politically powerful Western nations were working with Amnesty International to organize and advocate on their behalf. The Hmong veteran organization of registered participants in the CIA's Special Gorilla Unit (SGU), immediately began contacting Hmong elders and leaders across the United States. I sat in a Hmong church service in DFW when a man came to the podium to read a news report he had received from the SGU over this issue. After reading it he asked the church body to sign petitions and call their congressmen to act on behalf of "their people." The petition circulated from pew to pew during the sermon. Everyone that I could see signed it.

Weeks later, I revisited the church and asked if anyone had contacted their Senator. No one had, nor did they have plans to, including the man who read the announcement. He told me "they weren't very political," and that he reads every announcement sent to him out of respect for the clan members and elders who send them. Here we see how the politically active organizations, such as the SGU, use their clan status and kinship obligations to disseminate the call for political action across the United States. For the Hmong in DFW, merely signing a petition and passing on the message fulfilled their obligation to demonstrate kin support. However, the former military prestige of the SGU members from the larger communities was not enough to mobilize the DFW Hmong to further action. The local Texan attitudes of who was worthy of help and therefore of refugee status, had influenced DFW Hmong understandings of who was "authentic" refugee. This meant great skepticism toward the Lao-Hmong for whom the SGU was soliciting help. One Hmong community leader who felt comfortable speaking for the entire DFW group said:

> I think that most of the Hmong American community in Texas agrees that the Hmong refugees in Thailand are not real refugees, but who crossed the border from Laos to Thailand for different reasons. Some have very good legitimate reasons because they have been antagonized by the Lao government for many years, but most have been misled by some of their clan leaders or family members in the Western world, telling them they can get to the States and live better here. They follow this poor advice due to their lack of knowledge of how things really work. Some Hmong in Laos were quite established already, and on this poor advice chose to abandon everything and flee to Thailand. The Hmong in Texas, the majority of them, believe it is better for them to go back to their homeland. Because, after thirty-two years of changes in Lao government, I think there are foreign diplomats and embassies in and a lot of financial and technical assistance that is now being provided to assist the Hmong and other ethnic groups from the remote hills get on their feet who are far behind [less modernized]. We think it is better that they go back to their homeland.

This reluctance of the DFW Hmong to help the current Lao refugees is interesting in that they are making a very American distinction between economic and political migrants. Why this DFW group has made that distinction and not the Hmong in the larger communities, who are actively lobbying for the admittance of those held in camps to the United States, is assumedly shaped by local factors. Whether they were influenced by anti-welfare state ideology or anti-immigrant rhetoric, did not fully present itself during this research. One traceable opposition to helping them could be attributed to the atypically younger population in DFW with consequently few older members directly involved with the SGU (I met only one in my four years of fieldwork in DFW). That localized identification when confronted by different cultural-political forces in the diaspora still had to be tempered by more universally recognized Hmong cultural values of lineage reciprocity and face maintenance. In this way, culture *and* locality can both be seen as significant in understanding the political diasporic engagement of the DFW Hmong.

The same issue of Thai repatriation of refugees was aired in Germany over the German television news stations. It was the second-generation Hmong that mostly watched and understood these newscasts while the first-generation preferred to receive their news from the Thai satellite station or relatives overseas. The Thai station reported the repatriations from the perspective of the Thai government portraying the Hmong as illegal aliens. While in Germany, I was approached by a German human rights organization asking me to help them make contact with the local Hmong whom they assumed would get involved in what had now become an international human rights issue. I gave them several addresses of leaders from both generations and said they would have to take it from there.

When a letter in German from the agency arrived the Hmong recipient did not fully understand or know what to make of the letter. He thought it was official-looking, so, as he does with all official state mail, brought it to a trusted German neighbor for interpretation and advice. The neighbor did not connect the Miao, as they were called on the German TV news, to the "Vietnamese Mons" as they were known in Gammertingen, and therefore, deemed the entire plea for help with suspicion.

> Do you know any of these people personally? There are a lot of people trying to come to Germany as asylees now and most of them are turned away. Unless you know these people, I advise not getting involved in this. These people are probably just trying to get into a better country.

At the neighbor's suggestion, the Hmong did not respond back to the call for help.

Several months later, the same human rights organization re-contacted the Gammertingen Hmong community, but this time, wrote directly to a second-generation man in his early twenties. Having been raised in Germany, he was no longer dependent on the Germans for advice, and because he regularly watched the German news, was much more aware of Human Rights issues than his parents' generation. When he received the letter, his immediate assumption was that the story about the Hmong was "most likely" true. He not only rallied his peers together, he also convinced the first generation that it was a legitimate concern and that they should respond.

This young man said that the Hmong in Germany vote, but have not been politically active beyond that. "We have no interest. But, we would get involved if it is something coming from a Hmong. In that case, we would have an obligation to act"—obligation meaning rules of lineage reciprocity. What kind of action those allegiances called for would depend largely on the pre-resettlement experiences of those in Gammertingen. Deciding what action would be appropriate became complicated by the myriad backgrounds of the Gammertingen Hmong. Those who had been forcibly removed from their homes by the Pathet Lao tended to be more sympathetic toward the refugees, while those from Thailand and Laos who had lived freely without persecution were more suspicious. The ambitions of the human rights organization that wanted to make them into the face of their campaign in Germany further complicated matters. The Hmong were enjoying their position of relative anonymity, and did not want media attention. They became paralyzed by the thought that their portrayal, largely out of their control, might cast them in an unfavorable light to the broader Hmong diaspora. This desire to maintain control over their reputation combined with conflicting information from the neighboring Germans, Thai satellite TV, and contacts in the United States, led them to remain detached from the situation. Because it was a German human rights organization that had asked for their help, and not a Hmong directly, to whom they might have had obligations, the Gammertingen Hmong had a little room to stay uninvolved without directly insulting anyone.

To my knowledge, the Gammertingen Hmong's political diasporic engagement never took shape beyond these discussions. It remains to be seen if and to what extent, when called upon directly by a Hmong, they would get involved. The low level of diasporic political activism among the Gammertingen Hmong community indicates the scarcity of their international contacts directly asking for help, conflicting information on Hmong human rights issues, and the diversity of political allegiances that exist between the Hmong and the Thai or Lao government before resettlement. Similarly to the DFW community, these diasporic political engagements were filtered through the local situatedness of the Gammertingen Hmong. However, their response was not solely dependent on those localized identifications; it had to be filtered through Hmong cultural values of face maintenance, such as control of their reputation, and lineage reciprocity.

These examples of political engagement tell us something about the different way people envision belonging and interpret their responsibility to members in the diaspora. All of the forms of political activism discussed in this section can be seen as an active search for continuity and meaning linked to past roles, status, identity, and relation to homelands. But they are also efforts to make sense of these things in light of local emplacement. The Hmong in my two field sites were at the same time motivated and paralyzed by their worldview that prescribed allegiance to a web of kin relations and face saving restraint filtered through the complexities of their new life in the receiving country. Both forces, worldview and locality, dictated very different responses to diasporic political participation. In this way, there is a certain element of Hmong identity that lies in dispersion where Hmongness is a way of being between territories built around social networks. When competing ideas of political activism are expressed in diasporic spaces, spatial frameworks come into play as each position affects and informs the other. As a result, it is almost impossible for a localized idea of Hmongness to exist in a pure state when lived out in these third spaces where competing political identities become debated, challenged, and intertwined.

## Media Technology

The role of ethnic media and social networking technologies in global communication flows are steadily growing in importance to our understanding of diasporic communities. Anthropological focus on media has sought to analyze its social and cultural significance, its role in the formation of identities and communities, and its meaning to the lives of ordinary people (Askew & Wilk 2002). It is widely accepted that ethnic media contribute to group cohesion and cultural maintenance among diasporic populations permitting direct exchanges among scattered people.[3] Louisa Schein (2002) has demonstrated how ethnic media have become pivotal in securing, and even generating, forms of transnationality.

The relationship of media technologies as it pertains specifically to the Hmong has been examined in terms of Hmong-Chinese and Hmong-Thai identities (Leepreecha 2001; Schein 2002; Lee 2006), as a creator of ethnic solidarity in the large American Hmong communities of Minnesota and California (MacDonald 1997; Koltyk & Foner 1997), and as a generator of transnationalism and perpetuator of particular gendered ideas of Hmong women (Schein 2002; Lee 2006). This scholarship argues that communicator

---

3. See Riggins 1992; Naficy 1999, 2001; Cunningham & Sinclair 2000; Georgiou 2010; Hammond 1998; Kolar-Panov 1997; Everett 2002.

technologies "constitute a form of cultural reinvention that connects the Hmong together as a global community, and brings them a new changing identity, a new level of transnational group consciousness both in the diaspora and in the homeland" (Lee 2006:1). The following section adds to this body of literature by examining how global ideas of Hmongness communicated through circuits of video, satellite television, and Internet social networking, inform and contextualize the way the Gammertingen and DFW Hmong decide to use diasporic social spaces.

## Video

For the purposes of this study, I was interested in a particular genre of Hmong videos where people in the film directly address other Hmong across the diaspora creating pseudo social relations with the viewers and through them, transmit various ideas about cultural authenticity. There is a small, but important, body of work on identity making through transnational video consumption.[4] Naficy suggests that media production among displaced peoples is a particularly important site of identity reconstruction because it offers a "symbolic order and rigidity in the face of personal and social disorder and fluidity" (1993:118). Louisa Schein (2002) furthers this discussion implying that the way diasporic migrants "understand who they are and how they belong is inseparable from the kinds of media they consume." As Hmong videos are most often watched in groups, where typically people feel socially pressured to speak in terms of ideal behavior, watching these videos as a group in a particular locality has the potential to shape subjectification and foster particular values. From this lens, I will explore a few specific videos that I found widely circulated in DFW and Gammertingen to see how they have affected diasporic subjectivity.

We start with videos that purposefully try to construct a particular historical memory in the diaspora about an Asian homeland. This group of film represents the mountains of southwest China as the Hmong's mythologized land of origin. While they may be produced by Hmong in the United States exclusively for Hmong audiences, they are filmed far from the U.S. in the landscapes of Thailand and China. These videos are typically marketed at Hmong ethnic festivals throughout the diaspora, and other convenient outlets such as in ethnic grocery and video shops, or over the Internet.

---

4. See Appaduri 1996; Miller 1992; Schein 2002, 2004.

One example of how a specific narrative of historical identity is taking shape in DFW and Gammertingen involves the circulation of a popular video from this genre called *Taug Txoj Lw Ntshav: Keeb Kwm Hmoob Nyob Suav Teb* (Xiong 2000), or "Tracing the Bloody Path: Hmong History in China." The movie was made by an American Hmong who, as narrator, traces the migration of his co-ethnics southward across China then throughout the Southeast Asian diaspora. The film begins with the narrator looking into the camera directly addressing the viewers in Hmong:

> I'm a Hmong among the white peoples; I wonder where I come from and what is my history? The only one thing I have learned from my parents is that I was born in Laos and migrated to the United States, but our ancestors told that they originally came from China. I then traveled to trace my origin in China as told by our ancestors (translation).

The film climaxes with the loss of the esteemed Hmong leader's life, King Ci You, in a battle at the hands of the Chinese who drive the Hmong survivors further southward into Southeast Asia. The film ends with the narrator/producer standing in what he claims is the original Hmong town of Zhuolu, where he pays homage to a big statue erected in Ci You's honor. Once again, turning to the camera he addresses the diasporic audience urging them to make pilgrimages to this "original Hmong town" and "honor their ancestor."

This particular account of Hmong history has been widely distributed and viewed across the diaspora. I saw a copy of the video tape in several of my informant's homes in both DFW and Gammertingen. One German Hmong family said they received it from Hmong friends in France who had purchased it through relatives in the United States. Another German Hmong man, who was a marriage migrant from Thailand, said he had seen copies of it for sale at a Hmong New Year's festival in Thailand. According to those I spoke with in both field sites, the historical accounts depicted in the film were somewhat new to them. Like the majority of the Hmong who migrated into Southeast Asia one to two centuries ago, direct kinship ties or any memories of the Hmong in China had been long lost. This is important because, as pointed out in a previous chapter on Hmong history, legends have circulated among the diaspora of their origination from Mongolia, Siberia, Turkestan, Indonesia, and even as being the "lost tribe of Israel." Despite the ambiguous historical value of these origin stories, most Hmong refugees, prior to Laotian expulsion, had no unified notion of their homeland, although legends had always circulated about an eventual re-gathering of Hmong peoples by a messiah-type leader to a permanent Hmong land (Lee 2007). As we discussed earlier, there have been great efforts in the U.S. over the last thirty years to paint a section of Laos as this Promised Land. Yet after viewing this film, the viewers in Gammertingen and DFW accepted this historical narrative from China as factual and began repeating it in explanations to local nationals who questioned where they came from. For example, I was in Germany when the Hmong community was planning a thirty-year post-resettlement party to which the entire German village was invited. The proposed itinerary listed a showing of this film to be accompanied by one of the more bilingually fluent Hmong translating it into German. I was told its purpose was to explain their history to the Germans, saying, "We want them to know where we came from." Gary Lee (2007) suggests that such depictions of history are offered as alternative explanations for the many unconnected origins of the Hmong around the world looking to find a single explanation for their history. The Hmong in DFW and Gammertingen looked to this narrative circulated on video to piece together their own history, and then reproduced it to their local host communities as reality.

In DFW I was told about a group of Hmong inspired by the message of this and similar films who visited China on what they called a "heritage tour." The woman who told this story proudly showed off some souvenirs she purchased at the site that she referred to as cultural items from her homeland. She highly recommended that I watch this video if I "truly wanted to understand their history." Schein suggests that:

> In diasporic situations, physical dispersal and territorial uprooting regularly give rise ... to reconstitutions of primal kinds of identity, often fused with manufacturing of a homeland remembered as more timeless and essential than the actual place that was left behind (2002:230).

Simon During adds that these "organized collective memories" serve as a form of agency to correct "false representations of a community by outsiders—often for political purpose, especially in the case of marginalized oppressed groups in colonial contexts" (2005:59–60).

While this may provide explanation for why the DFW and Gammertingen Hmong have recently adopted this version of history as their own, the Hmong who have lived in Thailand, Burma, Vietnam, and Laos for centuries, and those in China for longer than that, may not have the same displacement incentive to adopt it. In these cases we should consider how economic capital and technological advancement privilege the U.S. Hmong communities of St. Paul/Minneapolis, Minnesota, and the California Central Valley to produce a particular version of history as "authentic" and disseminate it throughout the diaspora.

With the integration of media into educational materials over the past few decades, such videos are received around the diaspora with an air of authenticity that may not necessarily be warranted. While both the Gammertingen and DFW Hmong communities have access to the economic capital and technology to produce historical narrative videos of their own, their small size and relative isolation robs them of the social capital necessary to produce what would be considered legitimate ethnic videos within the broader Hmong community. Thus, the production of such narratives is not so much a Western privilege, as others have argued, as much as it is a specific localized privilege. While not all Hmong communities in the diaspora are involved in the production of this historical narrative, they are seemingly affected by its influence, demonstrating how the restructuring of economic and social capital as a result of flight can affect specific forms of identity in the diaspora.

Another group of videos produced by Hmong companies in Minnesota is a growing genre of documentaries that showcase the lives of other Hmong around the world. ST Universal Video, for example, the largest producer of Hmong films, has made documentaries that cover the Hmong in Burma, Laos, Vietnam, Thailand, and China. This series of diasporic documentaries calls its viewers into a "border-crossing sensibility" (Shein 2002:242). I was personally approached by the producer, after hearing of my research at a Hmong studies conference, and was asked if I would take them to the Hmong in Germany to shoot a film that would introduce them to the Hmong around the world. These videos include segments where an elder from the community speaks directly into the camera addressing the diaspora that would one day watch the film. For example, in one popular video seen in both DFW and Gammertingen, *China Part 3*, a Hmong Chinese leader addresses the diaspora saying:

> Today is a great day for all Hmong to get together. Not only that, but we have Hmong from around the world who have been apart for over 200 years.... We hope you take our words and images back to your country ... I hope that the heavens will help the Hmong, whether farming or working for a living, to survive throughout the world.

These videos are clearly generating discourses and practices of a broader Hmong identification that need to be reconciled with local ones. Because all these videos are produced and edited by Hmong-Americans in the larger communities of California and Minnesota, the packaging of the messages has been crafted through the gaze of their particular locality. In other words, they are about the Hmong in China, Laos, France, or Germany as seen and understood by the Hmong in the U.S. Undoubtedly, the final edited content is a reflection of the position of the privileged transmigrant Hmong, and not necessarily the diasporic population. Ultimately the viewership engages in what Schein calls "fashioning, even bounding, the local and impose this meaning of place on those who inhabit" other sites" (2002:235). It has been reasoned that these types of videos serve a therapeutic purpose for the forcibly displaced, helping them heal in grieving the loss of their homeland (Koltyk & Foner 1998:130). Yet, because of the films transnational circuits of distribution, the healing process of these U.S. refugees is played out on a diasporic stage, and its refugee-centric product gets disseminated as truth to others whose self-understandings may be very different.

The Hmong in Gammertingen, for example, found that the broader historical narratives of their Chinese origin helped them make sense of their own local Hmong community of co-ethnics from multiple countries. Small in number, the group also viewed the diasporic documentaries with a desire to be tethered to a larger group of people with whom they could identify and through whom they could operate as one people. In the case of the DFW Hmong, they shared the same experiences of expulsion as those producing the films. Because of this shared experience, they engaged the videos as a space for their own cultural memories and sentiments of loss. The more these videos circulate, the more adopting their narrative becomes an identifier for those who claim membership in this diasporic social network.

These stories of Hmong video consumption in Germany and DFW speak more broadly to the privileged position of Hmong within the large U.S. communities to construct a particular identity narrative and then draw others into its message. The privilege of the Hmong in this already economically powerful country, in relation to Hmong communities residing in lesser-developed parts of the world, is confounded by the integration of media into educational environments and Hmong cultural norms that dictate a certain deference to those in positions of prestige. This makes the documentary-style messages coming from these large communities in the West more likely to be accepted as "authentic" throughout the diaspora. As these videos find broader distribution in countries like China, where the Hmong may have contesting versions of history, it will be interesting to watch what kind of power, if any, these narratives will hold over local ones, and what kind of tensions they create.

Hmong video consumption in DFW and Gammertingen is also noteworthy in light of Hmong customs of reciprocity and collectivism that dictate a shared sense of communalism. While the resources of the larger U.S. Hmong communities give them the ability to produce videos that could situate Hmong identity in the United States, they do not. These videos reify the idea that Hmongness, while locally situated, is imagined in the diaspora. We cannot discount the influence of both locality and ethnicity in shaping the way the Hmong video industry has developed into a means of forming new relations between, and new understanding of, people defined as ethnically Hmong. These video documentaries are also creating tensions around identity and cultural authenticity. Those in the diaspora must reconcile the versions of history and Hmongness seen in the films with other localized experiences. Thus, identity making is not only a process experienced by refugees from their hosts, but also by forms of social industry within their own ethnic group.

## Satellite Television

Satellite television is another medium where identity and historical narratives are constructed and reproduced in the diaspora. With the proliferation of satellite dishes in the last ten years, Hmong television networks have sprung up in the U.S that broadcast into Europe and Southeast Asia, and Thai stations that capture intracultural markets beyond their borders. These stations are part of a larger trend of niche channels responding to the lucrative market of millions of foreign-born people that reside in Western countries (Frachon & Vergaftig 1995). While these medias are "primarily subject to the commercial logic of global media markets," their mission statements resonate with a clear diasporic tone of cultural continuity (Block & Buckingham 2007:64). For example, the mission statement for *Hmong TV* reads:

> To bring Hmong people together by working with other Hmong local TV stations, organizations, and businesses to provide a twenty-four hour Hmong TV channel for Hmong around the world. We want to share the talents of Hmong to the world Hmong community (*Zephyr Developers Inc.*, 2010).

I experienced this kind of cultural and identity reproduction firsthand when I was interviewed by *Hmong TV* about my work in Germany. They told me it would be broadcast to a satellite viewership of Hmong in America, Canada, France, and Southeast Asia. They asked me questions about the Gammertingen Hmong such as, "How did they get there?"; "Do they still speak Hmong?"; "Do they still eat Hmong food?"; and, "Do they have contact with other Hmong around the world?" His questions insinuated there was some understood threshold of Hmongness that his viewership would be interested in knowing that they still adhered to. The host seemed fascinated to learn about the asylees from the former socialist East who joined the group of refugees, saying "this is something we never considered."

The expense for these networks is high and travel budgets limited. Therefore, while the viewership is intended to be international in scope, they tend to produce one-way flows of material, from the larger U.S. Hmong communities, or from Thailand to other parts of the diaspora. The DFW Hmong have consequently expressed feeling marginalized in depictions of "U.S. Hmong" as what is projected across these networks is not necessarily representative of their community. Again, we see how those communities in an economically privileged position to disseminate information on, and images of, Hmongness, namely the large Hmong areas in California and Minnesota, also become the authoritative authors of that information. Additionally, satellite subscriptions are more costly than videos, so the poorer diasporic communities in Southeast Asia are not likely to view the programming, as are those in heavily regulated areas of viewership such as in Laos and China.

Thailand has its own competing satellite stations that are less expensive and more accessible to the Hmong in Germany. Most Hmong living in Gammertingen were not aware of the U.S. Hmong TV stations, and received their Hmong news and programming from Thailand. The Thai satellite TV tended to recycle older programming, and often showed translated martial arts movies. Most notably, the news it gave was Thai national in scope, and not representative of the minority Hmong groups that live in Germany.

These satellite stations exhibited the tensions of being Hmong in my two field sites. On the one hand, the familiar programming helped the displaced refugees combat feelings of isolation and enabled them to feel "at home" in their new environment, while on the other hand, the programing somewhat alienated them by not having any that reflected the realities of their current lives as Hmong in their locations. Nonetheless, these stations can be powerful mediums to reconstitute diasporic relations and subjectify its members to a single-sited portrayal of Hmongness. It exemplifies the disruption of what Block and Buckingham call "the seamless production to the 'imagined community' of the diaspora" (2007:66), and creates tensions between locally sited identities and those presented through satellite television participation in the diaspora. It is these multi-scaled identities that have to be renegotiated into a single imagination of Hmongness.

## Cyberspace

A final form of communication technology through which people engage the diaspora is on-line social networking. Much has been documented about the use of the Internet by diasporic groups and its potential not only to link people but also bind them and create emotional ties.[5] These transnational practices

---

5. See Karim 1998; Leepreecha 2008; Hiller & Franz 2004; Wong 2003; Ignacio 2004.

offer refugees links and engagement with their co-ethnics and thereby "negotiate a way of being and a way of belonging" (Levitt & Glick Schiller 2004). Jones argues that in cyberspace, "geography often appears irrelevant as a basis for interaction on electronic connectors" (1995:12). My data questions this. As will be demonstrated, the use of Internet technology has evolved differently in DFW and Gammertingen, and with very different consequences.

As previously discussed, the first group of refugees into Gammertingen had no experience with Western technology. Consequently, the kind of work they found there was in manual labor. Since their arrival, computer technology has become prolific, yet it had not become a part of the Hmong's everyday lives. Internet was first introduced into the community by the second generation in the early 1990s when they learned to use it in schools. It was a while before the children could convince their Schwäbischly frugal parents that such an apparatus was a worthy investment for the home. They did this by pointing out its benefits for communicating with other Hmong in France and the United States, where Internet use in the first generation had already taken off.

> I said, "Look here, you don't even have to know German. There are plenty of websites that are written in Hmong." It took them a while just to learn to move the mouse around. But they really enjoyed talking to other Hmong in the chat rooms. The other Hmong were always surprised to hear that we were here in Germany. My mom especially would tell them all about us. I think it really made her feel special, that people were interested in us.

By the turn of the century, Thailand was online and the Gammertingen Hmong found they could inquire about relatives and obtain material culture like plant seeds and traditional medicinal items from Thai Hmong websites. It was not long before all the Hmong homes in Gammertingen had a family computer.

Not unlike most of the world, when the German Hmong adults first connected to the World Wide Web, they spent a great deal of time in Internet chat rooms. Because their Schwaben counterparts socialized the Hmong women in Gammertingen to be Hausfraus, they did not work outside the home, and Internet chatting became a socializing connector to co-ethnics during the day when the rest of their families were gone. My informants said the men did not mind their wives doing this. In fact, they found it somewhat novel that they electronically talked with other Hmong. Then, something happened that changed everything.

> One day, one of the wives got up and left for America. She did not say anything to her children or anyone. When they got up one morning they found her gone. They soon learned she had left them for a U.S. Hmong man she had met on the Internet. They found that she had been Internet chatting with him for quite a while and was somehow convinced to leave everything for him.

This sent shockwaves through the small Hmong community. A few months later a similar incident occurred.

> One of our Hmong women was very depressed. She got joy from Internet chatting every day to Hmong in Thailand. This is all she did. One day, she left her family without a word—just abandoned her four children and husband—gone. They heard from others online that she had gone to Thailand to be with a man she had been chatting with. It was hard on everyone; her children especially. Sometime in the next half year the husband found another Hmong wife from France and brought her back to Gammertingen. They were married in the Hmong way [not a federally recognized civil service]. Shortly after, the other woman returned to her German family from Thailand. She said she had gone for medical treatments to heal her depression by a Hmong shaman since the German doctors had not been able to fix her there. But no one believes that. If it was just a doctor's visit then why didn't she discuss it with her family? Why leave so secretly? Why put your husband and children through all that worry and sadness? It is generally believed that she met up with a Thai man and, for some reason, things didn't work out so she returned. It was a big shame to her. Our Hmong here did not receive her back. All of her husband's relatives [clan] still won't talk with her. She had to go live in a German woman's shelter because no Hmong would take her in.

I have heard several different renditions of both these stories—including a conflicting version from the woman in the second story, who insists that her six-month-long visit to Thailand was purely for medical reasons. The content of the stories, or what is truth, is not really the issue here. The point is that this event, and the previous one, in whatever form they happened, led to a Hmong community-wide meeting where it was agreed that computer technology would "destroy their families," and was, therefore, bad. It resulted in an agreement to remove all computers from Hmong homes, that Internet usage be limited to school and work contexts, and that an explicit ban be placed on Internet chatting. The repercussions for going against these rules would mean the insinuation that someone is engaging in inappropriate sexual behavior which would result in a great loss of face and bring shame on them and their extended family. These taboos are still in effect as evidenced by a 2010 visit to the village by an American Hmong who was warned not to visit a particular Hmong because she was a "loose woman" who "Internet chatted all the time" and by talking with her she would be "polluted and drawn into her loose ways" and lose all credibility with the Gammertingen Hmong.

As time has gone by, the children of the refugees have challenged these taboos by insisting that their need for, and use of, a computer is required for schoolwork. Two of the second-generation Hmong men are even in trade programs for computer programming. The parents agreed to let the unmarried Hmong use a computer; as they are not married yet, the parents felt Internet-social networking offers a practical method for finding Hmong spouses outside of their small community. Once a youth marries, however, there is a great deal of social pressure by their parent's generation for them to get rid of their computers. I have personally witnessed women getting around this by either going to the public library and Internet chatting on the computers there, or if the second-generation husband allows, having a laptop that is put out of sight when members of their parent's generation come for a visit.

The consequences of all this has led to an active second-generation Gammertingen engagement with the Internet where it has played a significant role in connecting them to other Hmong in the diaspora. It is within these spaces that they are sorting through the traditional myths, legends, and histories disseminated throughout the diaspora. The second-generation has tapped into many journals and forums that have been established in the United States for Hmong who live in different countries to exchange photos, send messages, encourage activism, and write articles about their localized versions of Hmongness.

For the second-generation women in particular, whose courtship traditions leave them "waiting to be found," some have constructed rudimentary webpages devoted to marketing themselves to the diaspora. The content of these pages act within the realms of Hmong tradition, first communicating the basics for determination of potential marriage partners in their exogamous system, such as listing clan affiliation, a smattering of general information about what Hmong life in Germany is like, a list of likes and dislikes, and links to a photo gallery. The gallery is filled with uploaded pictures showcasing the girls in formal, business, and casual attire. These web pages also give e-mail contact information, should a potential suitor want to communicate further with them. One woman bragged about how many have visited her site. Another college-bound woman had forgotten about her site claiming she hadn't updated or visited it for over five years, insisting, "I don't have time for boys right now."

It has only been in the last few years that Facebook has come into fashion in Germany. It is now the place where the second-generation Hmong do the majority of their social networking with other Hmong around the diaspora. I have observed conversations between the Hmong in Gammertingen and France, French Guyana, the U.S, and Canada, and witnessed these conversations occurring in French, Hmong, German, and English. It should be noted that I am witnessing fewer and fewer conversations in these other languages as English is quickly becoming the de facto language on Facebook and in second-generation diasporic usage. It is also within these Internet social networking spaces that members of the second-generation are sorting out their situated identities and negotiating a collective Hmong narrative. Take for example this conversation that took place on Facebook:

1. [from the United States] It's said that there're more than 70 Hmong in Southern Germany, they all came from Laos (Thailand refugees' camp).... Once again, I'm so sad seeing our Hmong people are scattered everywhere in this world after the war ... so are the Vietnamese. Wondering if there any Hmong from Gammertingen here [on line]?
2. [from Germany] I've never seen any Hmong here before ... I didn't know they exist ... But aren't they one of Chinese ethnicity??? There are so many of them, why can't they just be called Chinese? I mean, Han is not the only Chinese so ...
3. [from the United States] Hmm ... the Hmong were once a nation too but were executed by the many Hans ... forced to assimilate. Once the Hmong and the Han were brothers; however Hmong were betrayed. Hmong can't claim to be Chinese.... the Hmong have their own uniqueness in the world. To claim to be Chinese would be what I call a traitor.
4. [From Germany] I am writing from Germany. Yes there are Hmong here. Maybe you should take a look at www.mxxxxx.de/sue for example. She is Hmong but also claims Chinese descent. It's a complicated story, ask her to explain it.
5. [from the German Hmong girl's website] "The Hmong came from China but we are not Chinese. Just like we live in Germany but are not German. We are Hmong. Hmong who lived in China until we were kicked out. The same story over and over."

6. [A German Hmong enters the Internet conversation] My mom and dad came from Thailand and Laos to Germany. This is the reason why I am here. I have 3 Sisters and 3 Brothers, but 2 Sisters are married in U.S. and France. Germany is very boring, because you have nothing to do.
7. [Hmong from the U.S] Dang that's amusing. I never knew there were Hmong in Germany. I will call you guys Nazis for fun.

January, 2011, I was sent a Facebook application from a German Hmong called "How Hmong Are You?" On this link you rate a set of questions, similar to a Likert scale, on how well you identify with certain statements like: "You like having lots of people around"; "Your family is huge"; "You know some things about the history of your people but you never really cared too much to study it"; and, "Hmong videos are hilarious, especially the really bad special effects." Even though this Facebook application was constructed by some American Hmong youth, it was sent to Hmong Facebook users everywhere. The Gammertingen Hmong that I follow on Facebook averaged a score of being "90% Hmong, meaning they enjoy the Hmong customs and abide to tradition. You speak the language frequently and can converse with the old folks without using English." The average DFW Hmong youth score of those I follow on Facebook was "10% Hmong meaning "Who are you fooling? You are not even a shade of yellow. H'mongs are from Mongolia aren't they?"

For the second-generation Hmong in Gammertingen, the Internet has played a significant role in enhancing their self-confidence and expressing their localized identity to co-ethnics outside of their small community, and in staking their claim as Hmong to those in the diaspora. The first-generation Hmong found the Internet to be a clandestine connector of co-ethnics that ultimately came between married people of their generation and a potential means to lose face in their community. However, their children experienced it as a necessity "to get ahead in life," and a means to connect to potential marriage partners.

By contrast, Internet usage was pervasive in the DFW Hmong community among both the first and second-generation. This can be attributed to the community's younger population, many with jobs that involve technology, and the ubiquity of computers in American life in general. In DFW I found that it was the first-generation men, and to a much lesser extent their wives, who regularly engaged in Hmong chat rooms, instant messaging, and other forms of networking. As a point of comparison, I told one first-generation man the story of computer prohibition in the Gammertingen community and asked if that situation had ever been a problem in DFW. He laughed and said:

> That kind of thing happens here too, but it usually involves the man, not the woman. Our wives are all working here, some even two jobs. Between that and their housework, they don't have a lot of Internet time. If anything, it is the men who are on-line, and sometimes it is them who go off with other women ... I guess because it's the man, it hasn't carried the same consequences here as in Germany. People may talk about it, yes ... but it just isn't the scandal that it would be if it were the woman.

He was referring to the often practiced gender roles of Hmong where the "authority is vested in men" (Donnelly 1994:170). In Laos, it had been tradition for a man to take several wives at will, but the wife was to remain loyal to the husband and her children. Since this disruption in family life was somewhat tolerated, though frowned upon, there have not been any Internet prohibitions in DFW.

The second-generation Hmong in DFW use the Internet, and especially Facebook, to regularly engage Hmong around the diaspora. Because there are more opportunities for the women to find marriage partners in the United States, this has not become one of its uses. A group of American-born female children of Hmong in a DFW focus group discussion told me that they use Facebook to connect with international Hmong, primarily out of curiosity for their different expressions of Hmongness and for travel. They described the use for travel as finding clan members of the same surname in different parts of the world that they would like to visit, and making arrangements:

> Our parents don't let us just jet around the world. They are distrusting [sic] of people who are not Hmong. But if I were to say that I was visiting a Hmong in another country, there would be no problem. They would even support my trip financially! The Hmong love to connect with each other. Our parents really encourage this. For our generation, we find this the easiest way to see the world and not get a lot of hassle from our parents.[6]

---

6. During the fall of 2010 I was following a young DFW woman on Facebook who connected with a Gammertingen contact of mine for this reason. She has just asked the German Hmong to connect her with one of their kin her age in near Paris, France. She is planning a trip abroad for next summer.

There are several important things we can understand from these cases about computer-mediated communication in the context of the migration experience. The first is that cyberspace territories, like real territories, provide a site where the meaning of ethnic identity is contested and shaped. The second is the realization that attitudes toward its use are drawn from the particular localized identities that develop in each site. The third is an understanding that both communities and generations of Hmong used computer-mediated communication to make contact with the broader diaspora, but it was both their locally defined (*hausfrau* model) and their ethnically defined (patriarchal) gender roles that shaped the consequences of this usage and the way in which each group expressed their identity to outsiders. From this we might understand that while computer-mediated communication can transcend the limitation of small and isolated diasporic communities to connect them to other co-ethnics, it is limited to those who possess the technology, and restrained by attitudes in relation to experiences with its use, and by ethnic traditions. Therefore, in opposition to what Jones (1995) has argued, locality *can* be relevant as a basis for interaction on electronic connectors because culture and people are sited in particular places. Moreover, while locality is important in considering migrant belonging, we cannot ignore that for some ethnic groups, like the Hmong, those places are influenced by ethnic identifications and cultural norms, such as lineage reciprocity and face maintenance that must be considered in an analysis of the relationship between diaspora and belonging.

## Celebration, Ritual, and Festival Performances

The final mode of diasporic engagement that this chapter will look at is public rituals, specifically New Years, weddings, and funerals. Ritual ceremonies and celebrations with a diasporic character have been the object of scholarly interest in both Europe and the United States.[7] When these performances have widespread participation from members of multiple diasporic groups they carry a great deal of practical and symbolic weight. Schrempf suggests that as "powerful vehicles for the objectification and representation of culture" (1997:92), these events convey a particular construction of identity while at the same time demonstrating a certain degree of cultural authentic-

---

7. See Bhachu 1995; Andezian 1986; McCarthy Brown 1991; Schrempf 1997; Gardner 1998; Byron 1999; Fortier 2000.

ity. Even as collectively performed traditions are staged in and modified according to new environments, the events serve as both a generator and potential risk for status based on how "authentically" one group performs them. As global networks increase and Hmong from around the globe collectively participate in ritual events, it is expected that complex social and face-saving relational work will be embedded in the experience. As some descendants lack enough ritual knowledge and discourse to perform these rites, what are the implications for Hmong subjectivities, both across generations as well as in resettlement locations? This section will consider how the experiences of the locality shape the character of Hmong participation and execution of practices. How do they construct discourses of authentic Hmongness in the diaspora? And how are tensions between co-ethnics, culture, and authenticity played out when Hmong with different local identifications get together at ritual events?

## Wedding Ceremonies

In previous chapters I have discussed the prevalence of Hmong marriage migrants in DFW, and especially in Gammertingen. Many anthropologists have noted the importance of getting married though a traditional Hmong ritual proceeding and its centrality to Hmong identity (Donnelly 1994; Lee 1981; Vang 1982). Seen as formally linking two clans, the entire process is considered a major event of interfamily relations and an important event during which each clan wants to put forward its best face (Lee 1981). Accordingly, any and all members of the clan throughout the diaspora with the available means try to attend the event. Due to a lack of technology and isolation of villages, this historically meant the event was attended by those from villages within walking distance of a few days. Because of the relative closeness of those getting married, the ritual ceremony was practiced similarly throughout their region. Today, as diasporic Hmong groups have become more spread out across the globe, and as traditions are passed down orally, the pervasiveness, traditionality, and uniformity of wedding rituals have disappeared. This fact is not lost among the Hmong (Hickman 2010). For example, fears of "Americanization" are widespread in the Southeast Asian Hmong communities. In instances where U.S. or other Western Hmong people don't know how to perform critical marriage ceremonies, those fears are substantiated, as displaying correct Hmongness at a wedding where co-ethnics from across the diaspora will be in attendance preserves face at these ritual events.

According to scholars, what is considered "traditional" Hmong marriage most likely went as follows: Before the wedding the groom's family presents a pre-arranged bridewealth to the family of the bride, traditionally an animal, providing a pledge that the woman be well taken care of. This also stands as social insurance for the bride, since her family could demand it back if wrongs are committed against her (Lo 2002). The wedding ceremony begins at the bride's home with a series of negotiations between representatives from each clan. The bride, however, is not present. She remains away dressing in specially prepared Hmong clothes representing the style and customs of her new husband's family. At the negotiations, both parties sit across from each other along a long table. Other family members fill the room sitting on each side. Placed at each seat are signs of wealth (traditionally opium) and small glasses to hold homemade liqueur. In the center of the table are plates of unseasoned cooked meat. As the two parties agree on the specific terms of the couple's future, such as who will take care of the children in the event of a death, who will financially provide for the couple in the event of joblessness, et cetera, they drink a toast that seals the commitment. The Hmong were preliterate peoples; therefore, all agreements were verbal (a tradition still followed today). Intermittently, representatives wave their cupped hands back and forth across the table, signifying a basket, symbolically sending baskets of good will to the other clan (Nibbs 2006). After all matters concerning their future and wellbeing are agreed on (a process that can take up to a week), a chaperone brings the bride to the ceremony where her parents formally transfer her from their clan to her husband's. This is followed by a time of feasting and formal presentation of the dowry, which is a display of wedding gifts purchased by the bride's family that should be closely equal in value to the bridewealth. Afterward, the bride leaves with the groom for her new life in his parents' home.

Today in Gammertingen, where cross-diasporic marriages are common and guests are present from myriad countries and communities, we can see how this plays out in its contemporary, localized version. Sue Lee (a pseudonym), from Gammertingen, agreed to marry Thao Vang (a pseudonym), from Thailand. Since this marriage will link the two Hmong clans together, the families choose representatives from their kin to enter into negotiations. These men were chosen for their prominence in the family and also for their specialized knowledge of this practice. The German Hmong bride's side of the family was represented by members in and out of her clan because there was only one other family in Germany who shared the same surname. Even though the specialist knew that these negotiations used to take place over a five- or six-day period of time, because of the German work schedule, he first thought it should be shortened to just one weekend day—a common compromise among the Hmong who have resettled in the West. He contemplated what Sue's family from Thailand would expect, and decided instead to save vacation days to accommodate the traditional lengthy process. Meanwhile, in Southeast Asia, Thao Vang's family was wondering how to hurry the process to accommodate the Westernized one-day event they had heard rumors of, and therefore expected.

When everything was set in order, the Thai delegation flew to Germany, a costly, but expected part of the process. Another member who was unable to attend the event took part in the negotiations by speakerphone. When the formal negotiations began, it was videotaped to be "witnessed" by other family members who couldn't make the journey. The groom arrived dressed in what he considered his "traditional" clothes, albeit they were traditionally Thai, not Hmong. The bride's family insisted that she wear Hmong clothes, but at the end of the negotiations, she was presented in a white German wedding gown.

At the negotiating table, there were German brand HB cigarettes placed in front of each delegate to represent the traditional opium, and German bottles of beer replaced what were traditionally small glasses of hard liquor. The negotiations proceeded without written agreement, just the sealing of each covenant with a toast between parties. At one point, the German Hmong parents insisted on an agreement that allowed their Christian daughter to attend church services and travel to Christian diasporic conferences even though her husband practiced animism. They argued for this clause, saying, "All the German Hmong are Christian and that is all she knows." The groom's family, knowing that the two were going to live in Germany and not Thailand, agreed.

After the negotiations, the entire Hmong community of all clans represented in Germany attended the feast, along with invited clan members from France, the U.S., and Thailand. They served a combination of Hmong dishes, German sausages, beer, and German wedding cake. The mother of the bride said:

> We wanted to serve familiar foods that all Hmong would like as well as show off some of the German things that we have come to enjoy.

The relatives from Thailand and France all helped with the food preparation, each adding their own localized distinctions to the dishes. Finally, the bride's parents displayed the dowry. It contained a combination of traditional items, such as a Hmong back basket, a hand-made silver necklace, traditional clothing, and more practical items such as an electronic rice cooker and a set of dishes. The Thai family of the groom inspected it, making sure the bridewealth had been appropriately used.

Afterward, the bride said her wedding had "more traditional" elements than some of the others she had attended in Germany.

> My husband is from Thailand and they are more traditional there and we didn't want to offend anyone.

On the other hand, the husband recalls how the wedding was less traditional and more Westernized than other Thai-Hmong weddings he had attended.

> This wedding was much shorter, attended by less people, and there were no animal sacrifices, or shamans, or Hmong music.

As I said previously, the pervasiveness and uniformity of wedding rituals has disappeared, and all groups have to some extent developed localized versions of "tradition." What is important is how the different perceptions of the bride and groom grew out of circulating ideas in the diaspora of refugee resettlement weddings being less "traditional" than those in Southeast Asia. This message places the Western Hmong communities on the defensive and requires them to practice a great deal of face maintenance in globally attended weddings. One man phrased these tensions like this:

> Our strong ties in the animist belief hold bondage over families because they have to perform correctly the ritual ceremonies for the clan. If you don't have anyone to perform these rituals for you or if the rituals are not performed in the right way you can be oppressed and can shame your family. Each family and extended family member is also affected by the reputation of the next, so maintaining close ties is a way of reputation maintenance. Reputation is very important to Hmong people; everyone is always looking out to see how the other behaves.

This is a strong example of how cultural values pressure members to display a particular or correct version of Hmongness at diasporically attended events. However, these pressures are not just constructed between countries where Hmong have settled. They must also be negotiated between localized identities.

I witnessed a similar blending of different localized versions of Hmong ritual at a wedding I attended in DFW between a local Christian woman marrying an animist husband from one of the larger and more traditional Hmong communities in the northern United States. As in Gammertingen, DFW weddings rarely occur along clan lines; rather, because of the small number of Hmong who settled there, they involve the broader conception of Hmong community as kin. As in Gammertingen, the preparations and food for this wedding became the joint responsibility and effort of all the DFW Hmong, and the bride's negotiators represented the collective body with at least one member chosen for his traditional knowledge in how to perform this ritual.

Because of the differing religious beliefs, the "traditions" were altered to accommodate both families. For example, prayers alternated between the Christian pastor of the bride offering thanks to their God and an animist offering prayers to the bride's ancestors, the slaying of chickens followed by the sign of the cross. Two dishes of each kind of meat were presented—one that had been offered as a sacrifice to the ancestors, and one that had not. The usual "strong drink" that sat on the table and was consumed by the groom and the negotiators throughout the ceremony was toned down to light beer "for the sake of the Christians." The bride did not participate in the negotiations, but was allowed in the room to watch. The parents of the bride and community members served an array of traditional Hmong foods to the guests alongside Coca-Cola, Subway sandwiches, and a tiered American wedding cake (Nibbs 2008).

None of the cultural adaptations at either the DFW or Gammertingen weddings were intended to be anti-Hmong, but evolved as constructive and logical responses to the circumstances and resources available in their resettlement environments. From these single sited contexts new patterns of wedding rituals have emerged and are becoming normalized at weddings between two local Hmong. Since the weddings are planned and officiated by the first-generation, the children of these refugees are inculcated into these new traditions. However, when performed in diasporic spaces, the ethno-communal consciousness of belonging to a broader diasporic people requires a certain amount of face maintenance that manifests itself through renegotiated ritual patterns involving co-acceptable levels of modernity and authenticity. What is most principally being offered at these diasporic weddings are alternative visions and narratives of Hmong authenticity and Hmong tradition.

## Funeral Rituals

Similar intersections of localized cultural formations can be seen in Hmong funeral practices. As stated in Chapter 1, this is widely considered the most complex and in depth of all Hmong rituals and is the final important rite of passage. For this reason its practice and participation, along with weddings, are considered quintessentially Hmong. As one Gammertingen woman told me, she identifies as "mostly Hmong" because she "still participates in Hmong funerals and weddings." As a people with a long tradition of a form of elder respect similar to other Asian forms of filial piety (Gap Min 1998), the Hmong go through a great deal of effort to make sure family members receive special funerals (Vang 2008). Before resettlement in Laos, a corpse was kept in the home of the deceased for a few days to allow clan members from far away villages to attend. Relatives and friends across the walkable distance visited the family and, out of respect, stayed up all night at the ceremony site. Historically, attendees contributed animal donations to help offset the significant funerary costs, to feed everyone and to perform the elaborate sacrifices to ancestors. Traditionally, ritual specialists offer multilayered rituals of chants, songs, drum beats, and sacrifices to collect all the souls of the deceased, guide them on a journey back through each place and time that person has lived, send them on to the other world, and provide those who remain with blessings and guidance for the future. A particularly significant part of the ceremony, for its ties to Chinese writing dated back to 3000 BC, is playing the Hmong musical instrument *qeej,* a mouth organ made out of hollowed-out bamboo reeds that is unique in that "every note or sound corresponds to a spoken word" (Vang 2008:55). Played by a cultural specialist, these melodies act as text that guides the souls to the afterlife. Specific burial rites for a kin group were historically distributed within a lineage group through word of mouth. Today, however, the dispersal of kin relations around the world has posed difficulties to traditional Hmong ritual networks, disabling the previous system of passing on expertise in a lineage group (Hickman 2010).

This disabling is evidenced in both Gammertingen and DFW, where there are no religious specialists or anyone who still knows how to play the *qeej.* Thus, in both communities, this thousand-year-old tradition has been eliminated. The Christian Hmong in both locations have also eliminated the ritual elements associated with animism and ancestor worship, although they maintain the same length of funeral service, guests are still expected to stay awake all night, and food is prepared and eaten in a similar manner as is done in traditional services. Whereas the children of the deceased are traditionally responsible for payment of the elaborate event, in the two small communities, similar to weddings, the entire community chips in to pay for and plan a funeral. The DFW Hmong have also moved their services from the homes of the deceased to rented funeral parlors, and following the German tradition, Hmong funerals in Gammertingen take place in a graveyard chapel.

Because of the ease of long distance travel, these events are attended by relatives and guests from across the broader diaspora. This often causes disagreements on how the ritual should proceed, especially when a family is split between multiple locations. For example, at one DFW funeral, a relative from a larger northern Hmong community insisted on paying for a *qeej* player to be flown into Texas, fearing a loss of face by those who would not understood its omission or cultural restraints of Texas.

In Gammertingen, as was discussed in a previous chapter, the Hmong community's conversion to Christianity was largely a response to the economic, legal, and social burdens of traditional ritual practices in their new German environment. The only Gammertingen Hmong funeral in thirty years of resettlement was a Christian church funeral done following the traditions of the German church. However, the Hmong there have spoken about traveling to France, America, Thailand, and Laos to attend Hmong funerals of other kin who have passed. They describe them as all being "Hmong" but also as being "different," indicating that they still carry important elements of Hmongness, while having noticeable adaptations to their different environments. What is significant in these small groups of resettled refugees is how their versions of funeral rituals are universalizing Hmong notions of what interconnectedness is. They expect all Hmong in the community to attend, regardless of clan or lineage affiliation. By doing this, they undermine the lineage group as a primary ritual necessity and a socially and geographically cohesive unit. This universalizing can be directly attributed to the cultural limitations of their locality.

The fracturing of Hmong families and kin groups around the world through marriage and displacement has led to two major trends in the Hmong diaspora. One is outsourcing certain parts of the ritual to more knowledgeable relatives. The second is a number of recent messianic movements that are trying to reimagine Hmong "tradition" and "authenticity." There are several independent movements going on in the United States and Thailand, that all characterize the Hmong complex ritual system as unnecessarily taxing, given their complexity, economic burden, and limited efficacy in the modern diaspora (Hickman 2010). The groups argue that residence in multiple locations and the fracturing of lineage groups makes it more difficult carry out older, complex, sets of rituals effectively. This was exemplified in the recent passing of Hmong General Vang Poa. The *Los Angeles Times* newspaper estimated thousands of pigs, ducks, cows and chickens were sacrificed in the proceedings (February 5, 2011). In answer to the cost and logistical complexities of such ritual events, these messianic groups are in the process of actively reformulating and standardizing what they argue will constitute the future canon of simpler Hmong rituals. One messianic group articulated their argument to one of my colleagues this way:

> What is better? To spend $50,000 at a funeral, or to invest in your children's education? Why do our ritual practices have to be so complex,

and require so many specialists? We offer an alternative where you can pay your respects to God and your ancestors, but without the unnecessary ritual and financial burdens.[8]

These adjustments are playing an important role in helping the Hmong like those in DFW and Germany deal with tensions that come from competing narratives and historical realities of displacement and belonging. They also demonstrate a form of embracing cultural values of Americanism. By locating tradition in the diaspora, these messianic movements are trying to consolidate the many forms of Hmong ritual practice that are fractured into their noticeably idiosyncratic state of local practices. While all the funeral practices discussed here offer somewhat competing versions of "authentic" Hmong tradition, they all serve similar purposes of making ethnic meaning out of the social reality of diaspora.

## New Year's Celebrations

Perhaps one of the earliest venues through which the Hmong engaged the diaspora was through Hmong New Year celebrations. Traditionally celebrated over the course of a month, these regional fests took place during the change of the lunar calendar throughout Southeast Asia in late November to late December.

> Hmong would celebrate the New Year by donning new clothes' offering gifts to parents and other elders in honor of their wisdom, age, and position; and traveling from village to village sharing news, visiting relatives, and arranging marriages for their children (Miyares 1977:220).

While no one knows the exact date or origins of the celebration, it is still celebrated by the Hmong in China, leaving researchers to believe it has its roots in the Chinese New Year and was adopted by the Hmong before their migration from the Han expulsion in 140 BC (Ranard 2004). These events have historically acted as diaspora conduits transcending particular localities and clan, albeit their globallity was limited to foot travel and geographically impeded by the mountainous terrain where Hmong lived. Modern versions of these events still exist throughout the diaspora today and are commonly accompanied by vendor booths selling videos, books, contemporary versions of traditional clothing, music, medicinal items, food, and story cloths. The German Hmong claim their population is too small to organize their own event, so they travel annually by car or train to the larger Hmong communities in France to take part in their celebrations. Both the first- and second-generation Hmong say this

---

8. This conversation was personally observed by Jacob Hickman in 2010 at the Hmong 4th of July Festival in St. Paul, Minnesota.

is a place where they can meet potential marriage partners. They often referr to their famous ball-tossing event that has traditionally provided an opportunity for men and women to meet members of the opposite sex in a speed-dating like fashion.

Today this ball toss is mostly played for symbolic reasons, but the Hmong still use the New Year festivities to find marriage partners. For example, a recently divorced German Hmong man in his fifties told me of his plans to fly back to Laos and Thailand where he will stay with distant clan members and attend their New Year celebrations. "I am looking," he said, "for a wife." Several other German Hmong couples, from both the first and second-generation, told me how they met at a French-Hmong New Year event.

These modern celebrations have also taken on elements of their respective localized identities. In DFW, for example, there is a live band and dancing after dinner, which inevitably draws equally large crowds to the floor for both the "Thai Happy Dance" and country line-dancing. Embedded in the festivities is a fashion show featuring several Hmong/Thai/Texan textile amalgamations. This is followed by a talent show, showcasing traditional Hmong dances, Thai dances, hip-hop numbers, country and western songs, and inventive combinations of multiple styles. At one event, a Hmong man dressed in cowboy garb took the microphone and sang "Yellow Rose of Texas" to his wife.

Figure 7.1 DFW Hmong man sings "Yellow Rose of Texas"

Photo courtesy of DN/Omega Productions.

Similarly, the Hmong in Germany describe the French New Year events they attend to be cultural fusions influenced by Hmong tradition, French fashion, and multiple cuisines, dance, and music styles. While the second-generation girls dress in a way that they hope brings them notice from potential marriage partners, the first generation is more preoccupied in face maintenance, and emphasize "just trying to blend in." Herein lies the tension. As found in wedding and funeral events, the Hmong are equally interested in how others are practicing Hmongness. They are in making sure they do not display a localized version of identity that casts them outside diasporically acceptable Hmong identifications. As one second-generation girl noted about her parents:

> They are always concerned about reputation. They don't want to offend anyone so they just melt into whatever is going on. Even if the Hmong in Germany do something different than those in France, they make a mental note of it, but they don't say anything. Everyone is doing that.

Here we see the some of the generational tensions within the Hmong diaspora. Individuality is not rewarded in Hmong culture the same way it is in the West. Members of the first-generation try to appear "authentic," and as practitioners of honored Hmong traditionalisms in the presence of other Hmong, while remaining humble and respectful and hiding distinct localisms. Parents bring their children to these events in hopes of socializing them into the importance of this balancing act—that to preserve family face, they must maintain their relationships with traditional culture within the diaspora. But for the second-generation in both field sites, who are brought up in a Western world with competing cultural models of self and morality, New Year's events serve as important places to showcase their own hybrid culture and seek Hmong marriage partners.

## Being Hmong: An Ongoing Formation

This chapter has highlighted some of the tensions within the diaspora between local identifications that have formed in response to dispersed resettlement, and Hmongness as a broader collective identity. The social dimension of these global spaces demonstrate an "ongoing formation of consciousness and positioning" (Siu 2005:4), in relation to what it specifically means to be Hmong. The diasporic contacts the Hmong in Gammertingen and DFW had served broader functions than just enhancing a sense of cultural continuity. These exchanges played a critical role in addressing the insecurities and uncertainties of otherness felt in isolated resettlement sites, and re-created a sense of belonging to a particular group of people at a particular point in time. The longings they had from sameness were at all times tempered by the realization that their various resettlements had made them different.

The diasporic experiences depicted in this chapter challenge theories that advocate meanings of home, identity and belonging as situated within "the natural order of things" in either the sending or receiving society (Malkki's 1992). This two-way, sending/receiving nation-state orientation becomes lost in cases such as the Hmong who have never had a singularly identifiable home country. For them, "home" is identified with a group of people with whom they feel ethnically attached, and not a singular geographic place. In this way, refugee diasporic research might be better served by conceptualizing these flows of culture and identity outside the bonds of a methodological-nationalist orientation to one that considers individual localities of various scales influenced by diasporic space as their units of analysis.

The second-generation's involvement in diasporic activities reveals new tensions of generational difference in balancing how they display parentally acceptable ideas of Hmongness and localized Western notions of individuality. In response to these tensions, they have shown a great deal of resourcefulness to use different structures as opportunities to continue meta-group belonging, as well as a great deal of agency regarding how they participate. The lives of the DFW and Gammertingen second generation Hmong also challenge theories that suggest that the diaspora is not a meaningful place of engagement beyond the first generation. As Thomas Faist (2000) suggests, transnational lives in themselves are increasingly becoming a strategy of survival, and as the children of Hmong refugees are demonstrating, a relevant space for finding marriage partners, world travel, and as an outlet for satisfying feelings of social responsibility.

In addition to theoretical challenges, these experiences highlight the different ways localized identities affect diasporic engagement. For those in the first-generation, political engagement seemed to hinge on how closely they were involved in the pre-exile military conflict, and on how much direct contact their current community members maintained with SGU veterans. For their children, political engagement was directly tied to exposure to human rights discourses in their countries of resettlement. Differences in attitudes toward computer mediated communication were also different drawing from the particular localized identities that had developed in each field site. In DFW computer chatting was used mostly by men who hailed it as ethnic continuity. On the other hand, in Gammertingen the Internet was used mostly by married women and was portrayed by the men as a source of ethnic discontinuity. For the second generation Hmong in both communities, the Internet was a social connector with other Hmong but, due to the isolated status of those in Gammertingen, it also emerged as an important space to find co-ethnic marriage partners. A final difference emerged in how the resources and experiences of the local environments shaped the character and execution of globally attended rituals. In these diasporic arenas the Hmong encounter other Hmong groups with different self-understandings that have risen from their position in differently scaled localities. Modifications in wedding, funeral, and New Year rituals strongly reflect local situatedness and bring each community's cultural authenticity, and therefore their right to belong as Hmong, into question. These tensions required each community to perform different measures of face maintenance that reposition aspects of their local practices back into some accepted norm. In this way, all members of the diaspora are at some point defining themselves in relation to the other diasporic members with whom they have contact, each diasporic member of which is also defining themselves, in part, by their local environments.

Equally important to these differences, the Hmong in DFW and Gammertingen demonstrated several notable similarities in how they engaged the diaspora and negotiated diasporic belonging. Engagement was seen as an active search for continuity and belonging linked to the past. They each created and maintained meaningful relationships that grew beyond those established before Laotian expulsion and beyond the first generation. Their sense of history and deterritorialized ethnic identity was directly influenced by diasporic interactions in physical geographical spaces and through virtual spaces such as video, satellite television, and Internet social networking. And when in doubt, they each used the diaspora as the main source of finding what they deemed "correct traditional knowledge." The diaspora was also a space where both communities practiced face maintenance by demonstrating to their fellow Hmong that their localized communities and families sustained a certain degree of cultural authenticity, and therefore, still belonged to the Hmong people. Diasporic belonging was important for clan reputation, being part of a global social safety net based on reciprocity, and for the opportunity to find spouses. The community in Gammertingen, for example, disregarded the video genre of Hmong films that highlighted war genealogies and flight, in favor of those that promoted the more global identity that fit their community's profile. The younger DFW Hmong community resisted the political activisms of the SGU claiming it was a holdover of status for those who had not been able to achieve the economic success that they had.

These commonalities raise several key issues about the way refugee groups negotiate belonging in the diaspora. First, this continuous and growing relationship between the global Hmong, as experienced in both field sites and across generations, suggests a relationship between worldview and diasporic identity that has not been addressed in migration research. Hmong principles of clan membership based on lineage reciprocity, the role of face maintenance as a form of social control, and Hmong cosmology had an undeniable influence on how and why the communities engaged the diaspora. If localized identities drifted too far outside of diasporically sanctioned constructs, there were social implications for reciprocity and marriage. Thus, the Hmong worldview gave each local community, and each generation within it, a powerful set of protocols to engage each other and to help shape the boundaries of who belongs, and what is "correct" and "right" and ethnically Hmong within it. Moreover, as ethnic belonging and cultural authenticity were negotiated through shifting contexts that often privileged information coming from communities with social clout and access to advanced technology, the power and privilege of some localities in migration research cannot be ignored. For this reason, both locality *and* ethnic worldview are important factors to be considered in our understanding of belonging. They are by necessity mutually opposed or contradictory forces, yet interconnected on an experiential level. It is because the Hmong are enmeshed in a global web of clan ties and alliances, that Hmongness in both field sites continues to be based, in part, on relations within the context of the diaspora. Being Hmong means belonging to the diaspora *and* living in a geographical location; therefore, it is almost impossible for a localized identity and a diasporic identity to exist independently of one another. For the Hmong, the local and the global are inseparable and the growing connectivity of Hmong groups across the diaspora will only continue to complicate these tensions. In this way, Hmong belonging is experienced as an ongoing formation of consciousness that invokes a greater importance in that which brings them together rather than in that which may drive them apart.

CHAPTER 8

# IMPLICATIONS: BELONGING, PLACE, AND SCALE

This study was conducted with the principal goal of understanding the process by which refugees reestablish their lives in the course of Western resettlement, and how the networks of social relations and social memberships, both locally and within what came to be defined as a Hmong diaspora, reflect Hmongness and world-wide circulating ideas of identity. It examined the often complex and intersecting relationships that accompanied this process by comparing two populations that originated from the same Lao hill people but resettled in communities with markedly different approaches to welcoming refugees, and by examining member-making institutions such as churches and government agencies as well as individual stakeholders who are not Hmong. While this ethnography stresses that the Hmong are not a homogeneous single actor, and therefore cannot be reduced to a single, essentialized identity, the findings do form the basis for discussions on broader issues of importance to anthropology; namely, the concept of belonging and its relevance for migration studies, social industries of identity making, the subjective positioning and rescaling of place by migrants, and the migrants as active agents in these processes. In so doing, it has produced a number of important insights.

The first is that the context of a specific locality matters in understanding social memberships. The paths to refugee belonging cannot be fully understood without situating them in the institutional structures, histories, and politics of a particular area. Gammertingen and DFW have very different characters, resources, ethnic populations, economies, ideologies, and historical relationships with the Lao refugees. The comparative distinctiveness of these two locations not only influenced how the Hmong were "made" into members, but also the strategies that they pursued in constructing their own sense of belonging. The data in this study set this research apart in that Germany and the United States were not the primary contexts for comparison; rather, the comparison was between one local place and another. Most refugee research does not directly address the place of resettlement itself. While it is clearly understood that nation-state policies are influential, by anchoring this research in locality it was able to reveal important differences in Hmong forms of belonging. Adopting this approach moves us beyond discussions of settlement in a particular place to what we might learn about how the position of being in a place informs belonging at different scales. This leads us to a second contribution.

Both the scalar size and positioning of the two resettlement sites mattered in terms of the types of structural opportunities and forms of social capital available. The small face-to-face relationships characterized by the village scale of Gammertingen provided a more intimate resettlement experience that resulted in more social capital, better access to language classes, enhanced employment opportunities, and the perceived ability to participate in local decision-making. However, the Hmong in Gammertingen also had to live out their struggles in a fish bowl of sorts, had less opportunity for co-ethnic community interaction, and had to rely on the locals. By contrast, the DFW city scale engulfed the refugees in a more autonomous living environment with a positive economy and plenty of low-skill work and low-income housing. However, they had to live with a negative public assistance discourse, the pressure to quickly become self-sufficient, and few opportunities for friendships with local nationals. These factors initially led to lower wage jobs, stigmatized housing, and few opportunities to gain social capital in the receiving community. Nevertheless, in both sites the refugees were able to read normative assumptions about what "fitting in" looked like and to formulate strategies around the available resources to position themselves in the mainstream of local belonging, while at the same time satisfying what they perceived it meant to belong to a group of co-ethnics and to the broader Hmong diaspora.

The way in which the two scales of settlement were juxtaposed does not imply, as some research has done, that a particular size of community, or a particular scalar positioning is better than the other; rather, it suggests that both contexts have specific structural constraints and opportunities causing different obstacles and opportunities for refugees. While size of the local host community has often been considered in migration research, as Glick Schiller and Caglar (2011) argue, scalar positioning is rarely a variable. The data in this study suggest that both are important and allow us to explore how local processes of belonging are informed by a nexus of hierarchical local, regional, national, and global social arenas.

This problematizes the way refugee resettlement policy is written in that it does not acknowledge the obvious structural and ideological differences between receiving societies, or regional variations within a single country. Resettlement in the United States, for example, is mostly done in cities where it is assumed that there are more resources to help the newcomer to make it. The village scale comparison in this study demonstrates that there are other political and economic resources in a smaller-scale context that may prove to be equally significant in facilitating the process of belonging. This leads us to the next contribution.

Despite the different structural opportunities, or lack thereof, refugee ingenuity and agency is an important and often overlooked tool in the process of belonging. While the two localities, through various stakeholders, were busy making the Hmong into acceptable members of the community, the Hmong were simultaneously orchestrating their own forms of capital and utilizing their traditional forms of kinship and reciprocity to negotiate success both in terms of Hmong and local values. Likewise, while the host religious institutions were operating as integrating mechanisms, the Hmong were using Western forms of Christianity as a transformative space for self-making where they held creative control. Therefore, I argue that the experiences of the Hmong demonstrate that a sense of belonging is shaped by a dialectical relationship between agency and victimization, and between "making it" and "being made." Allowing the refugees this agency departs from other studies that often focus on the newcomer's helplessness in the process of "being made." Refugee agency is also an often overlooked element in policy approaches aimed at cutting entitlements as an incentive to get the refugees to "do more," and could account for why these policies often result in government member-making strategies that facilitate, rather than discourage, long-term dependency, social isolation and stigmatization. What this adds to migration research is the knowledge that having access to resources and taking advantage of them, including those resources within a refugee's own network of co-ethnics and diasporic contacts, eases a path toward mainstream belonging.

Another salient outcome of this research is how historical forces and cultural practices shape relationships and, therefore, paths to belonging. This is most notably the case with the highland Hmong who have historically configured belonging not within the state-centered social, political, and legal impositions that are characteristic of the West, but through Hmong kinship ideology where loyalty and attachment have traditionally been directed toward members of their kin. Likewise, the lowland Hmong who had identities that included a form of state governance, influenced diasporic relationships with their political aspirations toward the formation of a Hmong state and sought recognition and legitimacy in waging this struggle. Forms of methodological nationalism that are standardly applied to migration research cannot adequately account for the hill tribe Hmong for whom nationality was not a known part of their social life. This methodology also misguides policies that define belonging in terms of national loyalties and legal passports. Only when we step back from it can we understand that formal ties established through citizenship rights do not necessarily bring about attachments of belonging; why formal ties affirm a condition of "being in" but do not automatically translate into feelings of "belonging to" a place; and why "making it" in a resettlement site may involve forms of cultural refusal as continued resistance to state-making.

The cultural underpinnings of Hmong kinship, residence patterns, supernatural belief, face maintenance, and reciprocity also cannot be ignored. Cultural consideration was essential in understanding how and why the Hmong interpreted concepts of relatedness and shaped the parameters of who does and does not belong. From this vantage point, we can understand how Christian conversion functioned as a site of improvisation for the Hmong to re-create, and to some degree redefine, their ethnic identity to one that fit both their individual local environments and sense of Hmongness.

Another important insight offered by this study is how the different modes of diasporic participation helped to illuminate the epistemology of the migrants and to map the shifting contexts of their belonging. The data suggest that for some refugee groups, this global space may be the core of their experience not the periphery. It is the place where multiple identifications and belongings get sorted out. Levitt has argued that while multiple studies have demonstrated that diasporic networks exist and have revealed a great deal about their characteristics in a specific setting, we as yet do not fully understand their relative weight or how they change in the face of different localized practices or the extent to which they remain salient beyond the first generation (2001:196). The refugees I met often had deterritorialized notions of belonging to the Hmong, which came with a global web of rights and responsibilities. The vastness of their connections and eager search to infinitely expand them, adds to our knowledge of groups who link themselves to a global diaspora as opposed to groups that remain more restricted to trans-state spaces. I argue that the refugee's global connectedness, and the constant negotiations that take place across space concerning what it means to be Hmong, are driven, in part, by their claim to a co-ethnicity can only be realized in the diaspora. In their own imagination, to be Hmong *is* to be diasporic. However, as the data from this research suggests, Hmong identities are more locally situated, thus the diaspora becomes the space where those local identities are contested. This research calls attention to the more complicated process of reconciling a diasporic identification with a localized one. The myriad identities that are formed match the simultaneity and doubleness that Hall described as occurring on different operating tracks. For this reason, I argue that the group identity of refugees needs to be analyzed as convergences of people, place, and perception of a shared past and local positioning, of structure and agency, of intersections and scale.

Conclusions drawn from the DFW Hmong's global participation follow other literature on scale that would suggest their local positioning is nested within the national and global hierarchical relations of power within communities of the United States. However, the literature on scale cannot fully explain the extensive diasporic engagements of the Hmong living in such a small isolated village as Gammertingen. Current thought would presume that migrants living in a village that makes little effort to position itself in relation to broader global hierarchies would be far less engaged with diasporic networks than migrants in larger, globally connected cities, like DFW. However, that was not necessarily the case. It was the Hmong who were trying to reposition themselves globally *despite* the lack of rescaling processes within the village. What might partially explain this is that the DFW Hmong have an intermediating scalar relationship with the larger Hmong communities of Minnesota and California. It is through these relationships that DFW area Hmong engage the diaspora—via their global platforms of videos, satellite television, clan based organizations, and hosting of major diasporic events. They have access to national scale social arenas and hence feel less compelled to enter the global arena. By contrast, for the German Hmong there is no comparable vital national arena, and hence the global networks are more vital to ethnic survival and identity. They jump scale directly to the diaspora. While this research is only suggestive, it does indicate that, for some refugee groups, ethnicity can impact scalar relationships, and that there is a relationship between the scalar positioning of the resettlement site and the different pathways to belonging.

As a final concluding point it is important to consider the analytical implications of using the concept of *belonging* in immigrant research. I would argue that this term accords refugees, and certainly migrants more generally, important agency while also giving weight to how a group simultaneously negotiates various memberships outside of the one-way connotations of integration. Whereas integration, assimilation, and incorporation often measure the effectiveness of structural support, the data in this study suggest that belonging is facilitated by an inseparable relationship between structure *and* agency. There has to be some sort of structure in place to which agency can be applied, and therefore migration research needs an analytical concept that affords equal weight to both and can account for interactions within a variety of social fields that encompass aid workers, local nationals, local co-ethnics, dispersed kin, and the broader diaspora. I argue that a concept such as *belonging*, defined as perceived togetherness, helps to capture precisely how an immigrant understands citizenship and membership and "fitting in."

The Hmong cases in this study viewed through this analytical lens demonstrate how refugee belonging is a multifaceted phenomenon that overlaps, intersects, and often conflicts with other social arenas where perceived togetherness is also desired. They demonstrate that the way in which these relationships play out is very contextual, and that they are shaped by the historic, economic, sociopolitical and cultural situations and characteristics of place of origin, destination, and diaspora. The data also suggest that refugees can construct a sense of belonging in ways that do not correspond to either local or national policies nor reflect notions of national identities. And most importantly, they demonstrated that for the newcomer, belonging is situated in a nexus between the local and the global and its multi-layered forms are continually negotiated in particular contexts at specific points in time. Thus, belonging offers not only a way to define incorporation via its actors, but also to develop a cross-national framework for thinking about perceived togetherness.

As refugees continue to settle in Western societies, debates surrounding "best practices" on how to effectively fit newcomers into a locality stand at the forefront of national policy agendas. The findings in this research carry implications for those policies and policy makers seeking to create flexible and creative incorporation programs for extremely diverse populations. By identifying the ideological and social factors that influence the process of belonging via its actors, and by considering locality and scale, resettlement programs can be more informed on how to handle the complex needs of incoming immigrants in a culturally sensitive manner. In this way, the significance of this research is not restricted to Gammertingen and DFW, or to the Hmong, but has implications for all refugees and Western societies in which they are settled.

# Appendix

| | 1st Generation Hmong Community Profile | | | | | |
|---|---|---|---|---|---|---|
| | **Dallas/Fort Worth** | | | **Gammertingen** | | |
| Distribution of Males and Females in the study sample | 10 Males | | 12 Females | 10 Males | | 12 Females |
| Distribution of families from a particular clan membership | Xiong 4 / Vang 4 | | Lo 4 / OH 4 | Xiong 4 / Vang 4 | | Lo 4 / OH 4 |
| Distribution of Hmong families by language dialect | White Hmong 11 | | Green Hmong 2 / Mixed 3 | White Hmong 9 | | Green Hmong 5 / Mixed 2 |
| Country of Birth | Laos 20 | | Other 2 | Laos 20 | | Other 2 |
| Geographic Region in Laos | Lowland 3 | | Highland 11 | Lowland 3 | | Highland 11 |
| Year Family Arrived in the West | 1st Wave 1975-1977 — 3 | 2nd Wave 1978-1985 — 10 | 3rd wave 1986+ — 1 | 1st Wave 1975-1977 | 2nd Wave 1977-1985 — 14 | 3rd Wave 1986+ |
| Average number of children per family | 5 | | | 5.3 | | |
| Highest level of education obtained before moving to the West | 0 – some primary school 11 | Some high school 2 | College 1 | 0 – some primary school 11 | Some high school 0 | College 3 |
| Housing Status as of 2009 | Rent 1 | | Own 13 | Rent 4 | | Own 10 |
| Heads of households currently working [13] as of 2009 | 99% (One family on disability SS, one retired, one looking) | | | 95% (one family unemployed and one retired) | | |
| Average time in the field site before employment | 1st wave - Less than 2 weeks; 2nd wave – one month | | | 13 months | | |
| % of families where the spouse works outside the home | 98% | | | Less than 1% | | |
| Family religion practiced before resettlement | Hmong Animism 8 | Christianity 5 | Other 1 | Hmong Animism 12 | Christianity 1 | Other 1 |
| Family religion practiced as of 2009 | Hmong Animism 5 | Christianity 8 | Other 1 | Hmong Animism 2 | Christianity 11 | Other 1 |

13. Figure represents the entire Hmong community, not just those in the sample. (Footnote original to chart.)

# References

Adas, Michael. "From footdragging to flight: The evasive history of peasant avoidance protest in south and South-East Asia." *The Journal of Peasant Studies* 1986: 13(2): 64–86.

Adelman, H., and S. Mcgrath. "To Date To Marry: That is the Question." *Journal of Refugee Studies* 2007: 20(3): 376–380.

Ahmary, Abdullah Azib, Al. "Ethnic Self-identity and the Role of Islam: A Study of the Yemeni Community in the South End of Dearborn and Detroit, Michigan." Ph.D. dissertation, University of Tennessee, 1998.

Alba, Richard and Victor Nee. *Remaking the American Mainstream: Assimilation and Contemporary Immigration.* Cambridge, MA: Harvard University Press, 2003.

Alber, Jens. "Germany." In *The West European Welfare States, vol. 2*, by P. Flora (ed), 249–353. Berlin: de Gruyter, 1986.

Aleinikoff, Alexander and Douglas Klusmeyer. *Citizenship Today: Global Perspectives and Practices.* Washington, DC: Carnegie Endowment for International Peace, 2001.

Alesina, Alberto, Edward Glaeser and Bruce Sacerdote. "Why Doesn't the United States Have a European-Style Welfare State?" *Brookings Papers on Economic Activity*, 2001: 187–254.

Alexander, Michael. "Comparing Local Policies towards Migrants," In *Citizenship in European Cities*, by Karen Kraal, Marco Martiniello, Steven Vertovec (eds), 57–84. Burlington, VT: Ashgate, 2004.

Andezian, S. "Woman's roles in organizing symbolic life: Algerian female immigrants in France," In *International Migration: the female experience*, by R.C. Simon and C.B. Brettell (eds), 254–266. New Jersey: Rowman and Allanheld, 1986.

Armstrong, John. *Nations before Nationalism.* Chapel Hill: University of North Carolina Press, 1982.

Askew, Kelly, and Richard Wilk (eds). *The Anthropology of Media: A Reader.* Malden, MA: Blackwell Publishers, 2002.

Balakrishnan, T. R., and Feng Hou. "Socioeconomic integration and spatial residential patterns of immigrant groups in Canada." *Population Research and Policy Review,* 1999: 18(3) 201217.

Barker, C. "Empowerment and Resistance: Collective Effervescence and Other Account." In *Transforming Politics: Power and Resistance,* by P. Bagguley and J. Hearn (eds). London: Macmillan, 1999.

Barnes, Diane. "Resettled Refugees' Attachment to their Original and Subsequent Homelands: Long-term Vietnamese Refugees in Australia." *Journal of Refugee Studies,* 2001: 14(4) 394–411.

Barns, J. A. *Three Styles in the Study of Kinship.* London: Tavistock, 1971.

Berghahn, M. "Women émigrés in England," In *Between Sorrow and Strength: Women Refugees of the Nazi Period,* by S. Quack (ed.) 69–80. Cambridge: Cambridge University Press, 1995.

Betts, Alexander. "Humanitarian innovation and refugee protection." Working paper series #85, Refugee Studies Center, University of Oxford, England, 2012. http://www.oxhip.org/wpcontent/uploads/wp85-humanitarian-innovation-091112.pdf, (accessed July 24 2013).

Bhachu, P. *Twice migrants.* London: Tavistock, 1985.

Blake, J. "Sponsorship: Its Changing Roles." *Hmong Forum,* 1990: 47–55.

Bloemraad, Irene. *Becoming a Citizen: Incorporating Immigrants and Refugees in the United States and Canada.* Berkeley: University of California Press, 2006.

Block, Liesbeth de and David Buckingham. *Global Children, Global Media: Migration, Media and Childhood,* Basingstoke. Hampshire: Palgrave, 2007.

Borjas, George J. *The economic integration of immigrants in the United States: Lessons for policy.* No. 2003/78. WIDER Discussion Papers//World Institute for Development Economics (UNU-WIDER), 2003.

Bourdieu, Pierre, and Loïc Wacquant. "La nouvelle vulgate planétaire." *Le monde diplomatique* 2000: 5 1–7.

Bowman, Glenn. "Migrant Labour: Constructing homeland in the exilic imagination." *Anthropological Theory,* 2002: 2 447–468.

Boyd, Monica. "Educational Attainments of Immigrant Offspring: Success or Segmented Assimilation?" *International Migration Review,* 2002: 1037–1060.

Bradley, Robert H. "Chaos, culture, and covariance structures: A dynamic systems view of children's experiences at home." *Parenting,* 2004: 4(2–3) 243–257.

Brah, Avatar. *Cartographies of diaspora: Contesting identities.* Routledge, 1996.

Brettell, Caroline B. "Bringing the city back in: Cities as contexts for immigrant incorporation." *American arrivals: Anthropology engages the new immigration* 163, 2003: 195.

Brettell, Caroline, and Deborah Reed-Danahay. *Civic Engagements: The Citizenship Practices of Indian and Vietnamese Immigrants.* Stanford University Press, 2011.

Brettell, Caroline and Deborah Reed-Danahay. "Introduction," In *Citizenship, Political Engagement, and Belonging: Immigrants in Europe and the United States*, by Deborah Reed-Danahay and Caroline Brettell (eds), 1–17. New Brunswick, NJ: Rutgers University Press, 2008.

Brettell, Caroline B. "Political Belonging and Cultural Belonging Immigration Status, Citizenship, and Identity Among Four Immigrant Populations in a Southwestern City." *American Behavioral Scientist,* 2006: 50(1) 70–99.

Briones, Claudia. "Our Struggle Has Just begun: Experiences of Belonging and Mapuche Formations of Self," In *Indigenous Experience Today*, by Marisol de la Cadena and Orin Starn (eds), 99–124. New York: Berg, 2007.

Brown, B. "Face-saving and face-restoration in negotiation," In *Negotiations*, by D. Druckman (Ed), 275–299. Beverly Hills, CA: Sage, 1977.

Brubaker, Rogers. *Citizenship and Nationhood in France and German.* Cambridge, MA: Harvard University Press, 1992.

Bryson, J. "Study in the GDR." *Die Unterrichtspraxis/Teaching German,* 1989: 22(1) 63–66.

Bureau, US Census. *S0201 Hmong alone or in any combination.* Selected Population Profile in the United States. Washington, D.C.: U.S. Census Bureau, 2008.

Byron, R. *Irish America.* Oxford: Clarendon Press, 1999.

Campbell, Randolph. *Gone to Texas: A history of the Lone Star State.* Oxford: Oxford Press, 2003.

Carliner, David, Lucas Guttentag, Arthur Helton, and Wade Henderson. T*he Rights of Aliens and Refugees: The Basic ACLU Guide to Alien and Refugee Rights.* Carbondale: Southern Illinois University Press, 1977.

Cashdan, Elizabeth. "Territoriality among human foragers: ecological models and an application to four Bushman groups." *Current Anthropology,* 1983: 24(1): 47–66.

Castaneda, Jorge. "La Matrícula Consular: Hay Que Buscar Aliados." *La Opinión* 8/17, 2003.

Castles, M. *The Power of Identity.* Oxford: Blackwell, 1997.

Castles, Stephen. *Citizens and Migrants.* New York: Routledge, 2000.

———. "Migration and community Formation under Conditions of Globalization." *International Migration Review,* 2002: 1143–1168.

Chen, Carolyn. *Getting Saved in America: Taiwanese Immigration and Religious Experience.* Princeton: Princeton University Press, 2008.

Chou, S. "Religion and Chinese Life in the United States." *Etudes Migrations*, 1991: 2(103)455464.
City of Gammertingen. "Bundestagswahl vom 27. September 2009." *Gammertingen Stadtinfos Nachrichten*, September 27, 2009. http://www.stadtgammertingen.de/stadtinfos/archivn.113.html (accessed April 5, 2010).
Clark, William. *Immigrants and the American Dream.* New York: The Guilford Press, 2003.
Clasen, Jochen. "Social Security: the Core of the German Employment-Centered Social State," In *Social Policy in Germany*, by J. Clasen and R. Freeman (eds), 61–82. New York: Harvester Wheatsheaf, 1994.
Clifford, James. *Routes: travel and translation in the late twentieth century. London:* Harvard University Press, 1997.
⸺. *The Predicament of Culture.* Cambridge, MA: Harvard University Press, 1988.
Cohen, Robin. "Response to Hathaway." *Journal of Refugee Studies*, 2007: 20(3): 370–376.
⸺. *Global Diasporas: An Introduction.* London: UCL Press, 1997.
⸺. "Rethinking "Babylon": Iconoclastic Conceptions of the Diasporic Experience." *New Community*, 1995: 21(1): 5–18.
Coleman, David A. "Partner choice and the growth of ethnic minority populations." *Bevolking en Gezin* 33, 2004: 27–34.
Comaroff, Jean, and John Comaroff. "Christianity and colonialism in South Africa." *American Ethnologist* 1986: 13(1) 1–22.
Commerce, US Department of. *1980 Census of population Detailed Characteristics Texas.* Washington DC: Bureau of the Census, 1983.
Connor, Walker's. "A Nation is a nation, is a state, is an ethnic group, is a …". *Ethnic and Racial Studies*, 2000; 1(4): 377–400.
Cooper, Frederick. "The Dialects of Decolonization: Nationalism and Labor Movements in Post-War Africa." Paper prepared for the Power Conference, Program in the Comparative Study of Social Transformations. Ann Arbor: University of Michigan. 1992.
Cooper, Robert. "The Hmong of Laos: Economic Factors in the Refugee Exodus and Return." In *The Hmong in Transition*, by B.T. Downing and A.S. Deinard eds. G.L. Hendricks, 23–40. New York: Center for Migration Studies, 1986.
Crul, Maurice and Schneider, Jens. "Comparative integration context theory: participation and belonging in new diverse European cities." *Ethnic and Racial Studies*, 2010: 33(7) 1249–1268.
CRS Report for Congress. *Refugee Admissions and Resettlement Policy.* Report, Washington D.C: The Library of Congress, 2002.

Culas C., and Michaud J. "A contribution to the study of Hmong (Miao) migrations and history," In *Hmong/Miao in Asia*, by J Michaud, C. Culas, G. Yia Lee ed. N. Tapp, 61–96. Chiang Mai: Silkworm Books, 2004.

Cunningham, Stuart, and John Sinclair (eds). *Floating Lives: The Media and Asian Diaspora.* St. Lucia: University of Queensland Press, 2000.

Daniel, Valentine and John Knudsen (eds). *Mistrusting Refugees.* University of California Press. 1995.

De Beauclair, I. "A Miao tribe of Southeast Kweichow and its Cultural Configuration." *Bulletin of the Institute of Ethnology*, 1960: 127–205.

De Certeau, Michel. "The Writing of History, trans." *Tom Conley (New York, 1988)* 101.

Delanty, Gerard, Ruth Wodak, and Paul Jones. *Identity, belonging, and migration*, Vol. 17. Liverpool University Press, 2008.

DeLuca, Laura, and Lauren Rhoades. "Nuer American Passages: Globalizing Sudanese Migration." By Dianna J. Shandy. *Journal of Refugee Studies,* 2009: 22(2) 250–252.

DeSipio, Louis. "Building America, One Person at a Time: Naturalization and the Political Behavior of the Naturalized in Contemporary American Politics." In *E Plurbis Unum? Contemporary and Historical Perspectives on Immigrant Political Incorporation*, by Gary Gerstle and John Mollenkopf (eds), 67–106. New York: Russell Sage Foundation, 2001.

DeWind, J. "Response to Hathaway." *Journal of Refugee Studies*, 2007: 20(3): 381–385.

DiPrete, Thomas and Patricia McManus. "Family Change, Employment Transitions, and the Welfare State: Household Income Dynamics in the United States." *American Sociological Review*, 2000: 65(3) 343–370.

Donnelly, Nancy. *Changing Lives of Refugee Hmong Women.* Seattle: University of Washington Press, 1994.

Dorais, Louis-Jacques. "Refugee adaptation and community structure: the Indochinese in Quebec City, Canada." *International Migration Review,* 1991: 551–573.

Duchon, D. "Home is Where You Make It: Hmong Refugees in Georgia." *Urban Anthropology*, 1997: 26(1): 71–92.

Dufoix, Stephane. *Diasporas.* Berkeley, CA: University of California Press, 2008.

During, Simon. *Cultural Studies: a Critical Introduction.* New York: Routledge. 2005.

Ebaugh, H.R. and J.S. Chafetz. *Religion and the New Immigrants: Continuities and Adaptations in Immigrant Congregations.* Walnut Creek, CA: AltaMira Press, 2000.

Eriksen, Thomas. *Ethnicity and Nationalism*. London: Pluto Press, 2002.
Evangelische Kirchengemeinde Gammertingen. *Gemeindeleitungsbericht der Kirchengemeinde Gammertingen anlaesslich der Visitation 2008*. Bishops Report, Gammertingen, Germany: Evangelische Kirchengemeinde Gammertingen, 2008.
Everett, Anna. "The Revolution Will be Digitized: Afrocentricity and the Digital Public Sphere." *Social Text*, 2002: 20(2)(71): 125–146.
Faist, Thomas. "Transnationalization in international migration: implications for the study of citizenship and culture." *Ethnic and racial studies*, 2000: 23(2) 189–222.
*Federal Law Gazette I*. N.d.: 1057.
Federal Ministry of Economic Cooperation and Development. *Partner Country Laos*. August 2008. http://www.bmz.de/en/countries/partnercountries/laos/zusammenarbeit.html (accessed January 27, 2010).
Fegan, Brian. "Tenants' non-violent resistance to landowner claims in a central Luzon." *The Journal of Peasant Studies*, 1986: 13(2) 87–106.
Ferrera, Maurizio and Martin Rhodes. "Recasting European Welfare States: An Introduction." *West European Politics*, April 2000: 1–13.
Fischer, Michael MJ. "Ethnicity and the post-modern arts of memory." *Writing culture: The poetics and politics of ethnography*, 1986: 194–233.
Fortier, A. *Migrant belongings: memory, space and identity*. Oxford: Berg, 2000.
Foucault, Michel. "The history of sexuality, volume I." *New York: Vintage*, 1978.
Frachon, C. and Vergaftig, M. *European Television: Immigrants and Ethnic Minorities*. London: John Libbey, 1995.
Franz, B. "Bosnian refugee women in (re)settlement: gender relations and social mobility." *Feminist Review*, 2003: 73, 86–103.
Fuglerud, Øivind. *Life on the outside: The Tamil diaspora and long-distance nationalism*. Pluto Pr, 1999.
*Gammertingen.de*. 1988. www.gammertingen.de (accessed May 18, 2009).
Gamson, W. A. *Taking Politics*. Cambridge: Cambridge University Press, 1992.
Gap Min, Pyong. *Changes and Conflicts: Korean Immigrant Families in New York*. Boston: Allyn and Bacon, 1998.
Gardner, K. "Deaths, burial and bereavement amongst Bengali Muslims in Tower Hamlets, east London." *Journal of Ethnic and Migration Studies*, 1998: 24, 507–23.
Garrett, W. "No Place to Run: The Hmong of Laos." *National Geographic magazine*, June 1974: CXLV.
Gazley, Phil. *Effective Evangelism: Refugee Ministry*, N.d. http://www.christiananswers.net/evangelism/methods/refugees.html (accessed July 26, 2010).

Geddes, W. *Migrants of the Mountains: Cultural Ecology of the Blue Miao.* Oxford: Clarendon Press, 1976.

Georgiou, Myria. "Identity, Space and the Media: Thinking through Diaspora." *Review Europeenne des Migrations Internationales*, 2010: 26(1): 17–35.

Getrich, Christina. "Negotiating boundaries of social belonging: second-generation Mexican youth and the immigrant rights protest of 2006." *American Behavioral Scientist*, 2008: 52(4): 553–556.

Gilbertson, G., and Singer, A. "The emergence of protective citizenship in the USA: Naturalization among Dominican immigrants in the post 1996 welfare reform era." *Ethnic and Racial Studies*, 2003: 25–51.

Gilroy, Paul. *There Ain't No Black In the Union Jack: The Cultural Politics of Race and Nation.* Hutchinson, 1987.

Glazer, Nathan and Daniel Moynihan. *Beyond the melting pot.* Cambridge, MA: MIT Press, 1963.

Glick Schiller, Nina and Aysa Caglar. *Locating Migration: Rescaling Cities and Migrants.* Ithaca. NY: Cornell University Press, 2011.

Glick Schiller, Nina, Linda Basch, and Cristina Blanc-Szanton. "Towards a definition of transnationalism." *Annals of the New York Academy of Sciences*, 2006: 645(1): ix–xiv.

Glick Schiller, Nina and Thomas Faist. *Migration, Development and Transnationalization: A critical stance.* New York: Berghahn Books, 2010.

Gozdziak, Elzbieta M., and Susan Forbes Martin, eds. *Beyond the gateway: Immigrants in a changing America.* Lexington Books, 2005.

Gozdziak, Elzbieta and Dianna Shandy. "Editorial Introduction: Religion and Spirituality in Forced Migration." *Journal of Refugee Studies*, 2002: 129–135.

Goffman, E. "On Facework." *Psychiatry*, 1955: 18, 213–231.

Goodenough, Ward. *Culture, Language, and Society.* Chicago: Aldine, 1971.

Goody, Jack. "Inheritance, Property, and Marriage in Africa and Eurasia." *Sociology*, 1969: 3, 557–556.

Grabska, Katarzyna. "Marginalization in urban spaces of the global south: Urban refugees in Cairo." *Journal of Refugee Studies*, 2006: 19(3) 287–307.

Grigoleit, Grit. "Coming Home? The Integration of Hmong Refugees from Wat Tham Krabok, Thailand into American Society." *Hmong Studies Journal*, 2006: 7, 1–22.

Grnseth, Anne Sigfrid. *Lost Selves and Lonely Persons. Experiences of illness and well-being among Tamil refugees in Norway.* Durham: Carolina Academic Press, 2010.

Guerra, Carlos. *Texans Go Hungry Because of Welfare Reform.* September 10, 2009. http://www.mysanantonio.com/news/columnists/carlos_guerra/Texans_go_hungry_be cause_of_welfare_reform.html?c=y&page=1#storytop (accessed June 3, 2010).

Gunning, Jan Willem. 1901 Evangelisatie of Christianisatie: Referaat mede naar aanleiding van reis indrukken in Indie, gehouden op de Nederlandsche Zending-Conferentie te s'Gravenhage op 18 Oktober 1901. (Evangelization or Christianization? A Lecture Presented with Reference to Travel Impressions of India, Held at the Dutch Mission Conference at s'-Gravenhage on October 18, 1901.) Mededeelingen NZG 45:297–344.

Hagedorn, H. *Wer darf Mitglied werden? Einbürgerung in Deutschland und Frankreich im Vergleich.* Opladen, 2001.

Hall, Sandra. "Hmong Kinship Roles: Insiders and Outsiders." *Hmong Forum*, 1990: 25–39.

Hall, Stuart. "The question of cultural identity." *Modernity and its futures*, 1992: 274–316.

———. "Cultural Identity and Diaspora," In *Identity: Community, culture, Difference*, by Jonathan Rutherford (ed), 222–237. London: Lawrence and Wishart, 1990.

Hammond, Joyce. "Visualizing Themselves: Tongan Videography in Utah." *Visual Anthropology*, 1988: 1, 379–400.

Hancock, Ange-Marie. *The Politics of Disgust.* New York: New York University Press, 2004.

Harrell-Bond, B. E. and E. Voutira. "Anthropology and the Study of Refugees." *Anthropology Today*, 1992: 8(4) 6–10.

Hathaway, J.C. "Forced Migration Studies: Could We Agree Just to 'Date'?" *Journal of Refugee Studies*, 2007: 20(3) 349–369.

Heisler, Barbara. "Immigrant Incorporation and Political Backlash: Four Papers and Some Questions," In *Beyond Exceptionalism: Immigration and National Traditions in the United States and Germany*, by James Hollifield and Detrich Thranhardt (eds.), In Press.

Henderson, Hilma. "New Immigrants a Tax Burden." *Dallas Morning News*, July 23, 1977.

Hickman, Jacob. "Of Traditionalism and Transnationalism: Constructing "Hmong-ness" in the Diaspora." *Annual Meeting of the American Anthropological Association.* New Orleans: November 17, 2010.

Hiller, Harry H., and Tara M. Franz. "New ties, old ties and lost ties: the use of the internet in diaspora." *New Media & Society*, 2004: 6(6) 731–752.

Hirschle, Edwin. "Wie geht es weiter mit den Vietnamesen in Gammertingen." *Amstblatt Der Stadt Gammertintgen*, August 29, 1980: 1.

Ho, David. "On the Concept of Face." *American Journal of Sociology*, 1976: 81, 867–884.

Hollifield, James and Dietrich Threnhardt. "Introduction: Immigration and Citizenship in Two Liberal Republics." In *Beyond Exceptionalism: Immigration and National Traditions in the United States and Germany*, by James and Dietrich Threnhardt (eds) Hollifield. n.d.

Horowitz, David. *Ethnic Groups in Conflict*. Berkeley: University of California Press, 1985.

Hudspeth, William. *Stone Gateway and Flowery Miao*. London: Cargate Press, 1937.

Ignacio, Emily. *Building Diaspora: Filipino Cultural Community Formation on the Internet*. New Brunswick, NJ: Rutgers University Press, 2004.

Isajiw, Wsevolod and Tanuja Perera. *Multiculturalism in North America and Europe: comparative perspectives on interethnic relations and social incorporation*. Toronto: Canadian Scholars' Press, 1997.

Jansen, Stef and Staffan Lofving. *Struggles for Home: Violence, Hope and the Movement of People*. Oxford: Berg, 2009.

Jary, David and Julia Jary. *Collins Dictionary of Sociology*, London: Harper Collins, 1991.

Jenkins R. *Rethinking ethnicity*. London: Sage, 1997.

Jenkins, S. (ed). *Ethnic Associations and the Welfare State*. New York: Columbia University Press, 1988.

Jones, S. "Understanding Community in the Information Age." In *Cybersociety: Computermediated Communication and Community*, by S. Jones (ed), 10–35. Thousand Oaks, CA: Sage, 1995.

Jones PR, and Krzyżanowski M. "Identity, Belonging and Migration: Beyond Describing 'Others'" In *Identity, Belonging and Migration* by Delanty, G.; Wodak, R.; Jones, P.R. (eds.), 38–53. Liverpool: Liverpool University Press, 2008.

Kammerer, Cornelia Ann. "Customs and Christian Conversion among Akha Highlanders of Burma and Thailand." In *Religion in Culture and Society*, by John Bowen (ed), 12–29. Boston: Allyn and Bacon, 1997.

Karanovic, Jelena Lyons, on Reed-Danahay and Brettel. "Citizenship, Political Engagement, and Belonging: Immigrants in Europe and the United States." *H-Net Review Publication*, 2011.

Karim, Karim H. *From Ethnic Media to Global Media: Transnational Communication Networks among Diasporic Communities*. Strategic Research and Analysis Canadian Heritage, International Comparative Research Group, 1998.

Karst, Kenneth, L. "Paths to Belonging: The Constitution and Cultural Identity, 64N." *CL REV* 1986: 303(306) 361–69.

Katz, Michael. *The Price of Citizenship: Redefining the American welfare state*. New York: Henry Holt, 2001.

Kelley, Tobias. "Returning to Palestine." In *Struggles for Home*, by Stef Jansen and Staffan Lofving (eds), 25–41. Oxford: Berg, 2009.
Kelly, Gail. "Coping with America: Refugees from Vietnam, Cambodia, and Laos in the 1970s and 1980s." *ANNALS, AAPSS*, September 1986: 138–149.
Keown-Bomar, J. *Kinship Networks Among Hmong American Refugees*. New York: LFB Scholarly Publishing, 2004.
Kinchen, David. *HMONG LAO UPDATE: 21 Hmong Lao Refugee Children Found Alive; Laos Refuses to Return Them to Their Parents*, April 17, 2007. http://www.huntingtonnews.net/national/070417-kinchen-hmong.html (accessed October 29, 2010).
Kolar-Panov, Dona. *Video, War, and the Diasporic Imagination*. London: Routledge, 1997.
Koltyk, Jo Ann, and Nancy Foner. *New Pioneers in the Heartland: Hmong Life in Wisconsin (Part of the New Immigrants Series)*. Allyn & Bacon, 1997.
Korac, Maja. *Remaking Home: Reconstructing Life, Place and Identity in Rome and Amsterdam*. New York: Berghahn Books, 2009.
Landolt, P. "Salvadoran economic transnationalism: embedded strategies for household maintenance, immigrant incorporation, and entrepreneurial expansion." *Global Networks*, 2004: *1*(3), 217–242.
Lanphier, C.M. "Refugee resettlement. Models in action." *International Migration Review*, 1983: 4–33.
Lavenex, S. "The Europeanization of Refugee Policies." *Journal of Common Market Studies*, 2001: 39(5), 851–874.
Leach, Edmund. "Concerning Trobriand Clans and the Kinship Category 'Tabu,'" In *The Development Cycle of Domestic Groups*, by Jack Goody (ed), 120–145. Cambridge: Cambridge University Press, 2004 [1958].
———. *The Political Systems of Highland Burma: A Study of Kachin Social Structure*. Cambridge, MA: Harvard University Press, 1954.
Lee, Gary. "Diaspora and the Predicament of Origins: Interrogating Hong Postcolonial History and Identity." *Hmong Studies Journal*, 2007: 8, 1–24.
———. "Dreaming Across the Oceans: Globalization and Cultural Reinvention of the Hmong Diaspora." *Hmong Studies Journal*, 2006: 7(1), 1–33.
———. "Minority Policies and the Hmong." In *Contemporary Laos: Studies in the Politics and Society of the Lao People's Democratic Republic*, by ed. M. Stuart-Fox, 1999–219. New York: St. Martin's Press, 1982.—*The Effects of Development Measures on the Socio-economy of the White Hmong*, Ph.D., Dissertaion, 1981.
Leepreecha, Prasit. "Kinship and Identity Among Hmong in Thailand." *Book*. Seattle: University of Washington, 2001.

_____. "Role of Media Technology in Reproducing Hmong Ethnic Identity," In *Living in a Globalized World: Ethnic Minorities in the Greater Mekong Region,* Don McCaskill, Prasit Leepreecha and Shaoying He (eds), 89–113. Bangkok: Mekong Press, 2008.

Lemoine, J,. *A Hmong village in Laos.* Paris: CNRS, 1972.

Levitt, P, and N. Glick Schiller. "Conceptualizing Simultaneity; A Transnational Social Field Perspective on Society." *International Migration Review,* 2004: 38(3). 1,02-10039.

Levitt, Peggy. *God Needs No Passport: Immigrants and the Changing American Religious Landscape.* New York: New Press, 2007.

_____. *The Transnational Villagers.* New York: Crossing Press, 2001.

_____. "You Know, Abraham Was Really the First Immigrant." *International Migration Review,* 2003: 37(3) 847–873.

Liang, Zai and Naomi Ito. "Intermarriage of Asian Americans in the New York City Region." *IMR,* 1999: 876–900.

Lieberson, S. and Waters, M. C. *From Many Strands: Ethnic and Racial Groups in Contemporary America.* New York: Russell Sage Foundation, 1988.

Ling, S. and Ruey, F. *The Miao Tribe of Western Hunan.* Taipei: Academia Sinica, 1947.

Lo, Kaying. "Across the ocean: The impact of immigration on Hmong women," PhD diss., University of Wisconsin, 2002.

Long, Lynellyn. *The Floating World: Laotian Refugee Camp Life in Thailand.* Stanford CA: Stanford University, 1988.

Long, Neil. "From Paradigm Lost to Paradigm Regained? The Case of an Actor-oriented Sociology of Development," In *Battlefields of Knowledge: The Interlocking of Theory and Practice in Social Research and Development,* by N. long and A. Long (eds). London: Routledge, 1992.

Lovell, Nadia. "Introduction," In *Locality and Belonging,* by Nadia (ed) Lovell, 1–24. London: Routledge, 1998.

_____. "Wild gods, containing wombs and moving pots: Emplacement and transience in Watchi belonging." In *Locality and Belonging,* by Nadia Lovell, 53–102. London: Routledge, 1998.

Lucassen, Leo. *The immigrant threat: The integration of old and new migrants in Western Europe since 1850.* University of Illinois Press, 2005.

Lucke, Joyce. *We All Agree: A study of cultural consensus in a Hmong community.* Milwaukee: University of Wisconsin, 1995.

MacDonald, Jeffery. *Transnational Aspects of Iu-Mein Refugee Identity.* New York: Garland Publishing, 1997.

Malkki, Lisa. "National geographic: the rooting of peoples and the territorialization of national identity among scholars and refugees." *Cultural anthropology* 1992: 7(1), 24–44.

———. "Refugees and Exile: From 'Refugee Studies' to the Natuonal Order of Things." *Annual Review of Anthropology*, 1995: 24: 495–523.

Mallison, Rodger. "Refugees prefer to turn welfare around and fare well." *Star-Tellegram*, December 1980.

Mangin, William, ed. *Peasants in cities: readings in the anthropology of urbanization*. Houghton Mifflin, 1970.

Mandel, Ruth. *Cosmopolitan Anxieties*. Durham: Duke University Press, 2008.

Mansfield, Becky. "Beyond rescaling: reintegrating the national as a dimension of scalar relations." *Progress in Human Geography* 2005: 29(4), 458–473.

Marfleet, Philip. "Making States, Making Refugees: A Review of Displacement and Dispossession in the Modern Middle East." *Journal of Refugee Studies*, 2013: 26(2) 302–309.

Martin, P., S. Martin, and P. Weil. "Best Practice Options: Mali." *International Migration*, 2002: 40(3), 87–102.

Massey, Douglas S., ed. *New faces in new places: The changing geography of American immigration*. Russell Sage Foundation, 2008.

Mavroudi, Elizabeth. "Diaspora as process: (de) constructing boundaries." *Geography Compass*, 2007: 1(3) 467–479.

Mayer, P. Townsmen. *Conservation and the Process of Urbanization in a South African City*. Oxford: Oxford University Press, 1961.

McAleavy, H. Henry. "Some aspects of marriage and divorce in Communist China." In *Family Law in Asia and Africa*, by JND Anderson (ed.), 34–38. London: Allen and Unwin, 1968.

McCarthy Brown, K. *Mama Loly, a vodou priestess in Brooklyn*. Berkeley: University of California Press, 1991.

McCarthy, J. *Report of a Survey of Sia,*. London: privately published, 1894.

McCoy, Alfred. *Politics of Heroine in Southeast Asia*. New York: Harper and Row, 1972.

McDonald, Archie. *The Texas Experience*. College Station: Texas A&M University Press, 1986.

Michalowski, Ines. "What is the Dutch Integration model, and has it failed?" *Focus Migration*, Bundeszentrale Fuer Politische Bildung, April 2005.

Michaud, Jean. "Handling mountain minorities in China, Vietnam and Laos: from history to current concerns." *Asian Ethnicity*, 2009: 10(1) 25–49.

Miller, D. "The young and the restless in Trinidad: A case of the local and the global in mass consumption," In *Consuming Technology*, R. Silverstone and E. Hirsch (eds.), London: Rutledge, 1992.

Millett, Sandra. *The Hmong of Southeast Asia*. Minneapolis, MN: Lerner Publications, 2002.

Miyares, Ines. "Changing Perceptions of Space and Place as Measures of Hmong Acculturation." *The Professional Geographe*, 1997: 49(2) 214–224.

Model, Suzanne and Lang Lin. "The Cost of Not Being Christian: Hindus, Sikhs and Muslims in Britain and Canada." *International Migration Review*, 2002: 1061–1092.

Moua, Teng. *Marriage and Family Therapy*. Masters Thesis, Stout, WI: University of Wisconsin-Stout, 2003.

Moua, Vang. *Hmong Christianity: Conversion, Consequence, and Conflict*. Olaf College: Northfield, 1995.

Naficy, Hamid. *An Accented Cinema: Exilic and Diasporic Filmmaking*. Princeton, NJ: Princeton University Press, 2001.

———. *Home, Exile, Homeland: Film, Media, and the Politics of Place*. New York: Routledge, 1999.

———. *The Making of Exile Cultures: Iranian Television in Los Angeles*. Minneapolis: University of Minnesota Press, 1993.

Nash, Manning. *The Cauldron of Ethnicity in the Modern World*. Chicago: The University of Chicago Press, 1989.

Neudeck, Rupert. *Wie hlefen wir Asian? order Ein Schiff fuer Vietnam*. Reinbek bei Hamburg: Rowohlt, 1980.

Ngo, Tam. "The "Short-waved" faith: Christian broadcasting and Protestant conversion of the Hmong in Vietnam." *Working Papers of the Max Planck Institute for the Study of Religious and Ethnic Diversity*, November 2009: 1–24.

Nibbs, Faith. "The Texas Two Step: A delicate dance between culture and ethnicity." *Hmong Studies Journal*, 2006: (7) 1–34.

Office of Refugee Resettlement. *Report to the Congress: Refugee Resettlement Program*. Washington, DC: US Government Printing Office, 1989.

Ong, Aihwa. *Buddha is Hiding: refugees, citizenship, the new America*. Berkeley: University of California Press, 2003.

———. "Cultural Citizenship as Subject-Making." *Current Anthropology*, 1996: 737–761.

Ortner, Sherry. "Resistance and the problem of ethnographic refusal." *Comparative studies in society and history* 1995: 37(1) 173–193.

Østergaard-Nielson, Eva. "Transnational political practices and the receiving state: Turks and Kurds in Germany and the Netherlands." *Global Networks*, 2001: 1(3) 261–82.

Ottino, Arlette. "Origin and ritual exchange." In *Locality and Belonging*, by Nadia Lovell, 103–124. London: Routledge, 1998.

Park, Robert. "Immigrant community and the immigrant press." In *Collected papers of Robert Ezra Park*, by Robert Park, 152–164. New York: Arno Press, 1974.

―――――. *Introduction to the Science of Sociology*. Chicago: University of Chicago Press, 1921.

Pass, Fred (ed). "The Texas Almana." *The Dallas Morning News*. Dallas: AH Bello Corporation, 1980.

Peterson, D. and J. Allman. "Introduction: New Directions in the History of Missions in Africa." *Journal of Religious History*, 1999: 23(1) 1–7.

Plascencia, Luis F.B., Gary Freeman, and Mark Setzler. "The Decline of Barriers to Immigrant Economic and Political Rights in the American States 1977–2001." *International Migration Review*, 2003: 37(1) 5–23.

Plotnicov, Leonard. *Strangers to the City: Urban Man in Jos, Nigeria*. Pitsburg, 1967.

Portes, A. and R. G. Rumbaut. *Immigrant America: A Portrait*. Berkeley: University of California Press, 1996.

Portes, Alejandro and Min Zhou. "The New Second Generation: Segmented Assimilation and Its Variants." *Annals of the American Academy of Political and Social Science*, Nov. 1993: 74–96.

Price, Charles. "Refugees and Mass Migration: Australia." *International Migration Review*, 1986: 20(1) 81–86.

Pritchard, Linda. "A Comparative Approach to Western Religious History: Texas a Case Study, 1845–1990." *The Western Historical Quarterly*, 1988: 413–430.

Probyn, Elspeth. *Outside belongings*. Routledge, 1996.

Prümm, Kathrin, Rosemarie Sackmann, and Tanjev Schultz. "Collective Identities of Turkish Migrants in Germany—the Aspect of self-Localization," In *Identity and Integration: Migrants in Western Europe*, by Rosemarie, Bernhard Peters and Thomas Faist (eds) 159–168. Burlington, VT: Ashgate, 2003.

Quincy, Keith. *Hmong: History of a People*. Cheney, WA: Eastern Washington University ress, 1988.

Ramsden, Robyn, and Damien Ridge. "'It was the Most Beautiful Country I have Ever Seen': The Role of Somali Narratives in Adapting to a New Country." *Journal of Refugee Studies* 2013: 26(2) 226–246.

Ranard, D. *The Hmong: An Introduction to Their History and Culture*. Center for Applied Linguistics, 2004.

―――――. *Hmong Self-Sufficiency: Community Differences*. Perspectives on Refugee Resettlement 1: 46, 1988.

Rapaport, R. "Political economy of migration: Pakistan, Britain and the Middle East." In *Migration, Workers and the Social Order*, by J.S. Eades (ed), 17–41. London: Tavistock, 1987.

Reed-Danahay, Deborah, and Caroline B. Brettell, eds. *Citizenship and Belonging: Immigrants in Europe and the United States*. New Brunswick, NJ: Ruthers University Press, 2008.

Reitz, Jeffrey. "Host Societies and the Reception of Immigrants: Research themes, Emerging Theories and Methodological Issues." *International Migration Review*, 2002: 36(4) 10051019.

Riggins, Stephen. "The Media Imperative: Ethnic Minority Survival in the Age of Mass Communication," In *Ethnic Minority media: An International Perspective*, by Stephen Riggins, 1–20. Newbury Park, CA: Sage, 1992.

Rivera-Salgado, Gaspar. "Migration and political activism: Mexican transnational indigenous communities in a comparative perspective." PhD diss., University of California, Santa Cruz, 1999.

Rosaldo, Renato and William Flores. "Identity, Conflict, and Evolving Latino Communities: Cultural Citizenship in San Jose, California," In *Latino Cultural Citizenship: Claiming Identity, Space, and Rights*, by William Flores and Rina Benmayor (eds). Boston: Beacon Press, 1997.

Rosaldo, Renato. "Social Justice and the Crisis of National Communities," In *Colonial Discourse/Postcolonial Theory*, by Peter Hulme and Margaret Iverson, eds. 239–252. Manchester: Manchester University Press, 1994.

Safran, William. "Diasporas in Modern Societies: Myths of Homeland and Return." *Diasproa*, 1991: 1 (1) 83–99.

Salazar, Jamie. *Legion of the Lost*. Penguin Group, 2006.

Savina, F. *Histories of the Miao*. Hong Kong: Society of Missions, 1924.

Sawyer, Lena. "Voices of Migrants: Solidarity and Resistance," In *Identity, Belonging and Migration*, by Ruth Wodak and Paul Jones Gerard Delanty, 241–260. Liverpool: Liverpool University Press, 2008.

Schein, Louisa. "Mapping Hmong Media in Diasporic Space," In *Media Worlds: Anthropology in New Terrain*, by Lila Abu-Lughod and Brian Larkin and Fay Ginsburg (eds). Berkeley: University of California Press, 2002.

Schrempf, Mona. "From "devil dance" to "World healing: some representations, perspectives and innovations of contemporary Tibetan ritual dances." *Korom, op cit, Ref* 5 1997: 91102.

Schuck, Peter. *Citizens, Strangers, and In-betweens: Essays on Immigration and Citizenship*. Boulder, CO: Westview Press, 1998.

Schulte, Bernd. "The Open Method of Coordination as a Political Strategy in the field of Immigrant Integration Policy," In *Managing Integration: The European Union's Responsibilities Towards Immigrants*, by Reta Sussmuth and Werner Weidenfeld (eds), 114–121. Washington, D.C.: Migration Policy Institute, 2005.

Scott, James. *The Art of Not Being Governed.* New Haven, CT: Yale University Press, 2009.

———. *Weapons of the Weak: Everyday Forms of Peasant Resistance.* New Haven: Yale. University Press, 1985.

Scott, James, and Benedict J. Tria Kerkvliet, eds. *Everyday forms of peasant resistance in South-East Asia.* Routledge, 1986.

Scott, George. "Hmong Aspirations For A Separate State in Laos: The Effects of the Indo-China War," In *Secessionist Movements in Comparative Perspective,* Ralph Premdas, S.W.R. de A. Samarasinghe, and Alan Anderson (eds.), 117. New York: St. Martin's Press, 1990.

———. *Migrants without Mountains: the Politics of Socio-cultural Adjustment among the Lao Hmong Refugees in San Diego.* Unpublished dissertation, University of California, San Diego, 1986.

Seeleib-Kaiser, Martin. "A Dual Transformation of the German Welfare State?" *West European Politics,* 2002: 55–48.

Shandy, Dianna. "Nuer Christians in America." *Journal of Refugee Studies,* 2002: 15 (2) 213–221.

Sheffer, Gabriel. *Diaspora Politics: At Home Abroad.* New York: University Press, 2003.

———. "Israeli-diaspora relations in comparative perspective," In *Israel in Comparative Perspective,* Barnett, M.J. (ed.) 53–83. New York: SUNY Press, 1996.

Siu, Lok. *Memories of a Future Home: Diasporic Citizenship of Chinese in Panama.* Sanford, CA: Stanford University Press, 2005.

Singer, Audrey, Susan Wiley Hardwick, and Caroline B. Brettell (eds.). *Twenty-First Century Gateways: Immigrant Incorporation in Suburban America.* Brookings Institution Press, 2009.

Smith, Neil. "Remaking Scale: Competition and Cooperation in Pre-national and Post-national Europe," In *State/Space: A Reader,* by Bob Jessop, Martin Jones, and Gordon Macleod (eds) 227–238. Malden, MA: Blackwell, 2003.

Steinbeck, John. *Travels with Charley: In Search of America.* Penguin, 1961.

Stepick, Alex. *Pride Against Prejudice: Haitians in the United States.* Boston: Allyn and Bacon, 1998.

Stepick, Alex, Terry Rey and Sarah Mahler. *Churches and Charity in the Immigrant City.* New Brunswick, New Jersey: Rutgers University Press, 2009.

Stewart, Angus. "Two Conceptions of Citizenship." *British Journal of Sociology,* 1995: 46(1) 63–78.

Stoler, Ann. "Plantation Politics and Protest on Sumatra's East Coast." *Journal of Peasant Studies,* 1986: 13(2) 124–143.

*Sueddeutsche Zeitung.* March, 2008.

Suhrke, Astri. "Indochinese refugees and American policy." *The World Today*, Feb 1981: 54–62.

Swyngedouw, Erik. "Neither Global nor Local: 'Glocalization' and the Politics of Scale," In *Spaces of Globalization: Reasserting the Power of the Local*, by Kebin Cox (ed), 137–166. New York: Guilford, 1997.

_____. "The Mammon Quest: 'Glocalization' Interspatial Competition and the Monetary order: The Construction of New Scales," In *Cities and Regions in the New Europe*, by Mick Dunford and Grigoris Kafkalas (eds), 39–68. London: Belhaven, 1992.

Tapp, Nicholas. "Hmong Places and Locality," In *Making Place: State Projects, Globalization and Local Responses in China*, by Stephan Feuchtwang (ed), 132–148. London: Cavendish Publishing Limited, 2004.

_____. *The Hmong in China*. Boston: Brill, 2001.

_____. *Sovereignty and Rebellion: The White Hmong of Northern Thailand*. Singapore: Oxford University Press, 1989.

_____. "The Impact of Missionary Christianity Upon Marginalized Ethnic Minorities: The Case of the Hmong" *Journal of Southeast Asian Studies*, 1989: 20(1) 70–95.

_____. *The Hmong of Thailand*. London: Anti-Slavery Society, 1986.

The Congressional Research SVC Library, *Review of US Refugee Resettlement Programs and Policies*. Committee on the Judiciary 96th Congress, 1st Sessionof Congress. Washington, DC: US Senate, 1979.

*The Nation*. September 6, 2007. nationmultimedia.com (accessed September 5, 2007).

Tiryakian, Edward. A. "Modernisation: Exhumetur in Pace (Rethinking Macrosociology in the 1990s)." *International Sociology*, 1991: (6) 165–80.

Thränhardt, D. "Einwandererkulturen und soziales Kapital. Eine komparative Analyse," In, *Einwanderer-Netzwerke und ihre Integrationsqualität in Deutschland und Israel*, by Ders./ U. Hunger (ed): 15–51. Münster/Freiburg: i.Br., S. 2000.

Tölöyan, Khacig. "The Nation-State and Its Others: In Lieu of Preface.' *Diaspora*, 1991: 1(1): 307.

Turner, Terence. "Representing, Resisting, Rethinking: Historical Transformations of Kayapo culture and anthropological consciousness," In *Colonial Situations: Essays on the contextualization of ethnographic knowledge*, by George W. Stocking Jr, 285–313. Madison, WI: University of Wisconsin Press, 1991.

Turner, Victor. *The Forest of Symbols: Aspects of Ndembu Ritual*. Ithaca, NY: Cornel University Press, 1967.

Ui, S. "'Unlikely Heroes": the evolution of female leadership in a Cambodian ethnic enclave," In *Ethnography Unbound: Power and Resistance in the Mod-*

*ern Metropolis*, M. Buraway, A. Burton, A. Arnett Ferguson, K. J. Fox, J. Gamson, N. Gartrell, L. Hurst, C. Kurtzman, L. Salzinger, J. Schiffman and S. Ui (eds), 161–77. Berkeley, CA: University of California Press, 1991.

UN High Commissioner for Refugees (UNHCR). *Convention and Protocol Relating to the Status of Refugees.* Geneva: UNHCR, 1968: Publication HCR/INF/29/Rev 23.

UN High Commissioner for Refugees (UNHCR). *Protecting Refugees and the Role of UNHCR.* Geneva: UNHCR, 2005.

van den Bergh, Pierre. *The Ethnic Phenomenon.* New York: Praeger, 1987.

Vang, Chia Youyee. *Hmong in Minnesota.* St. Paul: Minnesota Historical Society Press, 2008.

Vang, Her. *Dreaming of Home, Dreaming of Land: Displacement and Hmong Transnational Politics.* Dissertation, Sy. Paul, MN: University of Minnesota, 2010.

Vang, Kao. "Hmong marriage customs: A current assessment," In *The Hmong in the West,* Bruce Downing and Douglas Olney, eds. Minneapolis: Center for Urban and Regional Affairs, 1982.

Van Schendel, Willem. "Geographies of knowing, geographies of ignorance: jumping scale in Southeast Asia." *Environment and Planning D,* 2002: 20(6) 647–668.

Vermeulen, Hans and Rinus Pennix (eds). *Immigrant Integration: the Dutch Case.* Amsterdam: Het Spinhuis, 2000.

Vertovec, Stephen and Stephen Castles. *Migration, Diasporas and Transnationalism.* Aldershot: Edward Elgar, 1999.

Vertovec, Stephen. *Religion and Diaspora.* Oxford, England: University of Oxford, 2001.

———. "Three meanings of "diaspora," exemplified among South Asian religions." *Diaspora,* 1998: 6(3) 277–300.

———. "Migrant Transnationalism and Modes of Transformation." *International Migration Review,* 2004: 970–1001.

Viviano, F. "From the Asian Hills to a U.S. Valley." *Far Eastern Economic Review,* 1986: 132(42) 47–49.

Wahlbeck, Osten. *Kurdish Diasporas.* Hampshire, London: McMillan Press, 1999.

Wallman, S. "Ethnicity and the Boundary Process in Context," In *Theories of Race and Ethnic Relations,* J. Rex and D. Mason (eds.). Cambridge University Press: Cambridge, 1986.

Warner, Roger. "Blind Justice for the Hmong of Laos." *The Nation.* June 28, 2007. www.nationmultimedia.com/option/print.php?newsid=30037966 (accessed September 5, 2007).

Warner, Stephen and Judith Wittner (eds). *Gatherings in Diaspora: Religious Communities and the New Immigration.* Philadelphia: Temple University Press, 1998.

Weinstein, Gail. *From Mountaintops to City Streets: An ethnographic investigation of literacy and social process among the Hmong of Philadelphia.* Philadelphia: University of Pennsylvania, 1986.

Weissbrodt, D. *Immigration Law and Procedure.* Egan, MN: West Group, 1998.

Wiens, H. *China's march in the Tropics.* Connecticut: Shoe String Press, 1954.

Wimmer, Andreas and Nina Glick Schiller. "Methodological Nationalism and Beyond: Nation-State Building, Migration and the Social Sciences." *Global Networks*, 2002: 2(4) 301–334.

Wimmer, Leslie. "Voter turnout low for Fort Worth municipal elections." *Fort Worth Business Press.* May 18, 2009. http://www.fwbusinesspress.com/display.php?id=10211 (accessed April 5, 2010).

Wimmer, Andreas. "Binnenintegration und Außenabschließung. Zur Beziehung zwischen Wohlfahrtsstaat und Migrationssteuerung in der Schweiz," In *Migration in nationalen Wohlfahrtsstaaten Theoretische und vergleichende Untersuchungen*, Michael Bommes and Jürgen Halfmann. Osnabrück: IMIS., 1998.

Wong, L. "Belonging and diaspora: The Chinese and the Internet." *First Monday*, 2003: 8(4) 16.

World Relief. "Replanting lives: The Story of the church at Work." Baltimore, MD, 1988.

Xiong, Yuepheng. "*Taug Txoj Lw Ntshav: Keeb Kwm Hmoob Nyob Suav Teb*" or "Tracing the Bloody path: Hmong History in China." St. Paul, MN: Hmong ABC, 2000.

Yang, Doa. The *Hmong of Laos Face Development.* Vientiane: Siao Savath, 1975.

Yuval-Davis, Nira. "The citizenship debate: women, ethnic processes and the state." *Feminist Review*, 1991: 39, 58–68.

Zavella, Patricia. "The Tables are Turned," In *The New Poverty Studies*, by Judith Goode and Jeff Maskobsky (eds), 103–131. New York: New York University Press, 2001.

Zephyr Developers Inc. *Hmong TV.* N.d. http://hmongsatellitetv.com/ (accessed November 3, 2010).

# Index

Acculturation, 68, 239
Adas, Michael, 11, 227
Adelman, H., 227
Agency, 122
Ahmary, Abdullah Azib, Al, 227
Aid to Families with Dependent Children, 114
Alba, Richard, 227
Alber, Jens, 227
Aleinikoff, Alexander, 227
Alesina, Alberto, 227
Alexander, Michael, 227
Alienation, 75
Allman, J., 240
Andezian, S., 227
Anonymity, 86, 103
Armstrong, John, 228
Assimilation, 8, 201
Asylum, 64, 158, 168
Balakrishnan, T. R., 228
Ban Nam Yao, 29
Barker, C., 228
Barnes, Diane, 228
Barns, J. A., 228
Basch, Linda, 233
Basic Law, 66
"Being made," 12, 72, 89, 149, 150, 181
Belonging, 6
    Co-ethnic belonging, 153

Diasporic belonging, 13, 18, 68, 74, 159, 178, 179, 181, 182, 204, 209, 215, 216, 235
    framework, 4, 8, 9, 16, 85, 125, 126, 181
    identity, 4–6, 9, 12–14, 17, 18, 44, 57, 63, 66, 68, 69, 73, 74, 80, 81, 84–87, 125–127, 146, 150, 151, 153, 155, 159, 167, 168, 171, 174–178, 180, 185, 190–196, 202, 204, 205, 214–217, 229, 231, 233–238, 240, 241
Local belonging, 5, 10, 13, 18, 75, 76, 79, 80, 87, 89, 126, 143, 150, 177, 178
locality, 6, 12, 13, 80, 84, 87, 144, 178, 181, 188, 190, 191, 194, 195, 204, 205, 211, 217, 237, 239, 243
scale, 6, 12–15, 17, 18, 75, 80, 86, 150, 175, 177, 178, 202, 219, 242–244
National belonging, 5, 10, 13, 18, 61–87
Political belonging, 62, 63, 70, 71, 78, 80, 177, 181, 182, 189, 229, 235
Berghahn, M., 228, 233
Betts, Alexander, 11, 228
Bhachu, P., 228

Bishops Report, 135, 232
Blake, J., 228
Blanc-Szanton, Cristina, 233
Block, Liesbeth de, 228
Bloemraad, Irene, 62, 70, 228
Borjas, George J., 228
Boundary, 4, 6, 9, 12, 56, 80, 161, 165, 167, 168, 176, 178, 217
Bourdieu, Pierre, 228
Bowman, Glenn, 228
Boyd, Monica, 228
Bradley, Robert H., 228
Brah, Avatar, 228
Brettell, Caroline B., 229, 241, 242
Briones, Claudia, 229
Brown, B., 229
Brubaker, Rogers, 62, 65, 229
Bryson, J., 229
Buckingham, David, 228
Byron, R., 229
Caglar, Aysa, 233
Campbell, Randolph, 229
Canada, 5, 33, 62, 64, 196, 201, 228, 231, 239
Capital
    Economic Capital, 174, 193, 194
    Human Capital, 157, 159, 174
    Local Capital, 158, 159, 174
    Social Capital, 150, 194
Carliner, David, 229
Cashdan, Elizabeth, 229
Castaneda, Jorge, 229
Castles, M., 229
Castles, Stephen, 69, 229, 244
Catholic Charity, 70
Census Bureau, 119, 229, 230
Central Intelligence Agency, 61, 186
Chafetz, J.S., 232
Chen, Carolyn, 230
Chou, S., 230
Citizenship, 61–63, 68, 71, 75

Active, 4, 5, 10, 81, 86, 87, 136, 143, 172, 187, 189, 190, 200, 216
Advantages, 175
And belonging 85–87, 223
Cultural 89
Democratic 63, 65, 75
Diasporic 181
EU, 164
German Citizenship, 62, 65, 71–74, 131
Hmong Citizenship, 62, 73, 75, 77, 79, 86
And identity 81–85
And marriage 161–165
Policy, 6, 9, 15, 63–67, 228, 230, 241, 243
Political participation, 70, 75, 76, 79–81, 182, 190
Pragmatic, 74, 86
Rights 16, 67, 161, 222
State, 4, 5, 8, 10, 50, 57, 63, 65, 66, 68–71, 73–75, 77, 80, 82, 83, 85–87, 118, 135, 148, 153, 158, 159, 172, 177, 179, 181, 187, 188, 190, 212, 227, 229–231, 235, 236, 239, 242, 243, 245
US Citizenship 64–70
Vernacular, 78
And voting 81–81, 71–78
Clark, William, 230
Clasen, Jochen, 230
Clements, William 94, 95
Clifford, James, 4, 230
Cohen, Robin, 230
Coleman, David A., 230
Colonialism 7, 23–25, 193, 231, 236, 241, 243
Comaroff, Jean, 230
Comaroff, John, 230

Communism, 50, 63, 64, 155, 156, 238
Computer, 148, 175, 186, 191, 197–203, 215, 216, 234, 235, 245
Connor, Walkers, 230
Cooper, Frederick, 230
Cooper, Robert, 230
Crul, Maurice, 230
Culas, C., 231
Cultural formations 209
Cultural refusal, 84, 239
    Cultural local 181
    Cultural-national 181, 209
Cunningham, Stuart, 231
Daniel, Valentine, 231
De Beauclair, I., 231
De Certeau, Michel, 231
Death, 126, 127, 184, 206
    Funeral ritual, 126, 210–212
Delanty, Gerard, 231, 241
DeLuca, Laura, 231
DeSipio, Louis, 231
Development,
    Business 169
    Computers, 197, 198, 204
    Diaspora, 4, 5, 12, 14, 16, 18, 58, 68, 73, 74, 159, 165, 177–183, 186, 188–197, 201, 204, 205, 209, 214–217, 230, 235, 241
    Heritage tour, 193
    Housing, 111
    As multipolarity 178
    Neighborhood 55, 112
    Networks, 4, 6, 12, 14, 86, 159, 179–217, 235, 236, 245
    Political engagement, 63, 86, 188, 189, 215, 235
    Projects, 129
    Rural, 50
    Satellite television, 191, 196, 197, 216
    Social networking, 16, 190, 191, 201, 216
    Subjectivity, 14, 15, 191
    Technology, 83, 157, 159, 182, 190, 194, 197–199, 202, 204, 205, 217, 237
    Tensions in, 181, 195–197, 205, 208, 212, 214, 215, 217
    As a "third space", 17, 165
    Urban, 119
    Video, 179, 182, 191–196, 216, 236
DeWind, J., 231
DiPrete, Thomas, 231
Dispersion, 177, 190
Displacement, 3, 62, 78, 180, 182, 186, 212, 238, 244
Donnelly, Nancy, 231
Dorais, Louis-Jacques, 231
Duchon, D., 231
Dufoix, Stephane, 231
During, Simon, 193, 231
Ebaugh, H.R., 232
Education, 44–45, 129, 131, 211
    Hmong in Germany, 101–102, 157, 159, 163, 170
    Hmong in US, 70, 83, 121, 173, 176, 229
    Pre settlement, 24, 28, 29, 31, 61, 64, 80, 100
Elder, 143, 149, 157, 170, 171, 176, 177, 186, 187
Emplacement, 186, 190, 237
Employment, 16, 46, 74, 149, 153, 157, 162, 163, 173, 179
Entrepreneur, 11, 230
Eriksen, Thomas, 232
Ethnic associations, 70, 169, 235
Ethnic community, 6, 70, 77, 79, 155, 177, 194, 227, 230, 235
Ethno-nationalism, 180
Everett, Anna, 232

Exclusion, 7, 63, 90, 116
Extraterritoriality, 82
Face, 17, 40, 65, 158, 161, 165–167, 170, 174–175, 184, 186, 188–190, 200–205, 208–209, 214, 216, 222–223, 229
Faist, Thomas, 215, 232, 233
Federal Law Gazette I, 227
Federal Ministry of the Interior, 50
Fegan, Brian, 11, 232
Ferrera, Maurizio, 232
Festival, 17, 49, 191
Fischer, Michael MJ, 232
Fitting in, 3–4, 9, 17, 123, 142, 171, 220, 223
Flores, William, 241
Foner, Nancy, 236
Forbes Martin, Susan, 233
Fortier, A., 4, 9, 204, 232
Foucault, Michel, 232
Frachon, C., 232
Franz, B., 232
Franz, Tara M., 234
Freeman, Gary, 240
French Colonialism 12, 22–25, 47, 63, 169
Fuglerud, Øivind, 6, 232
Gammertingen, Old, 141
Gamson, W. A., 232
Gap Min, Pyong, 232
Gardner, K., 232
Garrett, W., 26, 232
Gatekeeper, 145
Gazley, Phil, 233
Geddes, W., 233
Georgiou, Myria, 233
Germany,
   Culture, 129,146, 154, 156, 165, 166, 177, 182, 188, 198, 205, 214, 215
   Dominant, 7, 79, 144, 149
   Economic, 172–174

Economy, 13, 162, 163
Hmong-German relations, 72–74, 77, 79–83
Ideology,
Refugee policy, 65–68
Religious, 125, 126, 137, 140, 150
Religion, 130, 132, 133, 141–143, 145, 146, 148
As a research site, 14–18, 29
Social, 66, 80, 85, 155, 187
Theories concerning, 62, 83, 84
Getrich, Christina., 233
Gilbertson, G., 233
Gilroy, Paul, 233
Glaeser, Edward, 227
Glazer, Nathan, 233
Glick Schiller, Nina, 233, 245
Globalization, 6, 13, 135, 180–181, 191
Goffman, E., 233
Goodenough, Ward, 62, 233
Goody, Jack, 162, 233, 236
Gozdziak, Elzbieta M., 233
Grabska, Katarzyna, 233
Grigoleit, Grit, 233
Grnseth, Anne Sigfrid, 233
Guerra, Carlos, 234
Gunning, Jan Willem, 234
Guttentag, Lucas, 229
Hagedorn, H., 234
Hall, Sandra, 234
Hall, Stuart, 177, 234
Hammond, Joyce, 234
Han Dynasty, 20–22
Hancock, Ange-Marie, 234
Harrell-Bond, B. E., 234
Hathaway, J.C., 234
*Hausfrau*, 46, 198, 204
Hayakawa, Senator (R-CA), 65
Heisler, Barbara, 234
Helton, Arthur, 229
Henderson, Hilma, 234

Henderson, Wade, 229
Heritage tour (see diaspora)
Hickman, Jacob, 212, 234
Hierarchy, 13
Hiller, Harry H., 234
Hirschle, Edwin, 234
Hmong,
   Highland, 23–28, 34, 41, 50, 61, 64, 73, 75, 84, 102, 221, 236
   History of expulsion, 20–33
   In Argentina, 64, 66, 72
   In China, 20–22, 38, 64, 127–128, 173, 175, 187, 191–196, 197, 201,
   In East Germany, 50, 155–159, 163, 169–170, 196
   In France, 16, 64, 72, 160–164, 169, 175, 179, 192, 198, 199, 201–203, 212,
   In French Guyana, 64, 161, 164, 201
   In Laos, 22–28, 37, 58, 81–83, 154, 156, 161, 163–164, 175, 283–191, 211, 113
   Lowland, 23–35, 63, 70–71, 102, 104, 155–159
   New Year, 39, 81, 126, 127, 175, 176, 192, 212–214,
   Thai-Hmong, 64, 74, 161–167, 185–190, 192–193, 199, 207–209, 213
Hmong American Planning and Development Corporation, 171
Hmong Veterans' Naturalization Act, 78
Hmong-Lao Radio, 84
Hmongness, 14, 84–86, 142, 145, 150, 153, 159, 165, 167, 168, 171, 173–178, 182, 185, 190, 191, 195–197, 200, 203, 205, 208, 211, 214, 215, 217
Ho, David, 235

Hollifield, James, 235
Horowitz, David, 235
Hou, Feng, 228
Housing, 35, 40, 51, 55, 130, 132, 135, 136, 142, 156–158, 179, 185
   Apartment, 46, 56, 157, 172
   Dorm, 51, 98–99, 101
   Home ownership, 46, 50, 104, 110–112, 117–119, 122, 124
   Hmong residence patterns, 37, 40–41, 61, 100, 118–119, 153, 156–157, 162–167, 175, 182
   Sponsors, 94–100, 102, 117
Hudspeth, William, 127, 235
Human Rights, 75, 85, 186, 188, 189, 215, 229
Identity,
   Children, 32, 37, 49, 55, 72, 73, 80–82, 85, 91, 95, 129–131, 134, 137, 160, 161, 163, 164, 171, 175, 176, 181, 182, 185, 198–200, 202, 203, 206, 209–212, 214, 215, 228, 236
   Ethnic, 5–7, 12, 14, 17, 18, 48, 54, 55, 65, 66, 69, 70, 74, 76, 77, 79, 80, 85, 138, 139, 143, 150, 151, 155, 157, 168, 177, 180, 181, 187, 190, 191, 194, 196, 204, 212, 215–217, 227, 230, 232, 233, 235, 237, 239, 241, 243–245
   Localized, 18, 65, 86, 146, 155, 165, 167, 168, 170, 171, 174–176, 178, 181, 182, 185, 188–190, 194, 196, 200, 202,
   Hyphenated, 83, 214, 204, 206–209, 213–217
   Personal, 16, 55, 56, 70, 76, 191
   Political, 9, 10, 25, 38, 62, 63, 66, 70, 71, 75–81, 84, 86, 122, 158, 177, 181–190, 193, 215,

252  INDEX

216, 221, 229, 231, 234–236, 239–241
Racial, 54, 80, 230, 232, 233
Relationship to belonging, 4–5, 9–16
Social, 4–6, 8–13, 16, 17, 28, 43, 56, 63, 70, 74, 80, 86, 125, 127–129, 132, 137, 143, 145, 150, 154, 157–159, 162, 163, 165, 168, 171, 173–175, 180, 181, 190, 191, 194–196, 200, 201, 205, 211, 212, 214–217, 230, 232, 233, 235–237, 240, 241, 245
Ignacio, Emily, 235
Immigration and Naturalization Service (ICE), 70
Inclusion, 4, 7, 8, 63, 110, 129, 135, 167
Income, 8, 56, 231
Individualism, 172
Indochina, 63–66, 136, 231, 243
Industry, 38, 44, 46, 195, 196
Inequality, 159
International Committee for European Migration, 33
International Rescue Committee, 30, 91
Isajiw, Wsevolod, 235
Ito, Naomi, 237
Jansen, Stef, 235, 236
Jary, David, 235
Jary, Julia, 235
Jenkins R., 235
Jenkins, S., 235
Jones, Paul, 231, 241
Jones, PR, 235
Jones, S., 9, 235, 242
*Jus sanguinis*, 65, 68
*Jus Soli*, 67
Kammerer, Cornelia Ann, 235
Karanovic, Jelena Lyons, 235

Karim, Karim H., 235
Karst, Kenneth, L., 235
Katz, Michael, 236
Kelley, Tobias, 236
Kelly, Gail, 236
Kennedy, Edward, 64
Keown-Bomar, J., 236
*Khaoxane*, 50, 63, 155, 159, 186, 189
Kinchen, David, 236
King *Ci You*, 192
Klusmeyer, Douglas, 227
Knudsen, John, 231
Kolar-Panov, Dona, 236
Koltyk, Jo Ann, 236
Korac, Maja, 10, 236
Krzyzanowski, M., 9
*kuv ti/kuv tyo*, 36
Landolt, P., 236
Language, 72, 97, 98, 123, 147, 157, 201, 202
ESL/GSL, 74, 90–91, 99, 109, 220
*Hmong Der*, 21, 24
Hmong Romanized Popular Alphabet (RPA), 54
Maintenance, 7, 180, 186, 188–190, 204, 208, 209, 214, 216, 217, 236
*Mong Leng*, 21–22
*Mon Njua*, 21
Shwaben identity and, 48
Lanphier, C.M., 236
Laos, 3, 38, 58, 61, 64, 70, 75, 77, 80–82, 139, 141–144, 148, 155, 156, 158, 161, 163, 164, 167, 169, 174, 175, 182–187, 189, 192, 194, 197, 201–203, 210, 211, 213, 230, 232, 236–238, 242, 244
Lavenex, S., 236
Leach, Edmund, 160, 236
Lee, Gary, 193, 236

Leepreecha, Prasit, 182, 237
Lemoine, J., 237
Levitt, Peggy, 68, 237
Liang, Zai, 237
Lieberson, S., 121, 237
Liminality, 28–33
Lin, Lang, 239
Ling, S., 237
Lo, Kaying, 237
Locality, 6, 12, 13, 80, 84, 87, 144, 178, 181, 188, 190, 191, 194, 195, 204, 205, 211, 217, 237, 239, 243
Lofving, Staffan, 235, 236
*Long Cheng*, 27–28
Long, Lynellyn, 237
Long, Neil, 12, 237
Los Angeles Times, 211
Lovell, Nadia, 174, 237, 239
Lucassen, Leo, 237
Lucke, Joyce, 237
MacDonald, Jeffery, 237
Mahler, Sarah, 242
"making it," 12, 87, 149, 150, 163, 181, 207
Malkki, Lisa, 238
Mallison, Rodger, 238
Mandel, Ruth, 238
Mangin, William, 238
Mansfield, Becky, 13, 238
Marfleet, Philip, 11, 238
Marriage, 16, 19, 127, 155, 159–162, 165, 167, 168, 174–176, 192, 200, 202, 203, 205, 206, 213–217, 233, 238, 244
    As ritual, 126, 127, 145–147, 149, 150, 182, 204, 205, 208–212, 239, 241, 243
    Cross diasporic, 186
    Divorce, 161, 176, 238
    Interethnic, 235
Martin, P., 232, 238
Martin, S., 236, 238, 242

Massey, Douglas S., 238
Mavroudi, Elizabeth, 238
Mayer, P. Townsmen, 238
Mayor, 49, 71, 79, 128, 129, 135
Mayor of Gammertingen, 71, 128
McAleavy, H. Henry, 238
McCarthy Brown, K., 238
McCarthy, J., 238
McCoy, Alfred, 238
McDonald, Archie, 57, 238
Mcgrath, S., 227
McManus, Patricia, 231
"member-making," 18, 89–122, 136, 150, 181, 219, 222, 128–139
Methodological nationalism, 12, 245
*Miao*, 127, 128, 188, 231, 233, 237, 241
Michalowski, Ines, 238
Michaud, Jean, 238
Migration, 4–9, 11–14, 58, 62, 66, 87, 125, 142, 155, 161, 167–169, 178, 182, 192, 204, 212, 217, 227–235, 237–241, 244, 245
    Hmong history of, 19–33
    Secondary, 155, 168, 178
Military, 14, 58, 63, 79, 155, 183, 185
Miller, D., 238
Millett, Sandra, 239
Miyares, Ines, 239
Model, Suzanne, 239
Moua, Teng, 239
Moua, Vang, 239
Moynihan, Daniel, 233
Naficy, Hamid, 130, 239
Nash, Manning, 239
Nation State, 76, 85
Nationality, 10, 81, 82
Nee, Victor, 227
Neudeck, Rupert, 239
Ngo, Tam, 127, 142, 239
Nibbs, Faith, 145, 239

*Nong het*, 23–24
*Nong Kahi*, 29
Non-governmental organization, 58
Office of Refugee Resettlement, 169
Ong, Aihwa, 149, 239
Ortner, Sherry, 239
Østergaard-Nielson, Eva, 239
Ottino, Arlette, 239
*Pa Ndau*, 133, 134
Park, Robert, 73, 240
Pass, Fred, 240
Pathet Lao, 50, 63, 155, 159, 186, 189
Patrilineal, 162
Pennix, Rinus, 244
Perera, Tanuja, 235
Peterson, D., 240
Phantasmagoric, 44
Plascencia, Luis F.B., 240
Plotnicov, Leonard, 240
Political participation, 70, 75, 76, 79–81, 182, 190
Politicians, 77–79
Portes, Alejandro, 240
Price, Charles, 240
Pritchard, Linda, 240
Probyn, Elspeth, 240
Prümm, Kathrin, 80, 240
Public assistance, 16, 158, 169, 172, 173, 232, 234, 236, 238
    Ideology, 66, 80, 85, 125, 126, 137, 140, 150, 155, 172–174, 187
    *Kindergeld*, 106–108
    *Muttersgled*, 106
    *Socialhilfe*, 106
Public discourse, 113, 120
Quincy, Keith, 240
Ramsden, Robyn, 240
Ranard, D., 240
Rapaport, R., 240

Reciprocity, 157–159, 165, 167, 170, 171, 174–177, 188, 189, 195, 204, 216, 217
Red Cross, 91–92, 100
Reed-Danahay, Deborah, 4, 9, 63, 80, 241
Refugee, 3, 5, 7–16,
    Asylee, 64, 158, 168
    Contingent, 66, 181
    Parole status, 63
    Refugeehood, 11, 63
Reitz, Jeffrey, 241
Relationships, 4–6, 9, 11–13, 43, 79, 85, 170, 178, 214, 216
    Face-to-face, 17, 45, 55, 86, 140, 150, 159, 220
    Friendship, 137, 143
    Hierarchical, 6,13,23,90, 99–109, 127, 144, 220, 223
    Horizontal, 100–105
    Vertical, 100–101, 105
Religion, See chapter 5, 217
    Animism, 130, 149, 150, 207, 210
    Baptist, 131, 138, 143, 146
    Catholic, 70, 128, 130, 136
    Christianity, 125, 127, 130, 137–144, 146, 149, 150, 211, 230, 243
    Evangelisch, 128, 129, 132–135
    Missionaries, 64, 128, 138, 139, 141
    kevcia tshiab, 142
    kevcia qub, 142
    Role in resettlement, 62, 126, 136, 137, 214
    Social change, 150, 154, 165
    Yeeb ceeb, 126
Rey, Terry, 242
Rhoades, Lauren, 231
Rhodes, Martin, 232
Ridge, Damien, 240
Riggins, Stephen, 241

Rivera-Salgado, Gaspar, 12, 241
Rosaldo, Renato, 241
Royal Lao Government, 58
Ruey, F., 237
Rumbaut, R.G., 240
Sacerdote, Bruce, 227
Sackmann, Rosemarie, 240
"safe villages", 27
Safran, William, 241
Salazar, Jamie, 241
Savina, F., 241
Sawyer, Lena, 241
Scale, 6, 12–15, 17, 18, 75, 80, 86, 150, 175, 177, 178, 202, 219, 242–244
    City, 6, 15, 43, 44, 46, 55, 61, 62, 72, 76, 105, 129, 150, 163, 177, 229–231, 237, 238, 242
    Global, 5, 6, 10, 12, 13, 15, 43, 64, 73, 135, 159, 180, 181, 190, 191, 196, 205, 214, 216, 217, 227, 228, 230, 233, 235, 236, 238, 243, 245
    meaning, 7, 8, 12, 69, 70, 73, 80, 81, 127, 159, 174, 189, 190, 195, 202, 204, 212
    National, 5, 6, 8, 10, 12–14, 18, 43, 53, 61–87, 125, 147, 161, 177, 181, 197, 220, 235, 238, 241, 244
    Village, 6, 13, 15, 17, 44, 46, 49, 51, 61, 62, 71, 79, 86, 128, 130, 131, 133, 135, 142, 143, 150, 156, 158, 165, 193, 200, 237
Schein, Louisa, 78, 190, 191, 241
Schneider, Jens, 230
Schrempf, Mona, 241
Schuck, Peter, 73, 241
Schulte, Bernd, 241
Schultz, Tanjev, 240

Schwabian Alb, 46, 48–51, 69, 80–86, 97, 112,
Scott, George, 242
Scott, James, 242
Second Generation, 159–162, 198, 215–216
Secret War, 25, 77
Seeleib-Kaiser, Martin, 106, 242
Self-identification, 50, 65, 67, 80, 81, 167, 171, 195, 216
Self-sufficiency, 27–28, 37, 92–95, 98, 115, 117, 119–122, 168–176, 220
Setzler, Mark, 240
Sexuality, 11, 16, 127, 149, 203, 204, 232
    Ethnicity, 5–7, 12, 14, 17, 18, 48, 54, 55, 65, 66, 69, 70, 74, 76, 77, 79, 80, 85, 138, 139, 143, 150, 151, 155, 157, 168, 177, 180, 181, 187, 190, 191, 194, 196, 204, 212, 215–217, 227, 230, 232, 233, 235, 237, 239, 241, 243–245
    Gender, 11, 16, 127, 149, 203, 204, 232
    Ideology, 129, 219
    Power, 10–13, 15, 18, 84, 126, 155, 162, 173, 178, 195, 217, 228–230, 243
Shandy, Dianna, 125, 231, 233, 242
Sheffer, Gabriel, 242
Sinclair, John, 231
Singer, Audrey, 242
Siu, Lok, 16, 181, 242
Smith, Neil, 242
Social Construction, 4
    Family, 15–17, 52, 58, 61, 62, 76, 83, 92, 127, 132, 136, 140–146, 149, 153, 158, 160–167, 169, 171, 173–175, 179, 184, 185, 187, 192,

198–200, 202, 203, 206–208, 210, 214, 231, 238
Identity, 4–6, 9, 12–14, 17, 18, 44, 57, 63, 66, 68, 69, 73, 74, 80, 81, 84–87, 125–127, 146, 150, 151, 153, 155, 159, 167, 168, 171, 174–178, 180, 185, 190–196, 202, 204, 205, 214–217, 229, 231, 233–238, 240, 241
Locality, 6, 12, 13, 80, 84, 87, 144, 178, 181, 188, 190, 191, 194, 195, 204, 205, 211, 217, 237, 239, 243
Mass media, 241
Social Democratic Party of Germany, 76
Social hierarchies (see hierarchy)
Social institution, 13, 70, 125
  Domains, 8
Social networking (see diaspora)
Social organization, 9, 50, 68, 85, 86, 127, 142, 149, 153, 157–160, 162, 167, 174, 175, 177, 190, 192, 203, 206, 209–211, 228, 234, 236, 237
Social safety net, 158, 174, 216
Sponsors, 58, 90, 103, 105, 129, 137, 156, 157, 173
  In Germany, 5, 14–18, 44, 46, 48–51, 58, 66–68, 72–74, 77, 79, 81–83, 130–133, 141, 143, 145, 146, 148, 155, 156, 159–166, 169, 171, 185, 188, 189, 193–198, 200–203, 206–208, 212, 214, 227, 230, 239
  In Texas, 5, 14–16, 53, 56–58, 61, 63, 70, 77, 78, 137, 143–147, 153, 168, 169, 171–175, 177, 185, 187, 211, 213, 238, 240

State, 4, 5, 8, 10, 50, 57, 63, 65, 66, 68–71, 73–75, 77, 80, 82, 83, 85–87, 118, 135, 148, 153, 158, 159, 172, 177, 179, 181, 187, 188, 190, 212, 227, 229–231, 235, 236, 239, 242, 243, 245
Statelessness, 18, 78
Steinbeck, John, 242
Stepick, Alex, 242
Stewart, Angus, 63, 75, 242
Stigma, 221
  Race, 8, 10, 76, 233, 244
Stoler, Ann, 242
Subjectivity, 14, 15, 191
*Sueddeutsche Zeitung*, 242
Suhrke, Astri, 243
Swyngedouw, Erik, 243
Tapp, Nicholas, 128, 142, 173, 243
Technology, 182, 190, 191
Television, 184, 188, 191, 196, 197, 216
Texas, 178–176
  Economy, 13, 56, 162, 163, 240
  Ideology, 66, 80, 85, 125, 126, 137, 140, 150, 155, 172–174, 187
  "Texas mystique", 57, 96
Thailand, 28, 38, 64, 74, 142, 148, 161–163, 175, 184–187, 189, 191, 192, 194, 197–199, 201, 202, 206–208, 211, 213, 233, 235, 237, 243
*The Dallas Morning News*, 234, 240
*The Nation*, 8, 57, 64, 65, 67, 68, 73, 74, 80, 81, 85, 86, 186, 201, 230, 233, 243, 244
Thirty Years' War, 46–47
Thränhardt, Dietrich, 65, 67, 243
Tiryakian, Edward. A., 243
Tölöyan, Khacig, 180, 243
Transnational, 190, 233, 234, 236, 244

Tria Kerkvliet, Benedict J., 242
Turner, Terence, 84, 243
Turner, Victor, 243
Ui, S., 243
United Nations High Commissioner for Refugees, 4, 10, 28, 244
University of Humboldt, 155
Urban, 7, 14, 55, 71, 155, 158, 163, 231, 233, 244
US Department of Alcohol, Tobacco and Firearms, 184
Van den Bergh, Pierre, 244
Van Schendel, Willem, 244
Vang, Chia Youyee, 244
Vang, Her, 244
Vang, Kao, 244
Vang Pao, General, 25–28, 32, 184
Vergaftig, M., 196, 232
Vermeulen, Hans, 244
Vertovec, Stephen, 244
Video, 179, 182, 191–196, 216, 236
Vietnam, 64, 65, 78, 175, 183, 193, 194, 238
Vietnam War, 65, 78, 183
Vietnamese, 48, 55, 63, 64, 67, 80, 135, 136, 188, 229
"boat people," 66
Village, 14, 46, 161, 185, 205, 210
Viviano, F., 244
Voluntary Resettlement Agency (VOLAG), 14, 91–94, 96, 99, 118
Vote, 64, 75–77, 79, 80, 85
Voutira, E., 234
Wacquant, Loïc, 12, 228
Wahlbeck, Osten, 244
Wallman, S., 244
Warner, Roger, 244
Warner, Stephen, 244
Waters, M.C., 121, 237
Weil, P., 238
Weinstein, Gail, 245
Weissbrodt, D., 245
Wiens, H., 245
Wiley Hardwick, Susan, 242
Wimmer, Andreas, 245
Wimmer, Leslie, 245
Wittner, Judith, 244
Wodak, Ruth, 241
Wong, L., 245
World Relief, 136–138, 245
World War II, 7, 24, 25, 46, 65–66
Xiong, Yuepheng, 245
Yang, Doa, 245
Yuval-Davis, Nira, 245
Zavella, Patricia, 245
Zhou, Min, 240
Zomia, 25–26

305.895972 N578    .    JIB
Nibbs, Faith G.
Belonging :the social dynamics of
 fitting in as experienced by the Hm
TEXAS ROOM
06/15